HENRY W. GRADY

AMERICAN NEWSPAPERMEN 1790-1933

RUSSELL FRANKLIN TERRELL

A STUDY
OF THE EARLY
JOURNALISTIC WRITINGS
OF HENRY W. GRADY

BEEKMAN PUBLISHERS INC.

NEW YORK   1974

Reprinted 1974 from the 1926 edition

Manufactured in the United States of America

Library of Congress Cataloging in Publication Data

Terrell, Russell Franklin.
    A study of the early journalistic writings of
Henry W. Grady.

    (American Newspapermen, 1790-1933)
    Originally presented as the author's thesis, George
Peabody College for Teachers, 1926.
    Reprint of the ed. published by George Peabody
College for Teachers, Nashville, which was issued as
no.39 of the college's Contributions to education.
    Bibliography: p.
    1. Grady, Henry Woodfin, 1850-1889.   I. Title
II. Series: George Peabody College for Teachers, Nashville.
Contribution to education, no. 39.
PN4874.G66T4 1974   070'.92'4   74-567
ISBN 0-8464-0006-5

INTRODUCTORY

The material upon which the discussion in the following pages is based comprises the early writings of Henry W. Grady. These writings, so far as can be ascertained, have not previously been collected nor published separately since their original appearance. What might seem to be an exception to this is the fragment of Mr. Grady's lecture, "A Patch Work Palace," which in a modified form appeared in Joel Chandler Harris' "Life and Works of Henry W. Grady." Joel Chandler Harris edited the lecture, but the fragment included here was copied from the original manuscript without any changes, hence the justification for its inclusion in the uncollected writings of Mr. Grady.

Practically all the articles included here were signed articles. As an early contributor of the *Atlanta (Georgia) Constitution,* Mr. Grady signed his articles with the *nom de plume,* "King Hans." Later he signed his name in full or just his initials, "H. W. G." Several of his unsigned editorials have been identified by cross references in the consecutive issues of the papers, and by references of his biographers to the titles and to the subject-matter of his editorials. The editorials here numbered 13, 14, 15, 16, 20, 21, 22, and 23 were identified by the style or phraseology. Two editorials, Numbers 18 and 28, were written by his co-editors, and they are included here merely for comparison.

The numbers from 1 to 67 in the footnotes refer to the writings of Henry W. Grady, designated as editorials in the appendix. The numbers from 200 to 346 in the footnotes refer to books, magazine articles, etc., containing information about Mr. Grady or general information on literary style. The editorials of Mr. Grady were copied directly from the files of *The Atlanta (Georgia) Constitution* and *The Atlanta (Georgia) Herald.*

This material has been studied in an effort to analyze Mr. Grady's literary style, his ability as an editorial writer, and his position among the outstanding journalists of his day in the United States. There is scarcely a doubt that his writings deserve more consideration than they have hitherto received. He was one of the journalists who has used his literary ability to promote journalism. The present study shows that Mr. Grady accomplished his work and became famous as a writer even while he was yet a mere boy. The selected writings are dated from May 28, 1869 to May 12, 1883. The task of analyzing Mr. Grady's writings as a mature man is not here attempted.

GENERAL INDEX

PART ONE

PART TWO

PART ONE

A Study of the Early Journalistic Writings of
Henry W. Grady

(From May 28, 1869 to May 12, 1883)

CHAPTER I

HENRY W. GRADY'S LITERARY STYLE

Saintsbury, in commenting upon newspapers, said that during the period of Addison and Swift newspaper-writing was not popular, and lent itself but slightly to literary production, and that Defoe's abundant journalism brought him more discredit than profit and praise. In commenting further upon this theme he calls attention to the change that took place after the French Revolution—the fact that the reading public read newspapers, and consequently people of literary merit began to write for the papers. Notwithstanding this change, in 1898 he makes this statement,

"—In fact, before our present period newspaper-writing was rather dangerous, was more than rather disreputable, and offered exceedingly little encouragement to any one to make it the occasion of work in pure literature, or even to employ it as a means of livelihood, while attempting other and higher though less paying kinds."[200]

While to-day much of our current literature finds its way to the public through magazines, it is possibly safe to say that even now many people discredit what they read in our great dailies.

THE SCULPTOR AND THE PAINTER

It is not the purpose of this effort to evaluate Henry W. Grady's literary style but to try to prove that he, in his early journalistic career, produced literature, and it is also the purpose to set forth some of the literary qualities that made him the great journalist he was. That he was an artist in his line no one can deny. Dr. J. W. Lee said of him,

"The genius of Henry W. Grady so far arose above the plane of ordinary talent that it was capable of transmutation into any of the fine arts. Had he lived in the thirteenth century he would have been an architect. Had he lived in the sixteenth century and in Florence he would have been a painter. Had he lived in the seventeenth, and in England, he would have been a poet. Living in the nineteenth, and in the South, he was an editor and an orator. In thought and spirit he lived in the boundless, the radiant, the beautiful. He saw visions as beautiful as Rubens' and temples as perfect as that of Phidias. But his genius was controlled by his heart. His sympathy for men was so constant and so universal that it denied his genius expression in the forms which only touched the few."[201]

If one will turn to some of his editorials one can see the justification of Dr. Lee's claims:

[200]Saintsbury, Geo. Edw.: A Hist. of 19th Cent. Lit., p. 445 (d).
[201]Lee, Dr. J. W.: H. W. Grady, Arena, 2: 9-23, Je. 1890.

"I noted at one of the resorts several days ago the handsomest woman I ever saw on the beach. She was tall and slender, but divinely formed. Her flesh was firm and dazzling in its whiteness. Her pretty head was poised like a queen's upon a swan-like neck that swelled into a snowy bust and shoulders. A bathing shirt loosely tied about the neck and without sleeves, gave perfect play to her superb body. Black silk stockings encased a leg of exquisite proportions, and feet that left perfectly outlined foot-prints set regularly in the sand at about thirty degrees divergence. There was something royal in the unconscious grace and beauty of this woman as she walked into the water the cynosure of a hundred eyes. Utterly dwarfing her escort, she seemed disregardful of his presence, and when the foam was clustering about her knees, she raised her gleaming arms above her head, and went like a flash into the body of an incoming breaker. The vision of that woman shines to this hour, as a serene star amid the crowding memories of this month, nor does the vision lose its luster when I reflect that she was an employe in the hotel, and her grace was the result of hard work and constant exercise."[64]

He sees what the sculptor would have seen had he been there, and presents in bold relief with only a few strokes of his magic pen the beauty of form and the grace of manner of this unsophisticated servant girl. But let us turn to a picture of a landscape painted as one grand cyclorama:

"Here we are on top of a hill—say 2,500 feet above tide water. Around is a scene the grandeur and beauty of which even the painter's brush could not put on canvas. To the front, right and left of us, are endless mountain ranges, their azure heads lost in the clouds. Breaking green surfaces of the outlying foot-hills are tiny gashes or miners' huts or swift and slender streams 'dropping like downward smoke.' To the rear of us is Dahlonega, showing up like a toy village in the skies."[63]

How true to art is he in this picture; the unimportant details are omitted. He has given us just enough of the details to make the important features stand out. This is a fine illustration of the economy of language. Not a phrase, not a word could be left out without marring the beauty of the picture. Painter says there is an art in the choice and marshaling of words. Such a choice is the adaptation of means to an end.[202] This story will illustrate Henry W. Grady's close study of words:

"Once he sent a scholarly member of the Constitution staff to an opera house to report a performance. In the course of his critique the reporter used the phrase 'well pleased' as signifying the reaction of the audience to the performance. Mr. Grady wrote the reporter a sharp note criticizing the phrase 'well pleased.' Mr. Grady said that if the man was pleased he was 'well pleased' and he asked the reporter his authority for the use of such a phrase. The reporter replied, 'It came down from Heaven in the sentence: This is my

[64]Edit.: Surf-Bathing, p. (a).
[63]Edit.: Gold in Georgia, p.
[202]Painter, F. V. N.: El. Guide to Lit. Crit., p. 9 (a).

beloved son in whom I am well pleased.'[203] Mr. Grady being generous to a fault, acknowledged his error."

Words are more than mere symbols of ideas to Henry W. Grady; after they have passed through his mind and have been warmed by his genial nature they become the expression of his personality.[204]

"Every great writer," says Winchester, "is a species by himself, and therefore his form is only the outward expression of an inward state . . . "[205]

From this standpoint, "Art is the spontaneous yet ordered overflow of life . . ."[206]

Winchester tells us that the literary artist must use concrete language—not abstract. He also hints at things he wishes to picture. He uses few words often, but arranges them artistically. He is not a mere stylist, but his writing is based upon substance and thought.[207] For instance, let us take the picture of the servant girl in surf-bathing and analyze the artistic touches of Mr. Grady. In the first place he prepares you for these artistic touches by telling you that she is the "handsomest" woman he ever saw on the beach. Then in the choice of words in keeping with the lines and curves of a piece of statuary he proceeds to tell that she is "tall and slender" and "divinely formed."[64] He might have said she had a beautiful complexion, but he didn't; he said her flesh was "firm," "dazzling" "in its whiteness." He chooses rather to give the most concrete adjectives in the language to describe the beauty of her physical appearance. In the next sentence he adds to the statuary effect by telling us that her "pretty head" was "poised like a queen's" upon "a swan-like neck that swelled into a snowy bust and shoulders." All of the womanly virtues and beauty are summed up in this one sentence. "Poised" and "queen's" are suggestive of virtue, and "swan-like neck" and "snowy bust and shoulders" suggest beauty in its simplicity; "swan-like neck" also suggests the beautiful curves we expect in a piece of statuary. "A leg of exquisite proportions," "and feet that left perfectly outlined footprints set regularly in the sand at about thirty degrees divergence" are clauses and phrases that suggest lines and curves and angles in a piece of statuary. "Royal" and "unconscious grace" are well-chosen descriptive words

[203]Hudgins, H. O. and C. P.: Life and Labors of H. W. Grady, pp. 61 (a), 62 (b).
[204]Rhodes, Chas. E.: Effective Expression, p. 38 (b).
[205]Winchester, C. T.: Prin. Lit. Crit., p. 223 (b).
[206]Winchester, C. T.: Prin. Lit. Crit., p. 291 (d).
[207]Winchester, C. T.: Prin. of Lit. Crit., p. 184 (a) (b).
[64]Edit.: Surf Bathing.

that call attention to the superiority of the woman. But
so far we have seen the woman in a passive state; Mr.
Grady used language suitable for such a state. How easily
he turns from a description of a passive person to that of
an active person. Look at his rhythmic words as he describes her in motion: "and when the foam was *clustering*
about her knees, she raised her *gleaming* arms above her
head, and went like a *flash* into the body of an *incoming*
breaker." In the description of the surf-bathing of the servant girl Mr. Grady shows the influence of the Greek masters upon his writings, not only in the chaste language but
also in the statuary effects of his descriptions.[64]

Let us analyze the view given above. Mr. Grady's viewpoint is on top of a hill; he prepares one for the picture
by telling of its grandeur and beauty. He gives one sweeping view, the "front," the "right," the "left," and the "endless mountain ranges," stretching in every direction in a
great cycloramic view with their "azure heads" lost on the
beautiful background of the "clouds." Then he very deftly
uses the artifice of contrast when he throws the "green surfaces of the outlying foot-hills, the tiny gashes, and the
miners' huts, and the swift and slender streams," all in
front of the mountain ranges. And finally he gives some
idea of the distance he is from Dahlonega by referring to it
as the "toy village in the skies." Some landscape painters
ruin their pictures by daubing on bold details. This cannot
be said of Henry W. Grady, especially in this picturesque
view. The background is made up of the mountain ranges
with their heads lost in the clouds, and the details consist
of mere tints, such as "tiny gashes," "miners' huts," "swift,
slender streams," and the "toy village in the skies." He did
not select merely what was obvious, but what was typical,
characteristic, and individual.[208] He is describing what he
has experienced and what his warm nature has colored,
therefore the picture is but a part of Mr. Grady's own
self.[209]

HIS DESCRIPTIVE VERITY

Mr. I. W. Avery, one of Henry W. Grady's co-editors,
said that his writings were characterized by their descriptive verity.[210] In one of his early editorials he draws a
picture of what he calls the majesty of the law in its cold
and unsympathetic attitude toward a poor family. The

[64]Edit.: Surf-Bathing.
[208]Canby and Others: Eng. Comp. in Theory and Practice (New Rev.) p. 266 (d).
[209]Gardiner, J. H.: The Forms of Lit. (Intro.), p. 3 (c) (d).
[210]Hudgins, H. C.: Life and Labors of H. W. G., p. 41 (b).

officers of the law were ejecting this poor family because
the rent had not been paid. This incident presents a very
vivid picture indeed:

"He (the father) had fought gamely, but the odds were piled up
against him, and cruel circumstances had dragged him to the dust.
So there he lay, deserted by friends, bereft of fortune—a panting,
gasping, fainting man. There officers of the law stood over him with
the terrible instrument of their office; his wife, weak and sorrowful,
and his hungry-eyed children were huddled around him, their eager
pangs dulled with wonder. The officer, in the name of justice, and
the majesty of the law, lays his hand upon the door lock and declares
that the scanty furniture is seized in behalf of the state, and that
the house must be vacated at once.

"The poor man rises from the bed on which he is sitting; his
children huddle around him and his wife leans weeping on his
shoulders; he gazes around upon what has been his home; then upon
the cold, cheerless snow; then upon his children. His lips quiver, a
red flush shoots into his face, flashes there an instant, and then dies
out again. He strokes his wife's head softly with his hand, and
murmurs tenderly into her ear: 'Cheer up, Bessie, cheer up; it will
all be right in a hundred years.' "[16]

What a suggestive picture! Not a word has been spoken
against our social order, and yet one cannot read this description without feeling a resentment toward the society
that permits such actions in the name of law and justice.[16]
Again Mr. Grady calls to his aid descriptive words—verbs,
adjectives and nouns—which make us see this pathetic picture. This father "had *fought gamely*," but the "*odds were
piled* against him," "*circumstances*," over which he had no
control, "had *dragged* him to the *dust*," and there he "*lay,
deserted by friends, bereft of fortune—a panting, gasping,
fainting man.*" The feeling of awe takes hold on one as he
views the officers with their "*terrible instruments* of their
office," and it is as soon turned to pity as he beholds the
"*wife, weak and sorrowful,* and the hungry-eyed children
huddled" around their poor, helpless father for protection
with "their *eager pangs* half *dulled with wonder.*" Then in
the next paragraph still other graphic phrases are used. As
the father rises from the bed "his children *huddle* around
him and his wife *leans weeping* on his shoulders." We see
the father "*gazing*" upon "*what was* his home," upon "his
children," and upon the "cheerless snow." His lips "quiver,"
"*a red flush shoots into his face, flashes* there an *instant,*"
and, then the pity of it, "dies out again." Then Mr. Grady
adds the most pathetic stroke of all, as he paints the husband all subdued trying to cheer his poor wife by the con-
soling words. "He *strokes* his wife's head *softly* with his

---

[16]Edit.: In a Hundred Years.

hand, and *murmurs tenderly* into her ear: '*Cheer up*, Bessie, *cheer up.*" Words have been in two's and three's to bring out the descriptive effect, such as "terrible instruments," "*panting, gasping, fainting,*" all of which has an accumulative effect. But more than all this Mr. Grady has selected connotative words, words that suggest sadness, words that are very close to life and have a place in the experience of the race.[211] Of course, they drive home the ideas Mr. Grady had in mind to present in this picture. It is not a forced effect, it is the portrayal of the feelings of a big, sympathetic heart.[209b] Such effect cannot be analyzed, it can only be felt by the reader. The simplicity of style and the imagination of the writer appeals very strongly to the emotional nature of the reader.

Let us contrast with this rather sad article another which has in it the Christmas spirit of the man. He loved children and this is why he wrote the following on Christmas Eve as he makes a plea for Santa Claus for the children:

"Let the young ones 'hang up their stockings.' It does not matter that you are not able to fill them with rare and precious gifts. That is not what the children hang them up for. It is the expectation and the mystery of the thing that makes it so delightful. A rag doll, or a penny whistle that comes to them across the frosty roofs, through the silvery air, behind the dancing reindeer with their crystal bells, in Santa Claus' magical sleigh, and then down the sooty chimney, is consecrated with wonder, wrapt in gorgeous glamour, that makes it better than silver and gold."[20]

The first few lines of the quotation is his simple plea for the children, but he ends with lines that are poetical in sentiment as well as in rhythmic beauty. How descriptive are these words of the feelings and experiences of child life![211b] "A rag doll, or a penny whistle *that comes to them across the frosty roofs,* through *silvery air, behind the dancing reindeer* with *their crystal bells,* in Santa Claus' *magical sleigh,* and *then down the sooty chimney,* is *consecrated in wonder, wrapt in gorgeous glamour,* that *makes it better than silver and gold.*" It is not necessary to point out the well-selected adjectives, nor the fitting nouns and verbs in the lines above. What could be more fitting for the effects he was striving for—the wonderful, the mystical, the glamourous?[212] If elegance is the adaptation of language to the thought and feeling in such a manner as to secure pleasing

[211]Rhodes, Chas. E.: Effective Expression, p. 77 (b).
[209b]Albright, Evelyn M.: Descriptive Writing, p. 29 (d).
[20]Edit.: The Little Ones and Their Stockings.
[211b]Winchester, C. T.: Prin. of Lit. Crit., p. 215 (d).
[212]Clark, S. H., Interpretation of the Printed Page, p. 253 (b).

effects, then is not Mr. Grady's plea for Santa Claus for all the children the acme of elegance?[213] Whatever the subject or the occasion Mr. Grady's language was pertinent to the thought or the feeling he wished his readers to experience. Goethe's dictum for artistic writing is very applicable to Mr. Grady:

"We should endeavor to use words that correspond as closely as possible with what we feel, see, think, imagine, experience, and reason."[214]

When one reads an editorial of Mr. Grady he is made to feel as Emerson said he always felt when he read the worthwhile thoughts of others—when he asked himself the question, "Why, that is just what I have often thought, but could not express. Why could not I say it?"[215]

Mr. Grady had a way of transporting himself into the very life and texture of his readers. He had had universal experiences, and he could depict things so vividly and insinuate his feelings so completely into the consciences of others that they saw and felt as they had never seen or felt before.

"This then is style," says Quiller-Couch.[216] "As technically manifested in the literature it is the power to touch with ease, grace, precision, any note in the gamut of human thought or emotion."[217]

The truth of this quotation will be illustrated more fully as we proceed to analyze his literary style. It is fully illustrated in the editorials appended hereto.

"Feelings must be exhibited, not described," says C. T. Winchester.[218] Mr. Grady's great heart beat in unison with those of the children as they had the experiences the beautiful language suggests. Walter Bagehot, in describing Shakespeare's power as a literary artist, said that he not only associated with men but that he was of men.[219] This is just as true of Mr. Grady in all his relations as a newspaper man. He was equally at home with all classes of men, and all ages. One of the finest tributes paid Mr. Grady by Joel Chandler Harris was his description of the great editor entering a circus with a gang of street urchins.[220] No wonder he could close his Christmas editorial with these words:

[213]Rhodes, Chas. E.: Effective Expression, p. 36 (c).
[214]Quiller-Couch: On the Art of Writing, p. 296 (b).
[215]Emerson, Ralph W.: Self-Reliance.
[216]Quiller-Couch: On the Art of Writing, p. 296 (a).
[217]Quiller-Couch: On the Art of Writing, p. 297 (a).
[218]Winchester, C. T.: Prin. of Lit. Crit., p. 239 (c).
[219]Bagehot, Walter: Literary Studies, Vol. I, p. 142 (d).
[220]Harris, J. C.: H. W. G. Life, Writings and Speeches, p.

"God bless the children all, and fill their stockings full!"

Let's take a look at this last paragraph in the Christmas editorial. It expresses so beautifully his paternal love:

"We know of a home, an humble one, too; where tonight while the pillow of a cradle is being warmed, a darling little rascal, barely able to toddle, and with just four teeth in his busy mouth, will work his way up to the mantle piece, and hang Grandma's woolen stocking— too big by half for his meager gifts—on the nail therein embedded! And happy will he be! Noble will he be! Great will he be, if in all the life stretching out before him, his heart is filled, and his impulses started by no meaner motives, than the sturdy faith, the honest hope, the abiding confidence that inspires him, as he pins the wrinkled old leggin to the chimney-board tonight."[20]

The force of this last paragraph lies in the simple concrete statement of facts which are so universal.[221] Each Christmas there are literally thousands of homes where such phraseology as this might be used: "While the pillow of the *cradle is being warmed, a darling little rascal, barely able to toddle,* and with *just four teeth* in his *busy mouth,* will *work his way* up to the mantle piece, etc." There is instinctively a reaction in every heart to such a description, and all mankind joins in with Mr. Grady when he writes:

"Happy will he be! Noble will he be! Great will he be, etc."

A host of people could say, "We too *knew* of a home" as their hearts swell with emotion at the recollection of the happy days long since passed. So long as people remain human such writings will have a powerful appeal to them.[222]

His Portrayal of Character

Someone has said that Henry W. Grady is the Christopher North of America, meaning by that that he is a writer of character sketches.[223] In such sketches he musters words to characterize the individuals. During a Congressional canvass he shows two politicians by means of comparison and contrast:

"Felton is the most finished orator, and has the most commanding presence and the highest culture. Lester is the most genial talker and the most versatile. His speech is all tears and smiles. It is delightful mixture of fun and eloquence—of humor and passion. Both are alert, quick as a flash and full of nerve. Both are well poised, adroit and imperturbable. Either catches the humor of the crowd on the instant and rides it snugly. Both are impassioned, or pretend to be. Either can dash his voice with tears or stiffen it with the

[20]Edit.: The Little Ones and Their Stockings.
[221]Rhodes, Chas. E.: Effective Expression, p. 78 (a).
[222]Clark, S. H.: Interpretation of the Printed Page, p. 251 (b).
[223]Huggins, H. C. and Co.: Life and Labors of H. W. G., p. 43 (b).

ring of the clarion. Lester is inimitable on anecdotes, Felton is matchless in certain kinds of raillery. I don't know which is the best 'stump-speaker.' If I were forced to give an opinion I should say both."[46]

In about one hundred and thirty words Mr. Grady has given us a vivid picture of two campaign orators. How has he done it? By contrast[224] and comparison, and by the choice and selection of fitting words, such as these in contrasting Felton with his opponent: "most finished orator, highest culture, most commanding presence, matchless in certain kinds of raillery"; and such as these to contrast Lester with Felton: "most genial talker, most versatile, all tears and smiles, delightful mixture of fun and eloquence—of humor and passion, inimitable on anecdotes"; and such as these compare the one with the other: "alert, quick as a flash, full of nerve, well poised, adroit and imperturbable, humor of the crowd, instant, rides it snugly, impassioned, dash his voice with tears, stiffen it with the ring of the clarion." He has thrown these words into proper order to secure the degree of connotation desired without the necessity of using many conjunctions; hence the sentences are vivid, forceful and easy flowing and the whole effect is eloquence. "Words fitly spoken are like apples of gold in pictures of silver."[225]

If Mr. Grady understood human nature as well as he could portray it, we can readily understand why he influenced men so much. Observe how he characterizes the Florida politician by the use of a few descriptive words:

"Pasco is a ridiculously yellow man of medium height. He has black whiskers that glisten, but do not grow thick. His eyes are lustrous jet, and he has the dreamy, far-away, listening-to-an-echo look, that I have heretofore supposed to be peculiar to husheesh eaters. His voice is soft and toned down, until it sounds something like a banana tastes. His hands are warm and feel like velvet. He is careful of his dress, wearing rich snuff color, reaching up to a modest maroon in the cravat, and dropping into a retired drab in the pantaloons. He carries his head well forward, his legs moving in short, quick steps, as if they were trying to catch up. I should say his favorite perfume is musk—his favorite cigar a cigarette—his favorite wine, Sillery; his favorite musical instrument, a flute. The idea he gives to an observer is one of—repression. He does not carry his claws peeled, to scratch himself with, as some bantish beasts do; but keeps them snugly sheathed, until he is ready to spring on the enemy. And then they flash out, cold and clean, like stilettoes in moonlight."[41]

---

[46]Edit.: The Saucy Seventh.
[224]Pritchard, F. H.: Training in Literary Appreciation, p. 10 (b) (c).
[225]Solomon: Prov. 25: 11.
[41]Edit.: Contested Election Returns in Florida.

Pasco is a man you would not choose for a friend, because Mr. Grady has portrayed his character so completely by a few well-chosen words. How these qualifying words characterize him: "ridiculously yellow man," "dreamy, far-away-listening-to-an-echo look," "bantish beasts," "claws, snugly sheathed," etc. The color of his clothes, his very motions, his cigarette, all tell you of his character. Every word at Mr. Grady's command does service and tells of his "brain children."

HIS IMPRESSIONISTIC DESCRIPTION

Mr. Grady used every kind of description, but possibly he excelled in impressionistic description.[226] In these descriptions is where one catches the moods of the man. Here is where his personal touches come to the front.[227] His power of suggestion is shown at its best in the following editorial:

"What a night that was! Out under the great live oak trees, that were drowsy with the hum of the cricket and the katydid. The stars gleaming in their tranquil depths—farther away and more steadfast than the city stars ever seemed to be; the lake lisping on the shore at the feet; the old house, larger than a cluster of modern houses, silent and desolate save where the overhanging boughs of the trees swept caressingly against it; the whippoorwill calling from the outlying woods, from vague and indeterminable points, as if some restless spirit of a bird were calling from a shifting, impalpable perch—the cows moving uneasily in their slumbers, and the geese, sweeping by as spectres through the pale byways of the night—the dogs crouching near where we sat—two city-bred youngsters huddled in our arms—and above all the ineffable hush, and peace, and expansion, depth, and breadth, and stillness of the starlit night in the country, into which no bustle can reach, and about which no limit is set. The stars, the trees, the earth, the lake, the house, the sky, water, brutes, and birds, and the watchers who sat beneath the trees seemed to be of one piece, and of one substance. The air that bound all these things together throbbed with one pulse and rose or fell with one breath. All things held kinship with all things else, and the incomparable quiet of the stars, the whisper of the lake and trees, and all the sounds and the silence of that restful night sank into the soul of men who lay beneath them and filled them with a peace that passes all understanding."[67]

The reader cannot help feeling the "restfulness of the night that sank into the soul of men." It is the suggestiveness of such words and phrases as these that suffuses the soul in peaceful quietness:

"The drowsiness of the oak trees, the hum of the cricket and the katydid, the stars gleaming in their tranquil depths, the whippoor-

[226]Rhodes, Chas. E.: Effective Expression, p. 292 (d).
[227]*Ibid.*, p. 84 ( ).
[67]Edit.: One Day's Fishing.

will calling from the outlying woods, above all the ineffable hush, and peace, and expansion, depth, and breadth, and stillness of the starlit night in the country," and all the rest of the words and phrases that go to make up the impression of the oneness of nature with man, is what fill the soul with the peace "that passes all understanding."

The impressionistic descriptive touches in the following remind one of Edgar Allen Poe's style:

"Bonaventure is an ideal graveyard—sort of Westminster Abbey. The tombs are massive, ancient and venerable, the grass is luxuriant and creeps over the graves. There the gray moss winds its arms about the limbs of the lusty oaks, and in the silent, eternal pressure chokes down the rising life of the trees, and represses the throbbings that else would burst into gay irreverent foliage—a solemn stillness holds all the scene, and so far away from the bustling world is the scene and its suggestions that one almost looks to see a hare leap adown the vast silence of the forest. Here in this deep solitude, the eternal past salutes the eternal future—and the present oppressed with cares and emotions, and the pains and ecstasies of the world and wooed by the infinite peace and restfulness of the scene, feels like falling down and praying that 'this fever called living may be conquered at last!' Really, one could find a pleasure in fleeing the maddening crowd, and lying down to dreamless and endless sleep in that placid city."[49]

Here Mr. Grady is striving to give his impressions of the grandeur of the scene as he meditates upon the vastness of eternity and observes that:

"Here in this deep solitude, the eternal past salutes the eternal future—"

and how our human nature reacts to his suggestions of the

"dreamless and endless sleep in that placid city."

HIS LOVE OF NATURE

Mr. Grady excelled as a descriptive writer, and an eminent litterateur of his time gave as his reason for claiming this, that he loved nature and the great outdoor world. The following is the estimate of this eminent writer:

"With every power of vigorous health and uninjured manhood, with a love of all natural sights and sounds, a love so poetical that at times past, with gun in hand, but with no thought of murder in his heart, we have known him to watch with curious delight the furtive practices of the unsuspecting squirrel, or, again, under the blossoms of the apple-tree, lull himself with the drowsy humming of the bees, or stop to listen and laugh slyly at the querulous wrangling of the jay birds, or stand while the glimmering landscape faded to the sight, and, with quiet joy, take sweet draughts of pleasure from that most charming of all hours and prospects—a summer sunset in the Georgia country. It is not surprising, therefore, that his allu-

---

[49]Edit.: The Ride to the Sea.

sions to the goddess at whose shrine he worships should be made with rare and charming felicity."[228]

All through Mr. Grady's writings and speeches this love of nature is continually manifesting itself. He sees the beauty of nature from the swiftly moving train and takes occasion to say:

"Already we have swept out of the murky atmosphere that over-laps Atlanta into sunshine. The muddy streets are replaced by brown slopes and forests full of rustling leaves."[62]

The following excerpt culled from an editorial on "Where Shall We Spend the Summer?" is written in his characteristic style:

"Or that magic vale, erst, the home of the wild-eyed Indian maiden —sweet Nachooche. Or Tallulah, with its hundred of spray-falls, filling the air with a delicious freshness, and the ear with a lullaby softer than mother ever sang to a sleeping babe. Or further, we might find joy and repose in the shades of Yonah, that great mountain, rising fresh and splendid from a setting of brooks and groves, its sides spotted by never a dust-fleck, defiled by no man's hand— primeval and pure just as God fashioned it."[24]

Someone has said that next to the great ocean he loved the mountains. If we are to measure his love for the mountain scenery by the beauty of his descriptions we would readily assent to this statement. But one can agree with the writer who said this of him:

"His soul felt a vitality in all beauty."[229]

That he was instructed by Nature in a most wonderful way, is very evident from his frequent references to the sounds and sights in the great out-of-doors. What is true of literary artists in general is certainly true of Mr. Grady individually:

"There is a deep and beautiful significance in this fundamental instruction of human nature; not out of books, but at the breast of nature by the sublime tutorship of living."[230]

He lived very near nature because, as one has said of Shakespeare:

"He looked out upon the green fields of England, and in his soul every blossom was mated with a word, every blade of grass and leaf and brook and living thing was tallied with teeming symbols of his brain."[231]

[228]Hudgins, H. C. and Co.: Life and Labors of H. W. G., p. 44 (a).
[62]Edit.: On to Florida.
[24]Edit.: Where Shall We Spend the Summer?
[229]Hudgins, H. C. and Co.: Life and Labor of H. W. G., p. 18 (b).
[230]Mabie, H. W.: Short Studies in Lit., p. 10 (b).
[231]Rhodes, Chas. E.: Effective Expression (R. H. Bell), p. 53 (d).

What was true of Shakespeare in his native land was also true of Mr. Grady in America. No sights or sounds ever escaped his perception if within his range.

If we were to make a hasty summary of the different kinds of descriptive writings that characterize Mr. Grady's style we would possibly best sum them up thus: the type that calls forth the idea of form and appeals to the intellect, as illustrated in the description of the servant girl in surf-bathing;[64] this might be designated as the aesthetic description.[232] The second would be designated the subjective type[233] in which the personality of the writer is projected, as is illustrated in the description of the ejection of the poor family from their home.[16] And the last outstanding type would be the impressionistic[234d] which enumerates the qualities of the objects rather than the parts, and this type is illustrated by the description of the restful night.[67] Of course he used variations and combinations of these different types.

The principal element in his descriptions is the sound element.[235] The peculiar effect is obtained by the rhythm as well as by the pictorial qualities of the words. He used the other senses comparatively little. Possibly color comes next to sound. He referred to the beauty of the women of Virginia as "a rosy glory in their complexion."[1] He referred to water in the St. Johns river in Florida as being "of a smart lavender color" which "trims out yellow." When it is in repose it is "a translucent maroon," when ruffled it is "a bright amber."[42] He describes a poor woman as having "shallow-blue eyes."[30] Notwithstanding the fact that he appreciated the value of color in description, he never painted any glowing sunsets; he used it merely to suggest and by way of contrast. He more frequently made use of the senses of taste and smell in a humorous strain.[2] He spoke of "ham and eggs," "ye savory correlatives." And he spoke of a fellow passenger as one who did not smell like "Eau de Cologne." While Mr. Grady appealed to the sense of hearing more than to all the other senses, nevertheless he could use and did use the other senses in suggestive writings when the occasion demanded.

---

[64]Surf-Bathing.
[232]Albright, Evelyn M.: Descriptive Writing, p. 5 (c).
[233]*Ibid.*, p. 5 (c).
[16]Edit.: In a Hundred Years.
[234d]*Ibid.*, p. 5 (d).
[67]Edit.: One Day's Fishing.
[235]*Ibid.*, p. 16 (c).
[1]Edit.: A Piquant Letter from the Univ. of Va.
[42]Editorial: Fair Florida.
[30]Lecture: A Patch Work Palace.
[2]Editorial: Marietta Fair.

Mr. Grady did not use description for its own sake; he used it in exposition, argumentation and narration to add interest, vividness, and force.[236]   Miss Evelyn Albright remarks that narration cannot be entirely lifelike without occasional recourse to description.[237]   Mr. Grady's journalistic writing prepared him for the masterful use of description in his famous speeches.[238]   There he used it as an argumentative device.   He used it for evidence and at the same time he used it for persuasion.   We are convinced by evidence which appeals to the intellect, but we act because our emotions are stirred.[239]   In the years that immediately followed the War of Rebellion the nation as well as the Southern states had become accustomed to react to emotional appeals.   The man and the moment, so to speak, met in Henry W. Grady.   It took the emotional appeal to catch the ear of the people.   Mr. Grady could make the emotional appeal by means of his descriptive power, and he used it for evidence as well as for persuasion for the sake of righteousness and universal peace.[26]   As Dr. J. W. Lee said, he might have succeeded in any of the fine arts, but being born in the South he became an editor and an orator.   Was he not truly the product of the age?[240]

His Poetic Nature

When we speak of Mr. Grady's poetic nature we do not necessarily mean that his thoughts were cast in poetic form, although he did use poetic phraseology often in his passages.   But we rather mean that the spirit of his writings was often poetic.

"There is no piece of literature," says Sherman, "properly so called, that is not the outcome of a purpose either to disseminate truth or impart enjoyment. . . . All literature is, therefore, in an important sense sentiment-literature, and is itself a record of what men have felt."[241]

Mr. Grady felt deeply and all of his writings were tinged more or less by deep feelings, and since he felt deeply he could touch the tender cords in the hearts of his readers. His poetic passages more often appealed to the sense of the beautiful.   What is more poetic than this?

"There is a sunrise, and a lark's song and an opening

[236]Albright, Evelyn M.: Descriptive Writing, p. 7.
[237]Albright, Evelyn M.: Descriptive Writing, p. 4 (a).
[238]H. W. Grady: Oration, "New South."
[239]Baker and Huntington: Argumentation (Prin.) Revised, pp. 9 (a) 10 (a).
[26]Edit.: A Platform of Peace and Good Will.
[240]Painter, F. V. N.: Elementary Guide to Lit. Crit., p. 8 (a) (b).
[241]Sherman, L. A.: Analytics of Lit., p. 354 (c).

daisy to every night."[16]   But in the next sentence he paints such a pathetic figure in contrast to the poetic beginning. "We saw a man today whose life was a failure." In the following quotation he is referring to "something a trifle spirituous," and by means of bright sparkling words which have a poetic tinge he produces the desired effect:

"We do not mean to suggest the drinking of that sharp and fiercer whisky which nips the nerves and twists them in its merciless fingers, sets the blood on fire and blears the eyes! Not at all. Rather that better article, drawn by deft machinery from the russet apple! —the liquid sunniness of a whole summer's shining, as it were, given up by the fruit as the swan pours out her dying song! This elixir, over which centuries have smacked their raptured lips, subjected into sugar, mellowed into marriage with fumy egg-foam, and spiced into nog; this is what we mean! O, nog! thou creamy golden joy! robbed of all the fierceness of intoxication, gently insinuating thy delicious aroma even into the elusive marrow of the bones; warming up, enfragranting, mellowing the whole corpus from top into toe, sending the rose into the lips, dimples into the cheeks, lazy sparkles into the eyes, and putting Christmas fairies to painting sunset pictures upon the summit of the enchanted nose."[21]

He never tires of giving poetic pictures of nature.   In answering the question, "Where shall we spend the summer?" he paints this beautiful landscape:

"There is Catoosa, with its matchless scenery, its silvery stream and grand old groves, where the jealous leaves, so green and cool, let in just enough of the sun's golden fretwork to enliven the scene, sweeter than a painted landscape."[24]

In his lecture on "A Patch Work Palace" he draws still another poetical picture of nature:

"One day in the spring time, when the uprising sap ran through every fiber of the forest, and made the trees as drunk as lords—when the birds were full-throated and the air was woven thick with their songs of love and praise—when the brooks kissed their uttermost banks, and the earth gave birth to flowers, and all nature was elastic and alert, and thrilled to the core with ecstasy of the sun's new courtship—a divine passion fell like a spark into Mr. Mortimer Pitt's heart. How it broke through the hideous crust of poverty that cased the man about, I do not know ought but that God put it there in his own sweet way."[30]

Professor L. A. Sherman in his "Analytics of Literature" makes this observation:

"Thus the essential difference between prose and poetry lies clearly beyond form, within the spirit, and can scarcely be categorically declared. When the ego may give itself wholly to delight, its literary diversions will be poetry."[242]

---

[16]Edit.: In a Hundred Years.
[21]Edit.: A Fat and Gentle Day.
[24]Edit.: Where Shall We Spend the Summer?
[30]Edit.: Lecture on "A Patch Work Palace."
[242]Sherman, L. A.: Analytics of Lit., pp. 363 (d), 363 (a).

So it is with Mr. Grady; he often, in the most common-place subjects, intersperses his writings with passages containing poetic flights, and what seems so strange these passages never leave any feeling other than their appropriateness. It is his poetic instinct that sees the eternal fitness of things and can throw them together carelessly without ever violating our sense of coherence.

While Mr. Grady does not call to his aid the ordinary forms of poetry properly arranged, he does use certain words and phraseology that poets use. For instance, in the editorial[16] quoted above we see the "sunrise" and the "opening daisy" and hear the "lark's song." All these phrases and words are suggestive of delights. In the editorial[21] quoted from above we have such poetic phrases as "drawn from the russet apple," "the liquid sunniness of a whole summer's shining," and "as the swan pours out her dying song." Later on we find these beautiful series of phrases: "sending the rose into the lips," "dimples into the cheeks," and "lazy sparkles into the eyes." In the same passage he reverts to "address" as a figure of speech: "O, nog! thou creamy golden joy!," etc., and thus he gives vividness to his editorial. We find in the passage[24] quoted above many adjectives used poetically, thus: "matchless scenery," "silver stream and grand old groves," "jealous leaves, so green and cool," "the sun's golden fretwork," and "painted landscape." And finally in the editorial[30] quoted from above these words lend a poetical setting to the passage: "uprising sap," "full-throated" "thick with their songs of love and praise," "gave birth to flowers," "nature, elastic and alert, and thrilled to the core," "the sun's new courtship," "a divine passion."

If the reader is interested in following up Mr. Grady's poetic spirit in later life, which is not being studied here, he may find it more nearly perfected in his speech before his fraternity in the University of Virginia, which Charles A. Dana called a prose poem.[243] Also his editorial, "A Perfect Christmas Day," which he wrote just one year before his death has been paraphrased into a poem.[244]

His Humor and Pathos

"His vein was incessant as a humorist. His presence was a light everywhere it came. Like the gushing character of his heart, it was

---

[16]Edit.: In a Hundred Years.
[21]Edit.: A Fat and Gentle Day.
[24]Edit.: Where Shall We Spend the Summer?
[30]Lecture: A Patch Work Palace.
[243]Hudgins, H. C. and Co.: H. W. G.—Life and Labors of, p. 60 (b).
[244]Harris, J. C.: Life, Writings, and Speeches of H. W. G.

constant and inexhaustible. Its range, under the guide of the most
rigid taste, extended from the reckless banter of the wayside—the
pun, the quirk, the brilliant repartee—to the polished jewel of wit
that would adorn the coronal of a queen of society. He was the
Rabelais of America."[245]

This is what a personal acquaintance of Mr. Grady
said about him. But one has only to read his editorials to
appreciate his rich humor. It is not of the explosive kind
but it is that kind that gradually insinuates itself into one's
very being.

"Wit is of the head, humor of the heart. Reflective writers, such
as George Eliot and Mr. Meredith, are more often witty than humorous. Analytical minds turn naturally to wit, impressionistic minds
to humor," says Shuman.[246]

Mr. Grady had an impressionistic mind. In fact, his
style was more impressionistic than otherwise. He made
one feel with him, and inevitably one laughs with him.
Mr. Grady says himself that one purpose of his writing is
to entertain his readers.[59]

"Entertainment as an end is concerned with amusement. It arouses
pleasant feelings, interests, mildly delights or produces hearty laughter."[247]

In the very first contribution to the *Atanta Constitution,* as a young man, one can find his characteristic humor.
This letter was written upon the occasion of the decoration
of the soldiers' graves. "Squeaky," the orator of the occasion, was making his address when it began raining and
Mr. Grady describes what took place as follows:

"Squeaky had to suspend—the ladies became 'frightened,' you
know—umbrellas were sought for and found—cloaks were jerked on,
dresses looped up, ankles began to flash delightfully, and the whole
thing grew exciting. Your correspondent having secured an umbrella,
made advances to a delicious little bunch of curls, cloaks, and calico,
that stood close by trembling prettily. The arrangement was consummated—curls cuddled up affectionately under our arm, and—this is
the way they dressed the soldiers' graves at the University of Virginia."[1]

And just a few months later he gives us a humorous
description of a Georgia fair and his predicament at the
fair:

"This fair, sir, is a lineal descendant of that one at which poor
Moses, the Vicar's son, was emparadised out of his three years' earnings, and I confidently assent that it is a most hopeful scion of so

[245]Hudgins, H. C. and Co.: *Op. cit.,* p. 16.
[246]Shuman, E. L.: How to Judge a Book, p. 75 (c).
[59]Edit.: Carping Critics.
[247]Phillips, Arthur E.: Effective Speaking, p. 23 (a).
[1]Edit.: A Piquant Letter Written at Univ. of Va.

hopeful stock. When a pinched up and ugly storekeeper asks you to buy an article, you can easily refuse him; but when a pair of deep blue eyes pleadingly glances into your face, when rosy-tipped fingers piquantly push an article at you, and an arch, silvery voice coquettishly begs you 'to buy'—and then, sir, I'll swear, you must buy even this, the article in question, be—a little Noah's ark, filled with very square animals."[3]

And after he has spent all of his money and evening comes he describes himself as follows:

"We can imagine nothing more delightful than promenading through this beautiful park with a fine lady on your arm—no money in your pocket to distract her attention from your discourse—the band throwing out most melodious love notes—to catch the flash of the bright eyes, as they peep shyly at you, or the glitter of the pearly teeth as they laugh love at your left shoulder; and not enough light to let any one see what you are saying—just privacy enough to stir up the passion in you, and just publicity enough to prevent your getting spoony; in short, just joy enough to fill you with glorious happiness, and not enough to dissolve you in ecstasy. Plump perfection! Come up and try it."[3]

If we jump down some four or five years later in his journalistic career we find Mr. Grady replying to the crematists of his time in an editorial entitled, "Shall We Bury or Burn?" in which he calls attention to Sir Henry Thomson's economic theory concerning our ashes and humorously agrees with him. Who else could get so much humor out of considering such a subject? It is ridicule rather of the humorous than of the sarcastic type. This is the way he says it:

"What, for instance, would give a tone and richness to a bed of garlic like bespreading it with the ashes of a dozen or so pronounced Italians? Where could flowers be found equal in brilliancy of color, sweetness of perfume, and gracefulness of carriage, to those springing in sweet resurrection from the remains of a well-ordered belle? From what could come a fairer crop of 'beats' than the ashes of a score of loafers captured in the free lunch saloons or slain upon the curb-stones? Who doubts but that the essence of an old smoker would give additional greenness to the nicotinous plant? or that the remains of a toper would give renewed pungency to the inspiring mint?"[22]

While Mr. Grady was editor of the *Atlanta Herald,* November, 1875, he wrote an editorial calling the attention of the people to the neglect of the Georgia press. The reports of what he called "The Okeefenokee Expedition" of the staff of the *Atlanta Constitution*—evidently a hunting trip—had been ignored. In commenting upon this trip he says:

"There is only one thing lacking in the report of this wonderful expedition, and that is the failure on its part to meet any wild ani-

[3]Edit.: Marietta Fair.
[22]Edit.: Shall We Burn or Bury?

mals. This lack is supplied, as best as it can be, by frequent references
to the trace of wild beasts. The public blood is frozen at frequent
intervals with such expressions as this, 'In the morning we went out
to where we heard the noise, and found where an American panther
had left his footprints.'   And if an American panther had passed that
way the next day, he would doubtless have found where an American
exploring expedition 'had left its footprints.'   We are promised 'a
picture of the scene from Mr. Hyde.'   We shall expect the foreground
of this picture to be two sets of footprints leading in opposite directions; the footprints of an American panther, and the footprints of
an American expedition—'led by Col. C. . .' "[34]

It was in the early part of the year 1880 that we find
Mr. Grady reminiscing from the editorial room of the *Atlanta Constitution* as he beheld the workmen razing the
building in which was formerly housed the *Atlanta Herald,*
the paper he once owned. He recounts his many experiences and names one by one his employes of former days.
But the most serious things, at least when they were hap-
pening, he pictures with humorous touches. This will illustrate his retrospect:

"It was in that building too that we prepared to fight all the
duels, that were afterwards not fought. Those were awful times!
The consultations we did have—the dueling pistols we did borrow—
the volumes of the code we did thumb, and the number of solemn
suppers we did eat, having them served from the restaurant because
we did not dare venture on the streets for fear of arrest.   It's a
wonder to me that we did not slaughter several men.   There is not
a field of honor on the borders of this state, or any other state for
that matter, that we did not intend at some time or other to dye
with the life blood of some one of our enemies.   We enjoyed them
just as much as if they had come to the most bloody termination, but
I can't help wishing that we had shot at somebody and missed him, or
that somebody had shot at us and missed—missed by a big margin."[52]

Few men could depict the foibles of mankind more
vividly than could this genius. Nor did his own escape
his description. In fact, great humorists very often depict
their own foibles. Foibles may be improved upon and men
will become stronger and over-ride such shortcomings, but
there are frailties in human nature over which mankind
seems unable to ride, and the contemplation of these frailties, as poor helpless beings are overcome by them, arouses
our sympathies. There is but a step between our foibles and
our frailties; likewise, there is but a step between laughter
and tears. Mr. Grady followed literally the Bible injunction, "Laugh with those that laugh, and weep with those
that weep."   In the early part of his editorial "On to Florida," Mr. Grady depicts the foibles of some of Georgia's
great men, such as United States Senator Ben Hill, and we

[34]Edit.: The Okeefenokee Swamp Expedition.
[52]Edit.: Leveled Landmarks.

laugh with him, but in the latter part of this same editorial he draws a very pathetic picture. He illustrates fully that he is a master of pathos in this description:

"Right across the car from me is one of the most touching figures in the car. A young woman of perhaps thirty years—with plain resolute face—alone. She wears that indescribable air of reserve and sadness that invest women who have lived their lives apart. She is dressed plainly and her well-worn habit tells of privation and struggle. She is probably a teacher, who, walking to and from her work in some bleak New England village, thinly clad and illy protected, the winds and storms of winter whipped into her slender form the seeds of disease. She has remained at her post too long—so long that death has already set its seal on her cheeks, and looks gaunt and inexorable out of her great clear eyes. It was probably poverty that kept her there—probably demands of a mother or a sister upon her small resources pinched them so that they pinned her to her martyrdom. And now at last, on the savings of many years, the price of her life, she comes to find balm and healing in the South. There is despair in her face, but there is no trouble there. Her great eyes are cloudless—her thin lips are peacefully closed—her brow is calm, and there is gentle resignation in every feature. Perhaps she looks with little regret to the end of life that has been hard and laborious and lonely and feels that God will give her at last the rest and peace so long denied her."[62]

Mr. Grady never selected his moods. His feelings are not forced. He saw the situation and his great heart responded sympathetically, whether with humor or pathos. He was true to nature and responded naturally. It was L. A. Sherman who said:

"Pathos of nature is always in order."[248]

HIS PERSONALITY

There is a force in every writer, whatever his writing may be, that is called personality. It is indefinable but it may be illustrated. There are just as many personalities as there are individuals in the world, hence an attempt at a definition would be futile. Everyone knows that there is something in each individual that differentiates him from every other individual. That intangible something is what we mean to refer to in this chapter. Mr. Shuman discusses it thus:

"Thus every work of art becomes a representation of an object or objects plus the artist's personality,—his temperament, his intellectual force, his culture, his religion, his philosophy, his love of his fellowmen, his attitude toward the things that are evil and the things that are lovely and of good report. All these elements of personality, taken together, determine a man's view of life,—deter-

[62]Edit.: On to Florida.
[248]Sherman, L. A.: Analytics of Lit., p. 351 (b).

mine the color of the world as seen through his eyes,—and this color will inevitably affect his written and spoken utterances."[249]

And Mr. Painter has this to say:

"Every literary work reveals, to a greater or less degree, the personality of the author. Every literary production may be regarded as the fruitage of the writer's spirit; and there is good authority for saying that 'men do not gather grapes of thorns or figs of thistles.' A book exhibits not only the attainments, culture, and literary art of the writer but also his intellectual force, emotional nature, and moral character. Wide attainments are revealed in the breadth of view and in the mastery of large resources. Culture is exhibited in general delicacy of thought, feeling, and expression. Literary art is shown in the choice of words and in their arrangement in the sentences, and paragraphs. The artistic sense, without which a finished excellence is not attainable, reveals itself in the proportion, symmetry, and completeness of a work."[250]

And Mr. Mabie also says in this connection that,

"So dependent upon personality, so bound up and identified with it, is art, that in literature a man's work approaches the very highest standard in the degree in which it expresses his personality."[251]

We quote from Shuman again,

" 'Literature,' says Pater, 'is the representation of fact connected with the soul.' An author's mode of presenting such facts will be affected by his attitude toward nature, man, and God."[252]

To a very great degree Mr. Grady's writings are colored by his personality. His broad sympathy for mankind is seen all through his writings; his keen sense of justice stands forth at all times; his love of nature and reverence for God is written in every page; his pervasive humor runs through almost every article written; his culture is his second nature; and his writings touching upon the great issues are all ethical. No people are too insignificant to attract his attention. For instance, turn to his editorial, "In a Hundred Years,"[16] and see how sympathetically he portrays this wretched family, and especially the father of this family:

"He had fought gamely, but the odds were piled against him, and cruel circumstances had dragged him to the dust. So there he lay deserted by friends, bereft of fortune—a panting, gasping, fainting man."[16]

Or look at the sympathetic picture of Mr. Mortimer Pitts in his lecture on "A Patch Work Palace."[30]

[249]Shuman, E. L.: How to Judge a Book, pp. 124 (d), 125 (a).
[250]Painter, F. V. N.: El. Guide to Lit. Crit., p. 19 (a) (b) (c).
[251]Mabie, H. W.: Short Studies in Lit. Crit., p. 36 (c).
[252]Shuman, E. L.: How to Judge a Book, p. 126 (d).
[16]Edit.: In a Hundred Years.
[30]Lecture: A Patch Work Palace.

"After a patient study of the responsibility that the statement carries, I do not hesitate to say that he was the poorest man that ever existed. He lived literally 'from hand to mouth.' His breakfast was a crust; his dinner, a question; his supper, a regret. His earthly wealth, beyond the rags that covered him, was—a cow, that I believe gave both butter-milk and sweet-milk—a dog, that gave neither—and a hand-cart in which he wheeled his wares about."

Mr. Grady tells of this man's love for his wife and children—how he, when he could give them no other comfort, kissed and caressed them. And finally at the last he pictures this poor man in his efforts to build for himself and family a home and makes this comparison:

"Mr. Pitts wanted a home. A man named Napoleon once wanted Universal Empire—Mr. Pitts was vastly the more daring dreamer of the two."

Now turn to his editorial on "John H. Inman."[55] Here Mr. Grady tells how a young man, John H. Inman, came out of the war between the States with less than a hundred dollars in his pocket, and how by the time he reached 36 years of age he had amassed a fortune. In the last paragraph of this editorial Mr. Grady makes this statement:

"I should like to strike a balance between the lives of John Inman, the merchant, and some one of our eminent latter day statesmen, when both are dead, and see which had done most and better work."

Mr. Grady sympathized not only with the poor and the rich, but he sympathized with the small and the great. In his editorial, "The Little Ones and Their Stockings," one can see him entering fully into the Christmas spirit with the children as he pens these words:

"God bless the children all and fill their stockings full!"[20]

One can see with what philosophy he discusses the problems of the great, and how sympathetically he discusses with Senator Ben Hill of Georgia his problems upon entering the United States Senate in 1877. If one turns to Mr. Grady's editorial, "Comment on Senator Benj. H. Hill,"[43] he will find this quotation:

"I have little doubt that Mr. Hill will find the true way, and imbed his name and fame in the very heart of the time in which he lives. He will remember that the leadership he acquired in the Confederate senate was won by the readiness and ability with which he improved a hundred opportunities which came unsolicited to his hands, and will appreciate the fact that he must now make his opportunity, as well as learn how to improve it."

[55]Edit.: John H. Inman.
[20]Edit.: The Little Ones and Their Stockings.
[43]Edit.: Comment on Senator Benj. H. Hill.

We all do honor to the man who has such broad sympathies and such a grasp of human nature.

Mr. Grady's philosophy was optimistic, and is best seen in his religious faith. Turn again to his editorial, "In a Hundred Years," and read the last paragraph and you will see that he predicts happiness in the great beyond for the poor man who has made a failure in this life and somehow he thinks the next world will compensate for our lack of happiness in this. This is what he says:

"And he will go on, and on through many a dismal day, and through many a struggle, thinking that it will all be right in a hundred years. And his eyes will grow brighter, and his blood will flush and die in the pale cheeks oftener, and the pinched features grow thinner, and the veil of flesh more threadbare, till he drops it altogether, and passing over the river lays him down on the golden banks and is baptized in immortal sunshine. And then, thank God, at last his 'hundred years are out' and it's 'all right' with him."[16]

He expresses the same thought again in his editorial, "On to Florida," and in the last paragraph of this rather pathetic description of some tubercular victims. He is contrasting the lives of a poor girl and a rich man. The one has had a hard life and the other has lived in affluence. His religious faith and philosophy are very clearly seen in this:

"Perhaps she looks with little regret to the end of life that has been hard and laborious and lonely and feels that God will give her at last the rest and peace so long denied her. Just beyond her there is a strong man chafing uneasily in the thralls of disease. His face is knotted with suffering and dread. His wealth, his strength, his resources—none of these give him the peace and content that has come to this frail, slender girl. Truly, there is no power like the consciousness of a life well spent, a duty fully performed, a mission accomplished, a martyrdom endured. To the girl across the way, death is but a falling to sleep—sweet, dreamless rest after a long and weary work."[62]

In his editorial on "Self-Made Men" he holds out to the young men of Georgia examples of men who have started this life with only their natural endowments and a will to succeed, and have finally won success. He tells

"Of men that have wrought their lives with their own hands—of whose brain and brawn their homes have been builded—men who, big-hearted and brave, with cool heads and steady nerves have marched to the front rank."[53]

Mr. Grady relates interestingly the story of hardships of these men who have forged their way to the front: Ex-

[16]Edit.: In a Hundred Years.
[62]Edit.: On to Florida.
[53]Edit.: Self-Made Men.

Governor Joe Brown, as a boy, hauled wood to the mountain town of Dahlonega: Milt. Smith left the ringing anvil to become governor of his state; Alexander Stephens repaid a charity society for his education with a noble life. Mr. Grady relates the incidents in the lives of many successful men, who started at the foot of the ladder. This old world to him was a good place in which to live and if one did not succeed in gaining a part of this world's riches he could succeed, as did the poor consumptive girl, in living a noble life of service, and receive the reward of the righteous in the life eternal. Misfortune to Mr. Grady was but a blessing in disguise. The last sentence is quoted from his editorial on "Self-Made Men," in which he gives his beautiful optimism concerning the loss of his own fortune:

"And to those named, and hundreds just as worthy who are unnamed—the self-made men of Atlanta—this hasty tribute is tendered by one who, starting life ready-made, speedily unmade himself and is now hopefully rambling along the road of regeneration."[53]

Had Mr. Grady expressed himself definitely, doubtless he would have said there is more of happiness, more of good, if not now there will be, than there is of misery and evil. His outlook upon the world was that of one who saw rainbows, and heard the music of the spheres. He could not be anything other than an optimist.

Mr. Grady thought of the material things as the embodiment of the spiritual rather than as something sordid to be grasped and held for their fleeting worth. The landscape to him was a thing of beauty; the eternal mountains furnished him a theme for meditation rather than a reservoir for the gold of the ages. One can all but see the sorrow on his face as he closes his description of the natural scenery in his editorial on "Gold in Georgia,"[63] in which he expresses this note of sadness:

"I hear, even now, the ceaseless pulse of the mills, the sudden roar of the torrent, the quickening ring of the machinery, and the pretty laugh and prattle of the miners, as the assault closes in on the everlasting hills. I see their great bodies gashed and pierced, their verdure stripped away piecemeal, their elixir stolen from their veins, their hearts rifted and torn. And I see the depths where silence has reigned since men first found voice, and with eager hands rifling the newly-opened veins of the slow-gathering wealth of the ages! And all for
    "'Gold! Gold! Gold! Gold!
    Bright and yellow—hard and cold.'"

[53]Edit.: Self-Made Men.
[63]Edit.: Gold in Georgia.

His idealization or spiritualization is also seen in his editorial on "Ben Hill Dead."[65] He likens Ben Hill's death to a beautiful sunset. Few figures of speech can be much more beautiful than this:

"I would dishonor the emotion that fills my heart in this sad hour if I attempted any study of the life that has just closed so solemnly or any analysis of a character that is idolized by universal grief. I shall write as one who loved him living and who mourns him dead, and as I look over the years through which he has passed and in which I knew him so well, I feel as one who has seen the sun move down the western sky, and after it has gone, stands gazing on the banks of clouds still luminous with its glory, and finds that it lives in the quivering afterglow, even after it has passed into the infinite."

Summary

No one can read Mr. Grady's editorials and not be impressed with the sincerity of the man. He spoke from his heart. There was no reservation or evasion whatsoever when he spoke. The beautiful descriptions he wrote could come, not from a man trying to produce fine writings, but only from a soul which was itself the very counterpart of the beauty it was pouring forth. Mr. Grady was in and a part of what he was writing about. Mr. Shuman says that:

"Imagination at its best must have the *glow, the fire,* the *spontaneity* that comes only through the fusing of materials of life in the furnace of the author's own earnest and sympathetic emotions. Only by first feeling the truth in his own heart can he conceive the beautiful imaginative forms that will convey the truth to our hearts."[253]

Turn to whatever editorial you please, if his writing is witty or humorous you perceive only Mr. Grady. If it is persuasion, it is Mr. Grady's emotions that move you; if it is logic, it is only the keen intellect of Mr. Grady that is pouring out its logical conclusions.

He had a purpose in writing. He said what he thought today against men and measures if he had to confess his error later. This one incident will show how he confessed his error. In "A Card"[17] written while he was part owner of the *Herald* he attacked Ex-Governor Joe Brown rather bitterly. He showed a wonderful power in the use of argument and sarcasm. But in an editorial some six or seven years later entitled "Leveled Landmarks" he has this to say concerning the attack upon Ex-Governor Brown:

"It was in that building that we tackled Joe Brown, and received encouragement in our fight against him from people who requested

---

[65]Edit.: Ben Hill Dead.
[253]Shuman, E. L.: How to Judge a Book, p. 83.
[17]Edit.: A Card.

that we should not let him know that they had encouraged us. I never knew exactly what we were fighting him for—and I do not think I exactly understood the fight, though I went into it heartily, until he smashed the paper out of existence, and we had time to reflect over it."[52]

Possibly the one purpose above all purposes of Mr. Grady's writing was to repair the breach that was made between the North and South during the Civil War. Later in life than the period this chapter has to deal with Mr. Grady said he had been criticized for his stand in this connection. Many times during his early writings Mr. Grady writes on the solution of the negro question and discusses the problem in a most sincere and honest way. He acknowledged very frankly the wrong of the slavery system and received criticism from some of the Southern people. In his editorial on "The New Solution of the Negro Question," written in 1875, he begged earnestly for an adjustment of the differences between the negroes and the whites. This he had to say to the Northern people:

"Why cannot these differences pass away, and this miserable struggle end forever? There is only one thing to prevent. The Northern people. And they cannot prevent it if they will only take a piece of advice that we can utter in two words. That is, 'Hands off.' "[27]

His sincerity of purpose was generally recognized; this is the best characterization of him that has been written:

"The sombre-winged vultures of hate, which had preyed on the remains of the lost cause, took flight at his approach, and the snow-breasted doves of peace lovingly nestled above the chasm in their stead."[254]

[52]Edit.: Leveled Landmarks.
[27]Edit.: The New Solution of the Negro Question.
[254]Hudgins, H. C. and Co.: Life and Labors of H. W. G., p. 13.

CHAPTER II

HENRY W. GRADY AS AN EDITOR

Possibly one of the greatest single forces in the rehabilitation of the South after the Civil War was the editorial pen of Henry W. Grady. His fame was the result of his great orations, but the greatest services he rendered to his people were the result of the high ideals of his life and the timely advice he gave them through his writings as a newspaper editor. The greatest need of the South and the nation after the Civil War was men who had ideals worthy to be followed, and who continually held them up before the people through a shining and forceful personality. It was Mr. Sherman who said:

"It is the elevation of sentiment that advances civilization."[255]

Mr. Grady not only presented beautiful and worthy sentiments, but he gave timely and wholesome advice to his people through his editorial pen. A contemporary of Mr. Grady had this to say about his journalistic career:

"It was no mere blind or idle chance which led him to adopt journalism as his life's profession. It was rather a decree of the same mysterious power which builds an Imperial highway among the stars. His wonderful vocabulary, his brilliant imagination, his invincible optimism, his infinite and fertile resources of mind all tended to impel him toward the journalistic pen. And in no other sphere of activity could he have rendered more effective service to the cause of Southern rehabilitation."[256]

It was Matthew Arnold who said that before there can be any great work produced there must be the meeting of two forces, "the power of the man and the power of the moment."[257] In this trying time of rehabilitation of the South Mr. Grady came forth with the "power of the man" to meet the challenge of the "power of the moment." He brought to this challenge the best elements of the "Old South" and the vision of a more glorious South. He had convictions and the courage of his convictions. In his early writings he was impetuous at times, but upon the whole he was sane.

HISTORICAL SETTING

In the evaluation of Mr. Grady as a journalist one must take into consideration the development of journalism in

---

[255]Sherman, L. A.: Analytics of Literature, p. 108.
[256]Knight, L. L.: Famous Georgians, Reminiscences of, p. 425.
[257]Arnold, Matthew: Essays in Criticism, p. 4.

America. Newspapers up to about 1850 were not what the name suggests, but they were for the most part "views-papers." The editors gave their views upon politics and advised their constituents how to vote. Mr. Neal says:

"Samuel Sullivan Cox, of the *Ohio Statesman,* was the first editor (May 19, 1853) to break away from the hampering traditions."[258]

He is referring to what he calls "human interest edi-torials" which he says have an "emotional appeal and ex-pect an emotional response." Another writer dates the modern newspaper from the firing upon Fort Sumter.[259] During the war the people back at home were not interested in the views of the editors but they were interested in the news from the front. After the war the reader still ex-pected news and the editor as a political spokesman found it necessary to adjust himself to the new situation. Mr. Grady began writing in 1869 just when this readjustment was taking place. The editors were gradually changing from dictators, and leaning rather to leadership. The edi-torial page became more and more a type of the open forum[259a] where the news and issues of the day were dis-cussed not so much in the vindictive spirit of former days but more in the spirit of friendliness. If one reads the editorials of the early seventies he will wonder how much worse the situation was in pre-war times. But reforms in the newspaper world, as in everything else, comes slowly. Friendliness did not always exist between the editors of rival papers in the seventies, but duels became less frequent, because, as one writer puts it, everybody had had their fill of fighting in the sixties.[260] But editors frequently en-gaged in "war of words." Charges and counter charges of dishonesty in the editorial management were very common. Mr. Grady himself, in 1869, while on the "Press Excur-sion"[10] accused an editor of selling out his editorial influence to Governor Bullock, the Carpet-bagger. Flint in speaking of the venality of the newspapers has this to say concern-ing their selling out:

"The charge that newspapers sell their influence to the highest bidder is seldom heard today, whereas fifty years ago it was a favorite criticism."[261]

In another statement Flint says:

---

[258]Neal, Robt. W.: Editorials and Editorial Writers, p. 142.
[259]Shuman, E. L.: Practical Journalism, p. 2.
[259a]Flint, L. N.: Conscience of Newspaper, p. 278.
[260]See note 320.
[10]Press Excursion.
[261]Flint, L. N.: The Conscience of the Newspaper, p. 294.

"That competing newspapers could live in peace, side by side, was almost an absurd idea in old-fashioned journalism."[262]

This was the period when a certain group of economists preached what they called the law of competition. The newspapers came in for their share of the practices. In 1873, Mr. Grady bought an interest in the *Atlanta Herald* which was competing with the *Atlanta Constitution* at that time. One of the most exciting episodes in Southern journalism took place shortly afterward.[263] Mr. Grady hired a locomotive engine in order that he might get the issues of his paper into Macon earlier than the *Constitution*. This episode appealed to Mr. Grady's emotional nature. To him it was more in the spirit of a contest, such as he had known in his school days; it did not appeal to his spirit of ill-will for he had none. But in all this rather dark setting Mr. Grady's journalistic career has to its account nothing but praise. Mr. Bleyer, writing of newspaper practices of more recent times, characterizes it thus:

"The 'Searchlight' journalism is thus giving way to 'Sunlight' journalism. 'Playing up' instead of 'down'."[263]

It is safe to say that Mr. Grady was on the side of those who started the "Sunlight Journalism," the "playing up" of his people and putting the optimistic spirit into journalism.

Here are his own words:

"I am proud to be able to say that in the ten years of my active service, I have never done any man a wilful injustice. It has been my pleasure to help rather than retard any fellow-journalist struggling side by side with me along a road that is tedious enough even when enlivened by courtesy and sympathy; to entertain my readers rather than gratify spleen or cultivate malice—to help build up our city and state and country, rather than tear down even the humblest character or hinder the slightest progress."[59]

One has only to read his editorials wherever found to verify this statement from his own pen.

A MAN OF CONVICTIONS

Mr. Grady was not sentimental; he had convictions tempered by justice. He acted upon convictions—not sentiments.[263a] While he was editor of one of the papers in Rome, Georgia, in 1869, the owner objected to his printing an editorial in which he arraigned severely the officials of the city government. Mr. Grady went across to the other paper and

[262]Flint, L. N.: The Conscience of the Newspaper, p. 290.
[263]Bleyer, W. G.: The Profession of Journalism, Introductory.
[59]Editorial: Carping Critics.
[263a]Hudgins, H. C. and Co.: Life and Labors of H. W. G., p. 41.

bought it, and to the surprise of the owner of the first paper the objectionable editorial occupied a conspicuous place on the editorial page next morning, and "Henry W. Grady" was flying at the masthead as editor.[264]   His convictions and ideals were of more value to him than his money.   In fact, Dr. J. W. Lee says:

"Not for money did he write, not for money did he care, but through writing would he make his life contribute to human weal. The newspaper became his brush and letters became his pigment. Through these he determined to make known what he felt for men, and what he wished for men."[265]

On September 4, 1869, Mr. Grady contributed a communication as correspondent of the *Atlanta Constitution* on the "Press Excursion," in which he expresses his opinions as follows:

"We are opposed to the motion to thank Governor Bullock from many reasons.   First the motion itself says, 'We wish to ignore all political matter whatever, etc.'   Well if you ignore politics altogether, Governor Bullock is thereby drawn from his political position, dwindles into the condition of a private citizen, and as such, deserves the thanks of nobody.   Secondly, because the people of the state are beginning to look upon the Excursion with suspicion, and this official homage to Governor Bullock will justly increase the suspicion. Thirdly, because we are opposed to truckling to a tyrant, or licking the hand that lashes us—and lastly, because Governor Bullock knew he was looked upon as an interloper by most of the press, from the very first; hence, should have had the good taste to have withdrawn, and because he did wrong and usurped Col. Hulbert's position and placed the press in a false position. . ."[9]

As an individual Mr. Grady was expressing his opinion of the Reconstruction governor of his state.   And on September 9, in answering a communication directed to him in the *Intelligencer,* a Georgia paper, he refuses to recant the statement that—

"We believe that bribery was attempted on the Press Excursion."[9]

This is his direct reply to the *Intelligencer* upon the demand:

"As to the withdrawal of the insinuations, we of course will do no such thing.   We believe Governor Bullock accompanied the Excursion with the intention of bartering Executive patronage for the control, or partial control of the editorial columns of the Democratic newspapers.   This belief is founded upon an opinion of Governor Bullock's policy in this direction as evidenced heretofore, and upon a number of little circumstances that we noted while upon the excursion."[10]

[264]Harris, J. C.: H. W. G., His Life, Writings and Speeches, p. 24 (d).
[265]Lee, Dr. J. W.: H. W. G., Editor, Orator, Man, Arena, 2: 9-23, Je'90.
[9]Editorial: Press Excursion.
[10]Editorial: Press Excursion.

Though a boy, he did not hesitate to hurl into the teeth of the Chief Executive of the state the charge of attempting bribery.

Other papers might barter their honor for filthy lucre, but the *Herald* and its editors would suffer bankruptcy before they would yield their inalienable right to free speech so long as it did not infringe upon the rights of others. There was an incident in the history of the *Herald* that illustrates this fact very clearly. At one time when the *Herald* was in financial straits, General Toombs, having learned this, very generously proffered to lend the *Herald* money to meet its obligations. At first this was declined, but later the *Herald*, through Mr. Alston, one of its owners, accepted a loan from General Toombs. This is what Mr. Grady has to say about the loan:

"Col. A. of course declined such impulsive generosity, for fear that later deliberations might produce regret. Subsequently, when the paper was in temporary trouble, he wrote General Toombs, recounting his generous offer and requesting the loan of four or five thousand dollars, stating, at the same time, that as he (Gen. Toombs) was a public man, the paper might frequently be called on to differ with him."[25]

The loan was secured, and the *Herald* followed out its policy of free speech. Mr. Grady, in commenting upon the loan and General Toombs' attitude, makes this observation:

"It was unfortunate for our relations that on nearly every public question which arose, the *Herald* took grounds against General Toombs."[25]

Notwithstanding the fact that General Toombs "loaned the money like a prince and collected like a Shylock," the *Herald* continued to speak its thoughts whether it pleased or displeased. Nothing short of death ever put an end to the message Mr. Grady had in mind for the people of the South. He had a message to deliver and, like the "Ancient Mariner," he button-holed as many as he could, but to the others he sent a flaming message from his red-hot pen, nor could threat or bankruptcy put an end to his writing. As soon as he found the *Herald* in bankruptcy he turned to other papers for an outlet. In a short while he was offered a position on the *Atlanta Constitution,* the former rival of the *Herald.*[265a] But so noble were his ideals that even his rivals could not afford to hold against him the fact that he had been a part owner of a competing paper.

Mr. Grady had views and convictions not only concern-

---

[25]Editorial: Gen. Toombs and *The Herald.*
[265a]Harris, J. C.: H. W. G., His Life, Writings and Speeches, p. 33 (a).

ing his personal affairs and local conditions, but his sympathies extended to the limits of his country. He could point out the faults and shortcomings of those he wrote about, and he could also praise when he saw anything to praise. It often takes as much courage to praise a person, and even more, than it does to find fault with the most criminal element. General W. T. Sherman, of all the men in the United States in his day the most *persona non grata* to the Southern people, found sympathetic comment at Mr. Grady's hands, for truth and love were ruling elements in Mr. Grady's nature. On January 1, 1881, he attended a theater in New York City where he saw General Sherman occupying a box. He became interested in the "sternest and most grizzled of soldiers," and this is what he had to say:

"I went up to the Fifth Avenue the other night to see Mary Anderson—that divine girl with a slouching stride of a race horse, play The Countess in 'Lov'. I found her the same thoroughbred she always was—the best product of the blue grass region."

.   .   .   .

"But it was not concerning the charming actress I started to write, but a very different person. In the stage box on the left, watching every curve of the milk-white neck, every uplifting of the glistening arms and every tremor of the red lips, sat General W. T. Sherman, sternest and most grizzled of soldiers."

.   .   .   .

"After the play was over I called at the Fifth Avenue hotel and spent a pleasant half hour with General Sherman."

"I doubt if there was a more conscientious soldier in the Northern Army than General Sherman. There is no sentimentalism about him. To his notion war meant cruelty—it meant death—destruction—and the sooner this was realized the sooner there was a chance for peace."[56]

For a Southern gentleman to seek a conference with General Sherman at this time, to the majority of Southern people, was unthinkable, much less a sympathetic write-up of the conference. It took a courageous soul to do it. Mr. Grady knew that real peace between the two sections could come only through a sympathetic understanding of each other. If it required the raising of the white flag he could do it. And on this occasion, as well as many others, he dared to follow the better impulses of his heart. He knew we live best and most when we live in accordance with the emotions of love and friendship. Mr. Winchester put it this way:

"For life is determined by the emotions. Our motives are never found in the realm of truth; only when such truths have been passed through the feelings can they take hold upon conduct."[206]

---

[56]Editorial: A Direct Question.
[206]Winchester, C. T.: Some Prin. of Lit. Criticism, p. 246.

The base motives could not receive the coloring of his soul, for he never permitted them to pass to the sanctity of his soul. So great was his love and sympathy for mankind that only the higher motives of human nature were compatible with his spirit. He lived above the sordid things of this world; he lived in the realm of the beautiful and the spiritual.

HE UNDERSTOOD PEOPLE

One of the greatest assets Mr. Grady had was his knowledge of human nature. His genial disposition gave him a peculiar advantage in getting into the good graces of those with whom he came in contact. He was an excellent conversationalist. If a person wants to get people to talk to him he must be a good talker.[266a] Through this intimate contact with people he learned what they were thinking about. An editorial writer must project himself into the life and experiences of his readers if he would influence them.[266b] Joel Chandler Harris, in speaking of this characteristic of Mr. Grady, said that he was as great a talker as Carlyle, with this difference[266c]: "Carlyle proposed his subject, while Mr. Grady talked on whatever his listeners were interested in." He was interested in all classes of people and would talk as readily to one class as another. Mr. Grady believed, to be successful, an editor must put himself into his writing, and he did not believe the editor could stay in the editorial sanctum all the while and be a success. He had this to say about one of his partners of the *Herald:*

"I have often wondered why Abrams never succeeded in maintaining a great paper. The first reason was that he never had the proper backing from the counting-room. In the next place I think he put too much of the journalist and too little of the man in his paper. In small cities there must be provincial touches in the journals —concessions that the journalist must make to circumstances. There was none of this in Abram's work. He wrote and edited as if he were running the *London Times,* and the result was a perfect piece of journalism—that appeared cold and unsympathetic, though, to the mass of its readers. This belied Abrams' real nature, too. He was tender, easily affected, full of good impulses, and clinging as a woman in his friendship."[52]

Mr. Grady knew human nature well enough to know readers liked to see the man behind the pen and feel his heart beat. The informal essay type of editorial has a greater appeal to the average newspaper reader than does the formal, logical type. Mr. Grady took advantage of this

---

[266a]O'Rell, Max: Lively Journalism, N. Am., R. 150: 364-69.
[266b]Quiller-Couch, Sir Arthur: On the Art of Writing, p. 297 (b).
[266c]Harris, J. C.: H. W. G., His L. W. and S., p. 26 (d).
[52]Editorial: Leveled Landmarks.

knowledge in all his writings. He said himself that he was
writing to please his readers.[59] In order to do this he must
know them intimately. The editor has an audience almost
in the same sense that a speaker has an audience. A writer
on effective speaking says:

"To best make known his opinion, he must know humanity, must,
in imagination, live the life of his listeners. Then will he know
what arguments come closest to their lives, what appeals come
nearest to their hearts. And knowing all this, living all lives, he is
able to distinguish that which appeals to all from that which appeals
to a few, and in great moments can touch with a deft sureness a
universal chord."[267]

In order that he might keep in close touch with the people Mr. Grady often went out as a reporter instead of sending some one. He went to Charleston, South Carolina, to
report on the earthquake in 1886. On this occasion he had
a reporter with him, but he himself did the writing up of
the report.[268] Thus by keeping in touch with the outside
world he was able to play with "a deft sureness" upon that
universal chord. It was to this habit as much as to any one
thing that Mr. Grady's easy-flowing style was due. Quiller-
Couch, in speaking of style, said:

"It comes of endeavoring to understand others, of thinking for
them rather than for yourself—of thinking, that is, with the heart
as well as the head."[269]

Seeing through others' eyes presupposed a sympathetic
understanding of their viewpoint. This comes best by social
contact. Book knowledge will not suffice.

"What separates an author from his readers, will make it pro-
portionally difficult for him to explain himself to them."[270]

Notwithstanding the fact that Mr. Grady lived and
wrote in an age when the personal editor was passing, his
editorials were far from being impersonal.[270a] He knew his
readers and was known by them. If perchance the readers
did not know personally the people of whom he was writing,
they knew these people were very much alive after they had
read his editorials. To Mr. Grady these people were personalities and he passed them on as such to the newspaper
world. Other newspapers might have suffered from a lack
of personal contact and a personal understanding between

[59]Editorial: Carping Critics.
[267]Phillips, Arthur E.: Effective Speaking, p. 36 (d).
[268]Harris, J. C.: H. W. G., Life, Writings and Speeches, p. 63 (b).
[269]See Note 266a.
[270]Bagehot, Walter: Literary Studies, Vol. I, p. 139.
[270a]Mabie, Hamilton W.: Short Studies in Lit., p. 35.

the editorial writers and the readers, but this was not true when Mr. Grady wrote.

One should look at Mr. Grady's character sketches if he would like to see his grasp of the subject of human nature. He should take, for instance, his editorial on "In a Hundred Years"[16] and see how sympathetically Mr. Grady has portrayed this family of the poorer classes. He sees them in their very agony, but he understands the reading public so well that he picks out the very elements of their natures which appeal most forcefully to the emotion of pity. If one should turn from this sad sight and behold the man and his pitiable family in Mr. Grady's lecture on "A Patch Work Palace,"[30] he would see how thoroughly he understood the longings of the human heart as he portrays this poor man working so earnestly to build for himself and family a home. In these circumstances Mr. Grady showed that he understood the emotions of those poor wretches and, even more than this, he knew the chords in the universal nature of mankind which were most susceptible to his appeals.

In his editorial, "Comment on Senator Benj. Hill,"[43] Mr. Grady jumps to the other extreme and gives a description, so to speak, of the soul of this great man, and by this means typifies to us the great in general. Then a few years later he is writing on "Ben Hill Dead."[65] With only a few strokes of his pen he again shows us this great man in his home, in those most sacred relations to his family, and at the same time one sees laid bare the souls of his whole family. His thorough understanding of human nature gave him the grasp of the English language to such an extent that he, in a very few words, draws a picture all but sublime. It would be hard to say just to what extent his portrayal is due to his art, and to what extent it is due to his understanding of human nature and the world around him. One is inclined to believe that much of what is called art is due to insight into these deep spiritual things.

But Mr. Grady showed that he understood human nature, not only in his portrayal of character, but also in the very things he wrote about. He was immensely interested in "the big business of living," and he talked and wrote about the things he knew touched the lives of his people most intimately—such things as love, home, family ties, money and

[16]Editorial: In a Hundred Years.
[30]Lecture: A Patch Work Palace.
[43]Editorial: Comment on Senator Benjamin H. Hill.
[65]Editorial: Ben Hill Dead.

honor.[270b]   Herein lies the force of his writings, and of his speeches.

HIS MODERN VIEWPOINT

For a proper appreciation of Mr. Grady's attitude toward life in general and newspaper editing in particular we must take a view of the age in which he was born and reared—and the attitude of the intelligentzia of the South. From Colonial times down to and immediately following the Civil War every parent who was able to give his son a college education looked forward to a career for his son in politics.[270c]   The institution of slavery, so long as it obtained in the South, destined Georgia to be an agricultural state.   Therefore, a career as a politician was about the only thing left for the ambitious youth.   Possibly the war changed Mr. Grady's career, and his public expressions were in accord with this changed condition.   His biographers claim, however, that he loved politics.[271]   He took an interest in government, but it does not appear that he had any desire to write about the dirty practices of those who administered it.   He thought he knew more about such things than the general public did, hence as an editor he wrote to point out the things that were right and proper.   He wrote about politics because the subject came down to him as the dominant idea in the newspaper world, but he did not let it dominate him in his newspaper writing.   In the very first communication to the *Atlanta Constitution* he expressed himself in no uncertain terms about politics.   Here is what he had to say:

"By the way, this system of college politics is a hard nut to crack.   Boys, like apes, are imitative in their actions; hence you will find every canvass within our college walls the same electioneering trickery, the same party combinations, and the same stump speaking which characterize the campaigns of older politicians.   We have our caucuses—secret and open; we have our party issues and every candidate must define his platform and we have all the bluffings and villainies and chicanery that you will find in the outer world.   In fact, so strongly are we tinctured with the mad spirit of the age, that our elections are getting to be such affairs of importance, that an explosion is soon inevitable."[1]

As a college boy evidently college bluffings and villainies did not appeal to Mr. Grady.   The spirit of contest, however, did appeal to him immensely, but his nature loathed the petty practices in which politicians indulged.   Later in

[270b]Bleyer, W. G.: Intro. the Profession of Journalism, p. XIII.
[270c]Harris, J. C.: H. W. G., His Life, Writings, and Speeches, p. 11 (c).
[271]*Ibid.*, p. 29.
[1]Editorial: A Piquant Letter Written at Univ. of Va.

life he turned from the subject as often as the exigencies of
the circumstances would permit, and would exclaim:

"To the deuce with politics."[53]

Then Mr. Grady would tell us of the "self-made men"
of his acquaintance, and how they were honoring their day
and nation. After the defeat of Hancock for the presidency
he again expresses himself in no uncertain terms, and one
must conclude that he does not put a very high estimate
upon politics, especially from the standpoint of the development of the South, which he was most interested in from a
material standpoint. Listen to what he says:

"We are able to do without federal patronage. The defeat of
Hancock will be a blessing in disguise if it only tends to turn our
people from politics to work. We have the best country in the world.
The sun shines on us kindly, the soil yields us abundant crops, the
earth gives us gold, iron and coal at every fissure. How grander a
mission it is to develop this section into its full power and production
than to win a share of public patronage. What we need is fewer
stump-speakers and more stump-pullers—less talk and more work—
fewer gin-mills and more gins—fewer men at the front and more
men at the hoe. One plow is worth twenty politicians. In the old
days of slavery it was a passion with us to lead in politics—in these
days of close competition, he should be the best man who can lead
in the corn-row. Let us crystallize within our heart the sacred
principles of our faith—and then turn about bravely and build up
the South; make it thrill and swell with growth until it has compassed the full measure of the destiny for which God intended it."[54]

Mr. Grady realized the changed conditions and, journalist that he was, he was an opportunist. His policy was to
let the "dead past bury its dead"; he believed in the living
present. But this position was not taken by the vast majority, if any, of the editors who lived at the same time Mr.
Grady lived. Mr. Spencer, writing recently upon this topic,
says:

"Worse even than this, the editorial writer has refused too much
to concern himself with topics touching the immediate, personal interests of his readers. He has refused persistently to learn that the
American nation has changed from a politically governed republic
to one controlled by economics, and that in consequence the major
interest of the general reading public is no longer in politics. He
has not appreciated the way in which the interests have been vastly
broadened and humanized."[272]

If this criticism is just, then one must conclude that Mr.
Grady was a modern journalist in every sense of the word.
He turned more than fifty years ago from the sterile politi-

[53]Editorial: Self-Made Men.
[54]Editorial: I Told You So.
[272]Spencer, M. L.: Editorial Writing, p. 6.

cal type of journalist to the humanized editorial writer, for he touched upon every problem of the South as a whole and upon every problem of every man individually. Every great man lives in what he does and says many years ahead of his time. And as a great editorial writer, Mr. Grady was far ahead of his time. How many of his editorials would make good reading today! He struck a universal note because he struck at the root of our social structure. Nor did he leave our people wrapt in the sordid material universe and permit their souls to dwindle away, but he spiritualized everything he touched.

"Because of the condition the South was in after the war this material was the most pressing and immediate. He would put truth in every mind, the flower of charity in every heart, honor and fairness in every relation, and consolations of religion in every spirit," says Dr. Lee. . .

"Thus through men he would embody all over the South the ideas which he saw. He would put them into cattle upon every hill. He would put them into a home for every family. Around every home he would plant orchards and vineyards. Over every door he would trace vines and flowers. In the center of population he would put great cities, for distribution and help. Thus he would paint a picture standing over men and under men and blessing men. A panorama filled with the actual things men need rather than the representation."[273]

He lifted their eyes heavenward, while he kept their feet firmly planted upon the earth.

HIS HUMAN INTEREST TOPICS

"There was literally no item in the catalogue of Southern resources on which he failed to enlarge."[274]

Mr. Grady traveled all over the South and he came in contact with all sorts of people, and, as has been said elsewhere, by his wonderful ability as a conversationalist he talked to the people and deftly drew from them the things they were interested in. By his powers of observation and by his love of, and insight into the natural world, he was able to picture to the people the abounding resources of the South, and to show them how they could, by marshaling their own forces, harness the forces of nature and make the South the garden spot of these United States. This was his theme from the very first; even on the "Press Excursion," he called attention to the great mineral wealth of North Georgia.[5-10] His editorial on "Globes of Gold,"[40] in which

[273]Lee, Dr. J. W.: H. W. G., Editor, Orator, Man—Arena, 2: 9-23, Je'09.
[274]Knight, L. L.: Reminiscences of Famous Georgians, Vol. I, p. 425.
[5-10]Press Excursion, Editorials.
[40]Editorial: Globes of Gold.

he refers to the oranges in Florida, and his editorial on "Gold in Georgia,"[63] show how interestingly he wrote on the extraction of these satisfying things from "mother earth" in Florida and Georgia. He never tired of calling attention to the bounties of nature, and by so doing he interested people in other sections of our country in the advantages of the "Sunny South," and through his efforts there are many immigrants living in the South who came because of his representation of the natural resources. He reminded the Southern people of the fact that more men were needed in the agricultural pursuits than in the professions, especially that of politics.[54] In his editorial on "Where Shall We Spend the Summer?"[24] in enumerating the desirable resorts, he mentions this one as his preference:

"There is still another resource for the man who really seeks rest for the summer, and respite from its troubles. To strike a bargain with some sturdy old farmer, who has a spare room, and 'will board a couple for a while at $12.50 a month.' If you select the right sort of a farmer you are sure to find his house a roomy, drowsy nest, perched on the shady side of the hill, filled with marmalade, pickles, cordials, preserves, etc., which with supplements of chicken knocked from the trees, butter yet trembling from the agitation of the churn-handle, lambs killed at yester sunset, milk poured from jugs that live in the spring branch, are all yours to eat and revel in, for the modicum mentioned above. The family you will find affable and pleasant—capital listeners, and yet full of information that strikes you like a revelation. The beds are downy, and all the surroundings full of pleasantness and peace. This we prefer to any other style of summer resort. It is worth a hundred dollars to lie on the hay stack every evening in the balm of the falling dew, and watch the daughter, always a buxom and comely lass, milk the cows and feed the calves."[24]

Many were Mr. Grady's writings on the different phases of farming. He emphasized truck farming. And he called attention, from time to time, to the advantages of diversified farming. In the early years of his newspaper work he and some other men of Atlanta established a farm paper, and the records show that he contributed to this paper on subjects suitable for such a publication; these publications, however, could not be found. The fact is that he was very much interested in farming, because he knew his readers for the most part were identified more or less with the farming interest; he therefore wrote about farming from the practical standpoint as well as from the imaginative. He was an ideal editor for an agricultural magazine, and would be today a superior editor for our best farm papers.

[63]Editorial: Gold in Georgia.
[54]Editorial: I Told You So.
[24]Editorial: Where Shall We Spend the Summer?

Mr. Grady, in his character sketches, held up as examples of true worth some of the noble sons of the South and other sections of the United States. The South had been cut loose from her earlier ideals and many young men were adrift on the perilous sea of life without a rudder. There were many casualties in the South after the war. There was a great need for such ideals as Mr. Grady set before the young men of his section. He showed how plodding youths had left their homes of penury and had set their faces firmly toward the front, and by brain and brawn had succeeded in amassing fortunes, all the while fighting against odds. Then by a wonderful touch of his imagination he showed how these fortunes, in many instances, had been used for the advancement of mankind. In the accumulation of great wealth he showed how happiness was gained more from the proper spending than from the amassing. Nothing from his standpoint was ever done just for an end in itself, but it was just a step forward in making the world a better place in which the great mass of people should live and have an opportunity to realize themselves more fully.[274a] He not only preached that we are our brothers' keepers, but he practiced his preaching. In his editorial on "Self-Made Men,"[53] Mr. Grady recounts how some young men, starting with nothing but the scanty clothes on their backs, had, after years of struggle, gained success, and in their success had blessed humanity.

"The truth is, Atlanta," he goes on to say, "is full of these self-made men. They enrich her blood, quicken her pulses and give her vitality, force and power. I have always known them to be the strength of our goodly city, and I have always honored them in my heart. They have won fame and fortune by no accidents of inheritance, nor by capricious turn of luck, but by patient, earnest, heroic work. They have wrought much out of nothing—have compelled success out of failure—have been exemplars to their fellows, and have set hopes in the hearts of struggling youth. They have sunk the corner-stones of the only aristocracy that America should know—the distinction of honest and intelligent labor crowned with its inevitable results."[53]

In a previous passage reference to John H. Inman has been made in connection with Mr. Grady's ideas as to the worth of our present-day statesmen. Of course, Mr. Grady evaluates Mr. Inman's life and services to mankind much more highly than the statesmen, so-called. He did not think everyone would make a success in the same sense that Mr. Inman did, but he did think under proper conditions the

[274a]Lee, Dr. J. W.: H. W. G., Editor, Orator, Man,—Arena, 2: 9-23, Je'90.
[53]Editorial: Self-Made Men.

possibilities were great. Just this sentence in that connection:

> "To be sure, there will be few who can hope for such success—but nothing is surer than that a young man who starts with clean habits, a clear head and faithful soul, and works earnestly and devotedly can get far enough along this road to come into sunshine, while yet the flowers on the wayside are wet with the dew and the air of the morning embalms the earth."[55]

Few writers have ever used more appropriate words and better illustrations in directing the young men to the way of success. The only thing anyone can do in lecturing on success is merely to point to the way of those who have traveled the road of success, and this Mr. Grady did in a most excellent manner.

Let us turn to some character sketches in which he points to the happiness gained by serving mankind with the fortunes amassed by successful men. In commenting on Peter Cooper, he tells how he started with nothing and by hard work and persistent effort gained great wealth. He recounts sympathetically Mr. Cooper's struggles up from poverty to wealth and then tells how he longed to build an institution to help poor, struggling boys such as he himself was. The Cooper Institute was the fruitage of this desire. Mr. Grady introduces Mr. Cooper as follows:

> "For a model life let me commend you to that of Peter Cooper.
> "Ninety years of age, enthroned in the bosom of his family and the love of his people, he waits in his peace and content for the end. He lived to see all the dreams of his youth realized. His inventions have been made useful, his philanthropy has proved a mercy and a profit, his schemes have all prospered, his children have grown up in honor and prosperity around him and their children clamber on his knees, and with a stingless conscience and a heart that still glows beneath the snow of age, he will round a noble life with a Christian's death."[58]

In a short time after the editorial quoted from above was written Mr. Grady contributed another on the same theme. A Mr. Seney had given a donation to the public—possibly it was the Science Hall at Emory College in Georgia—and Mr. Grady draws a beautiful lesson from it. Evidently the recollection of the previous article was still lingering in Mr. Grady's brain, for he again refers to Peter Cooper.

> "It is this lesson that Mr. Seney teaches that is more valuable than his donations," says Mr. Grady. "How many men fall under the influence of this greed of which he speaks, and live and die in

[55]Editorial: John H. Inman.
[58]Editorial: A Noble Life.

its blighting shadow! It will be worth while for any man who reads this article to look about him and see how many really rich men of his acquaintance are happy and contented men. He will see that the few he selects are men who have done good with their money—who have helped public enterprises, and dealt in private charity—who have fought off the miserliness that too often comes with wealth.

"To illustrate, who will weigh the happiness of Peter Cooper, who at the close of a long and honorable life, meets death placidly without a fear, and goes into the next world with the consciousness of having done his duty in this, with the life of a man who, having pinched and starved himself for years, crouches among his money bags at the approach of death, and finds the pangs of his dissolution sharpened with the knowledge that he has never soothed a human sorrow or gladdened a human heart. Which has lived the happier life? To which has money brought most joy? Which man leaves the best legacy to his children—the man who dies with the blessings of his people on his life and leaves a moderate fortune, an honored name and beloved memory, or the man who leaves a mass of money and the taint of a selfish and miserly life?"[60]

The treatment of these two topics was from an emotional standpoint,[274b] and naturally all hearts respond except those that are selfish and miserly.

His Patriotism

Mr. Grady's was the patriotism of peace. All through his writings one will find this stressed. He fully believed in peace and he practiced the power of suggestion in his writings. When people elsewhere were stirring up strife he was calling attention to the fact that the sections were coming closer and closer together. He lamented the strife that the "fire-eaters" of both sections were bent on keeping alive. As early as April, 1875, Mr. Grady wrote an editorial on "A Platform of Peace and Good Will,"[26] in which he cites the attitude of some legislators from Connecticut and Ohio in trying to stir up sectional animosity, while Gordon and Lamar of Georgia insisted on peace. I quote from this editorial:

"Gordon and Lamar ask for peace and concord and are willing to buy it by acquiescing in the results of the war. Eaton, of Connecticut and Allen, of Ohio, insist that the Bourbon flag shall again be raised even at the cost of perpetuation of strife between the sections. Almost every Southern man we have talked to confesses that the negro is free, and that he must remain free. They acknowledge that he has the right of suffrage, and propose to guarantee him the enjoyment of that right; and yet we hear of an absolute certainty that the two newly elected congressmen of New Hampshire deny the validity of the amendments, and propose to open the very dead question again. We predict that at the National Democratic Convention of '76 the Southern delegates will advocate the adoption of a platform

[60]Editorial: A Life Worth Living.
[274b]Spencer, M. L.: Editorial Writing, p. 175 (c) (d).
[26]Editorial: A Platform of Peace and Good Will.

upon which the sections can be reconciled and the country rehabilitated, and that the Northern delegates will insist upon disinterring
the issues which were settled at Appomattox, and have been since a
dozen times buried.

"The truth is the Southern people want peace and quiet. They
are tired of this miserable sectional strife which is checking the
growth of either section, and paralyzing the energies of both. We
respectfully request that we be allowed to 'rally around the flag.'
This republic is of our own making."[26]

Continuing his discussion, Mr. Grady enlarged upon the
idea that this republic is of our own making by emphasizing
the part our Southern forefathers played in establishing the
national government—the part Jefferson, Washington,
Patrick Henry, Andrew Jackson, Clay and Calhoun played
in making possible this government—thus appealing to
Southern patriotism. These are the names all men conjure
with when they would make us all patriotic, and he was
appealing especially to Southern patriotism. In the last
paragraph of this same editorial he says:

"We want to see the Centennial Canvass fought upon a platform
that is in harmony with the year and its suggestions and memories
. . . We are anxious to see the best government the world ever
saw enter its second century under the right sort of auspices."[26]

If one were to search all of the writings at this time,
it would be hard to find more beautiful sentiments expressed
about our government, or more unaffected expressions of
loyalty to our government.

In a half playful spirit Mr. Grady writes an editorial
on "The War Between the States," in which he mentions an
effort of the city of Atlanta to raise money for the young
men's library which, by the way, was the beginning of the
splendid Carnegie Library that is the pride of the city now.
The editorial begins thus:

"Last night, at seven o'clock exactly, was begun in this city, the
second war between the States of the Union.

"Not a war similar to that one which, born in sectional hate,
begun at Fort Sumter, desolated the South, wasted a generation of
men, put the Republic to mourning, and ended beneath the Apple
Tree of Appomattox. Not such a war, with its desolating savagery,
but a war of friendliest emulation. . .

.   .   .   .

"The representatives of each State rally manfully around their
new methods of war. We see much that is auspicious in the present
occasion with its rival of old memories, its renewal of old associations, and its reawakening of old revolutionary traditions. It is a
fit opening to a great Centennial of next year, and the pervading
interest taken in our little side-show gives a token that the old

[26]Editorial: A Platform of Peace and Good Will.

sectional partisan hate is dying out, if indeed, it is not already dead."[33]

In 1877, when Senator Benj. H. Hill was elected to the United States Senate, Mr. Grady reminded this great Senator of his opportunities; he said:

"The sentimental is passing out of our politics—sectional prejudices are about to die a death from which there will be no resurrection. The great men of the future must become the authors of and champions of some intelligent and reformatory progressive movements."[43]

Thus we see that Mr. Grady preached peace from the very earliest days of his journalistic writings. He believed that it was impossible for the country as a whole to prosper while the people of the two sections were harboring sectional hatreds in their hearts. He wished all people to read what he wrote, but he knew his papers were local and consequently reached only a very few people outside of the South, therefore he talked for the most part to the Southern people in an effort to get his people to accept the right attitude in the matter. It is impossible to estimate the good he did in restoring the proper attitude between the sections —North and South. Some one has said that peace between the North and South was an inspiration with Mr. Grady, and resulted in his projected plan for harmony.[275]

His Political Editorials

As has been remarked elsewhere, Mr. Grady was not dominated by politics, but he dominated politics. He says himself that he helped General John B. Gordon into the United States Senate while he was part owner of the *Atlanta Herald*.[52] He contributed several articles on the campaigning of Lester and Felton in the race for Congress in the Seventh Congressional District of Georgia.[45] While his bias was for Lester, he wrote about this campaign more because of the general interest it was attracting than from a personal interest. It was the human interest part of it and not his interest in politics specifically that made him write about these lively campaign speeches. It was true that he went to Florida in 1876 to write on the Florida Election Frauds; it is also true that he was keenly interested in what he was reporting, but who was not? The play of his imagination and the characterization of the men

[33]Editorial: The War Between the States.
[43]Editorial: Comment on Senator Benj. H. Hill.
[275]Hudgins, H. C. and Co.: Henry W. Grady, Life and Labors of, p. 12 (c).
[52]Editorial: Leveled Landmarks.
[45]Editorial: Lester and Felton.

on the Commission took as much and even more of his time than did the political features of the reports. His characterization of Ex-Governor Joseph E. Brown of Georgia,[37] while he was sick at this crucial moment, and his description of the dance in an adjoining room to that in which Ex-Governor Brown lay sick, were more to Mr. Grady's liking than the political aspect of the situation. Think of a man sent as a special reporter on such a mission as the Florida Frauds; then read this extract from one of his reports:

"You may imagine that the democrats were very blue, when he (Gov. Brown) was at his worst. Although I have a great deal to do with the ex-Governor—although he took occasion once to rise up and 'sit down' on an enterprise with which I was connected with a vigor and emphasis only equaled by that with which Humpty Dumpty sits down on the inflated baby in the play, I never knew until he was sick what mental power the man had. He lay there in the bed, with two fly-blisters pulling torture out of his breast, and every breath he drew cutting his lungs like a knife, and surrounded by a pile of law books, which were being read to him, made up the skeleton of a legal argument on which the democrats will rest their case tomorrow. On Thursday night there was a ball in the dining room which is separated by a single wall from his room. The clamor was fearful. A brass band was blowing its brains out through some exceedingly noisy horns. A half dozen greased elbows were sawing across as many resonant fiddles, and the shouts and laughter were literally ear-splitting. I expressed the fear that it might make him worse by keeping him awake.

" 'Oh, no,' said he, 'I can will myself to sleep at any time I want to.'

"And almost straightway he shut his eyes and did so. I arose and looked at him with wonder in my eyes. A sort of smile came to the sleeping face, and I have no doubt he was dreaming that he was snoozing away after a hard day's work in that old log cabin at Canton, the winter's air pattering drowsily on the shelving house-top, and the wind sobbing huskily against the stout oaken-door!

"I started out of the room on tip-toe foolishly thinking of waking the sleeper. Jeff, his faithful attendant, laughed at my caution and said:

" 'You might shoot your pistol off right in the Governor's ear, and he wouldn't wake less he wanted to.'

"I solemnly believe that Jeff was right."[37]

In another report,[41] in a semi-humorous strain, he describes Pasco, "a ridiculous yellow man." In the interval he gets away from the political scenes at Tallahassee and writes up his trip on the St. Johns river under the title of "Fair Florida."[42] One would never think from his beautiful descriptions and his humorous allusions on this trip that he was a special reporter for one of the most interesting political episodes in American history. And in his communi-

---

[37]Editorial: Florida Frauds.
[41]Editorial: Florida Frauds.
[42]Editorial: Fair Florida.

cation on "Globes of Gold"[40] he shows that he has gotten
away from a politically-governed America to an economical-
ly-governed America, and despite the stormy national situation he manifests his abiding faith in the industrial development of this Southland of ours whichever way the political situation might turn.

Mr. Grady was a democrat, as all the leaders in the
South were—they could not get a hearing otherwise—but
he discussed the situation nationally more from the standpoint of political economy than from a partisan viewpoint.
He preferred honest principles and failure from a party organization to party power without the principles.   And in
his editorial, "I Told You So,"[54] in 1880, he recounted the
national political situation and pointed out the weaknesses
in the position of both political parties. The "Radicals"
were determined to keep the South from gaining power under any pretext, and the democrats were grabbing at every
straw in an effort to get in power. The contentions of the
one were illogical and the efforts of the other sacrificed
what he regarded as principles. He evidently had been
pointing out to his constituency the weakness of the democratic position. His editorial was written after an extended
trip through the North, and he again is discussing the prop-
osition from close range rather than from the editorial
room. It is hard to pick any one paragraph that expresses
his view in short, but the following sums it up pretty well:

"The South has but one thing to do, and that is to stand firm to
the principles upon which democracy is based—the rights of states
—to supremacy of civil law—a free ballot and honest money. It is
better to be beaten forever upon this platform than win by abandoning it. With these principles surrendered there is nothing left
worth fighting over, and our party contests will then become mere
struggles over patronage. We have lost too much already by compromise. Point after point has been yielded, this man and that has
been followed, until it really looks as if we only wanted to get into
power and did not care under what leadership or what platform.
If the South is true to her traditions, she is brave enough to stand
by the right regardless of the results. If she is worthy of herself,
she will stand firm even if the national democracy should dissolve—
and amid the dissolution will see this faction or that depart, with
tranquil determination, and when the last has gone will raise the
flag of eternal protest against the destruction of the states, and
will stand by the old guard of constitutional liberty."[54]

Of course, Mr. Grady wanted to see his party in power,
but he did not wish to see it sacrifice principles in order to
get into power. He did not endorse his party, right or

40Editorial: Globes of Gold.
54Editorial: I Told You So.

wrong; principles to him were more than party affiliations. He believed his people, and the people of the United States should know the true situation, but he did not believe in dealing in personalities—berating the leaders in order to fill up the columns of his paper with reading matter. He was not guilty of writing "political bunk" merely for fillers. From this standpoint he was very different from the ordinary editorial writer of his age. He made an effort to direct the attention of the nation to principles instead of men.

One of Mr. Grady's characteristics of writing was to cite examples and make comparisons. In his editorial on "Honest, Happy England,"[23] he used his wonderful power of suggestion in dealing with some fundamental principles of political economy, choosing again rather to leave out all personalities. He is adopting the role of teacher in an effort to get his people to think on some important question pertaining to our own situation. Observe the economic themes he suggests in the following paragraphs concerning the political situation in England:

"Free sugar, a penny off the income tax, and six millions surplus. With this triune of glories, Johnny Bull can well afford to sit down in his solid comfortable sort of a way, and laugh at perspiring, push-ahead, enterprising, but always poor America. Ease and wealth across there—shoddy and sham over here. Honesty and prudence at the helm over there; rings and cliques wrecking the government over here. High salaries and good men in office there; low salaries and perquisite hunting bummers in office here. An oak tree the emblem of the kingdom over there; a mushroom the pride of our nation over here.

"With all of America's boasted progress in the science of governing, she might find something of practical profit in the study of that government, where defalcation is the exception and not the rule; with all her boundless resources and her remorseless income, she might find something new in the theory of taxation in that country where each class yields its equitable proportion to the general exchequer; in the study of English politics she might at least see the propriety of eliminating Butlerism from her own governmental affairs."[23]

He hit upon two of our faults of government. In the Constitutional Convention, 1787, our forefathers took a niggardly attitude toward the salaries of governmental officials. Some even argued that the United States Senators should receive no pay at all.[275a] It was an appeal to patriotism. There had been very little change in salaries since the adoption of the Constitution, but a great change in the purchasing power of our dollar. Mr. Grady pointed out the fact

---

[23]Editorial: Happy, Honest England.
[275a]Papers of Madison, Vol. II, p. 1020 (b).

that our country did not have the best men in office because of the poor pay. He also called attention to the inequalities in our taxation system. The ideas he was dealing in were principles then and they are principles now. Many questions he discussed then are engaging our political scientists today. It was not partisan politics.

So, if the critic would do Mr. Grady justice he must say that he discussed governmental questions not in the same sense that the old-fashioned editor did—not from the standpoint of the professional writer of political editorials, but from the standpoint of one who treated of these ideas as the exigencies of the case demanded. He never debated such issues for the sake of mere politics, but he wrote about them because they constituted a part of the topics which the reading public needed to know something about.[275b] Then, too, he never wrote from that partisan bias that is so often objectionable in other writers on these subjects. Few editorial writers have ever attained to such heights of journalistic writing.

His Newspaper Ideals

"When I was eighteen years of age, I adopted journalism as my profession. After thirteen years of service, in which I have had various fortunes, I can say that I have never seen a day when I regretted my choice. On the contrary, I have seen the field of journalism so enlarged, its possibilities so widened, and its influence so extended, that I have come to believe earnestly that no man, no matter what his calling, his elevation, or his opportunity, can equal in dignity, honor and usefulness the journalist who comprehends his position, fairly measures his duty, and gives himself entirely and unselfishly to his work. But journalism is a jealous profession, and demands the fullest allegiance of those who seek its honors or its emoluments. Least of all things can it be made the aid of the demagogue, or the handmaid of the politician. The man who uses his journal to subserve his political ambition, or writes with a sinister or personal purpose, soon loses his power, and had best abandon a profession he has betrayed. . .

.   .   .   .

"Therefore, devoted as I am to my profession, believing as I do that there is more of honor and usefulness for me along its way than in another path, and that my duty is clear and unmistakable, I am constrained to reaffirm in my own mind and to declare to you the resolution I made when I entered journalism, namely, that as long as I remain in its ranks I will never become a candidate for any political office, or draw a dollar from any public treasury."[276]

This quotation is taken from a reply of Mr. Grady to his friends who wanted him to run for Congress in 1882. He declares in this same letter that he has no higher ambition than to serve his people in such a way as to make "a better

---

[275b]See Note 274b.

[276]Harris, J. C.: H. W. G., His Life, Writings and Speeches, p. 10 (d) 11 (a).

and grander Georgia." No one ever held his profession in higher esteem than did this peerless journalist hold his. He acknowledged the great responsibility and his work as a journalist stands as a monument to his faithfulness to the obligation he took upon himself. He was, indeed, wedded to his profession.

Mr. Grady gives a pretty concise statement of his opinions of the editorial writers in his "Southern Newspaper Writers."[29] He says that the Southern editors had too many responsibilities to accomplish very much as writers. They wrote their editorials and then set up the type; they solicited advertising, and did anything else that was to be done on a paper. He says:

"The result of this overwork is, very legitimately, to depreciate the quality of the work done. The editor being required to furnish editorials upon at least two, and frequently half a dozen dissimilar topics daily, of necessity, hardly reaches the bottom of either one of his subjects. No editor who hopes to make an impression upon his age, should write more than three a week. None of the editorial writers upon the New York papers do more than this, and most of them do less. As a consequence, the editorials of the New York papers, and particularly the *World* and *Tribune* are models of style and power. The drudgery that the Southern editor is forced to do is telling upon Southern journalism."

.   .   .   .

"The most noticeable effects of the hurry and embarrassment under which our Southern journalists are forced to write is, that it affords them no leisure in which to look over their work, to spy out its defects, and determine upon the points at which it should be corrected. As a consequence, the defects become fixtures, the mannerisms are confirmed, and the style becomes more and more fixed and monotonous day after day."

.   .   .   .

"Now there is Mr. Watterson, of the *Courier Journal*, who is perhaps the smartest writer on the Southern press. He did some very brilliant and earnest work in the Greeley campaign, doing the best writing that was done in that desperate and sentimental campaign. But he has not written a dozen great editorials since. His work is all flippant, thinnish, and without any sturdy backbone of purpose. He is pert always, entertaining usually, and brilliant sometimes. But there is a slouchiness and slanginess about his editorials that even a perusal of his proof on his part would eliminate. He is not doing himself justice. With two-thirds of the work that he is doing taken off his shoulders he would be in two years at the head of his profession."[29]

Evidently Mr. Grady believed in a very high grade of work for Southern editorial writers. He did not believe an editor should dissipate his powers in trying to write on so many dissimilar subjects. He would have the editors to

[29]Editorial: Southern Newspaper Writers.

think through their subjects before giving their opinions to the world. Not only should they study their subjects carefully, but they should take time to correct what they wrote before publishing it. Good style to him was an important asset to the editorial page, but mannerisms were a liability. He knew the disadvantages of not revising, for it is stated that he never revised.[277] He wrote under pressure. It might be said, in practice, he did not live up to his ideals, but he, too, was overworked.

But there was one thing he believed in and practiced. He believed that the editor should know intimately his readers in order to make himself felt. He criticized St. Clair-Abrams, one of his partners on the *Atlanta Herald*, because he put too much of the journalist into his paper and too little of the man.[52] Then, judging from his practices, he believed in making his readers laugh, making them weep, making them think, making them look out upon the great, wide, beautiful world and behold the beauties of nature and the love of God. He said in one editorial that his purpose was to please his readers.[59] He meant more than merely to entertain; he meant to make his paper worth while and thereby please his readers. He always had a purpose in writing. His humorous editorials often taught very deep lessons.

For instance, turn to his humorous editorial on "That Jones."[31] the reporter who was continually making such glaring mistakes in the use of his tense-forms. He tells how he sent Jones away on a vacation with instructions to "brush up" on his grammar. Jones fell in company with a newspaper boy from the *New York Herald* who taught him what Mr. Grady calls the "Gerraceous Hevings" method of journalism. This is the way he writes about Jones:

"The first morning after he came back to work, the local page was sprinkled about with headlines until it looked as if the advertisement had gotten drunk and jumped over the column-rules. A little girl was bitten by a dog near Mr. Castleberry's. Jones worked it up into a column article, and started it out with the harrowing title—'The Fatal Fangs; or the Sleuth-Hound of Castleberry's Hill.' A negro man tickled another's ribs with a pen-knife. Jones regaled us the next morning with 'A Bucket of Blood; or a Carnage in the Glare of the Gas Lamp.'"

.   .   .   .

"We have a man of lymphatic temperament, who sleeps in the ice house and feeds on cold potatoes, whose duty is to follow this blazing fiend of a reporter and crush the fire and passion out of Jones' headlines, just as tradition tells us there are old women who ride across the sky on broom-sticks and sweep up the sparks from the tracks of the comets. This man is a sort of Babcock fire extinguisher, and he plays a perpetual stream on Jones."

.   .   .   .

"We shall try to keep his fiery shape, in the shadow of the fish-blooded phantom that plies in his wake; and if he at times flashes before the public we beg them to close their eyes until he is again put in the eclipse."[31]

Mr. Grady was playing up what to him was not ideal journalism. In all the issues of the papers examined— either the *Herald* or the *Constitution*—nothing similar to what he was describing in Jones appeared. There were no sensational headlines in his papers. Had the type been the same as that used in the present day the paper would have had very much the same appearance as the present-day newspapers.

The *Atlanta Herald* from 1873 to 1875 was influenced principally by Mr. Grady's suggestion as to its general make-up. Of course, general news came first; there was a space for national topics as opposed to state topics; there was a space for local and state topics; there was a space for international topics; there was a space specifically for the discussion of literary topics, often chapters quoted from current publications on literature, corresponding to the Sunday magazine section of today; then there was space given once a week to sermons of the different pulpit orators of the city reported by a special reporter. The writers for these different departments were men of ability. For instance, those who were interested in literary criticism were treated to discussions by Chancellor Lipscomb of the University of Georgia. And Mr. Grady himself discussed the theater; you can see his ideals set forth in such contributions as "The Stage,"[57] in which he so interestingly discusses the rendition of Uncle Tom's Cabin in Washington. He also gives us an interesting criticism of Mary Anderson, in his contribution on "A Direct Question."[56] Betsy Hamilton, a famous Southern woman, who wrote on questions of general interest, was one of his contributors at times. In fact, Mr. Grady was surrounded by, and was a part of, a group of famous newspaper writers of the South. He and his partners were responsible for the writings of many of these.

---

[31]Editorial: That Jones.
[57]Editorial: The Stage.
[56]Editorial: A Direct Question.

Editorials Point to Famous Orations

Mr. Grady's famous speeches were but the crystallization of ideas expressed from time to time in his editorial
writings. His speeches, like Webster's reply to Hayne,
were made years before and put into an auger hole for safe
keeping, but his speeches were first written as editorials and
the fragments were collected into his beautiful oratory in
later life. The style in his speeches is not different from
the style used in his editorial writing. He became the master of the metaphor as a writer before he startled the world
with his eloquence. His descriptive writings were valuable
to him later when he wanted to picture conditions in the
South in his orations. His pictures of the loyal old slave
standing guard over the defenseless women and children of
the South during the war, which he gave in his speech before the New England Society in 1886, is but a variation
of the picture he gave in his editorial on "The New Solution of the Negro Question"[27] in 1875. The following is a
quotation from his oration on the New South:

"We remember with fidelity for four years he guarded our defenseless women and children, whose husbands and fathers were
fighting against his freedom. To his eternal credit be it said that
whenever he struck a blow for his own liberty he fought in open
battle, and when at last he raised his black and humble hands that
the shackles might be struck off, those hands were innocent of
wrong against his helpless charges, and worthy. to be taken in loving
grasp by every man who honors loyalty and devotion."[278]

A similar expression is also found in his oration at Dallas, Texas, on "The South and Her Problems," which was
delivered in 1887. It follows:

"I want no truer soul than that which moved the trusty slave,
who for four years while my father fought with the armies that
barred his freedom, slept every night at my mother's chamber door,
holding her and her children safe as if her husband stood guard,
and ready to lay down his humble life on her threshold. History has
no parallel to the faith kept by the negro in the South during the
war."[279]

Compare the quotations given above to this one taken
from his editorial on "The New Solution of the Negro Question":

"We doubt if history will furnish a parallel of such absolute faith
on the one hand, and such superb loyalty on the other, as was furnished in those terrible days, when the mother of the household in
Dixie, with her little children huddling around her, her husband and

[27]Editorial: A New Solution of the Negro Question.
[278]Harris, J. C.: H. W. G., His Life, Writings and Speeches, p. 89 (d).
[279]*Ibid.*, p. 97 (d).

sons on the battlefields, would place her only gun in the hands of the very man they were fighting to enslave, and bid him sleep on her doormat and guard the house through the night. For his fidelity and forbearance then, and by the memories of the long-gone, peaceful and harmonious years, which later differences have not effaced, the white man of the South is today ready to unite with the black man in an honest attempt to build up his fortunes and work out for himself a future."[27]

These are but variations of the same sentiments, and the one is as beautifully expressed as the other. One is as eloquent as the other. The same heart pulsated in the breast of the maturer man. The same sentiments glowed and were expressed as beautifully at one time as the other.

Again in his Dallas, Texas, oration he has this to say about the negro's voting:

"The clear and unmistakable domination of the white race, dominating not through violence, not through party alliance, but through the integrity of its own vote and the largeness of its sympathy and justice through which it shall compel the support of the better classes of the colored race,—that is the hope and assurance of the South. Otherwise, the negro would be bandied from one faction to another. His credulity would be played upon, his cupidity tempted, his impulses misdirected, his passions inflamed."[280]

Compare this, if you please, with another quotation from his editorial on "The New Solution of the Negro Question":

"The true solution of the negro problem is to eliminate from our politics all questions on which he can be massed against the whites. He must divide his vote. He may vote freely and openly, but he must take himself out of the hands of the foolish and wicked leaders who use him for the purpose of corruption. He must watch the drift of public affairs, and judge for himself as to what principles or what candidates he shall support with his ballot. Instead of letting others, who have proved themselves incapable and treacherous, think for him, he must think for himself. He must not follow the whispered command of some midnight league, but he must hear the truth spoken openly and bravely in the sunlight, and become its champion."[27]

It would be very easy to point out many more similar passages in his editorials and orations, showing that the thoughts expressed in his orations are but the crystallization of his earlier writings. In the making of the editor, the orator was evolved.

Not only do we see the orator using the same materials and sentiments the editor used, but we also see the same devices of style in the one as in the other. Mr. Grady's use of the character sketch as an editor, and his beautiful descriptions in earlier life, helped to make him the vivid and

---

[27]Editorial: A New Solution of the Negro Question.
[280]Harris, J. C.: H. W. G., His Life, Writings and Speeches, p. 99 (d).
[27]Editorial: The New Solution of the Negro Question.

brilliant orator that he was, for some of his greatest appeals as an orator were his characterizations of Southern incidents and the impressionistic presentation of his themes. There was not a single element of the orator that was not in the editor.

SUMMARY

One writer on journalism has said that there are three "absolute essentials" in the making of a journalist. In the first place, the aspirant must have the aptitude for the profession; in the second place, he must have an unconquerable persistence; and in the third place, he must have a good nature.[281] By training and by natural endowments, Mr. Grady was adapted to the journalistic career. He had a broad collegiate education, and he loved above all professions that of journalism. He inherited a handsome fortune, but before he was twenty-five years old he had spent it all in two newspaper enterprises, both of which were financial failures. But his optimistic spirit would not be dampened by such a trifle for he says himself in commenting upon "Self-Made Men":

"This hasty tribute is tendered by one who, starting life ready-made, speedily unmade himself and is now hopefully rambling along the road of regeneration."[53]

His good-natured humor was always a most potent influence in his newspaper work.

He was born in a time when it was easy for him to lay aside the old-fashioned journalistic writing—the politically-dominated editorial writing. He, therefore, devoted himself to the regeneration of his stricken section, giving in this connection timely editorials on "human-interest" topics. Young as he was, he wielded a power in the reuniting of the North and South after the war. His patriotism was unchallenged, and he longed to see his section reunited in spirit to the government of their making. He was a man of deep convictions, and he had the courage to express his convictions whenever it was necessary to advance the cause of righteousness. He lived at the time of the awakening of the consciences of the literary men to the condition of the down-trodden element of humanity.[282] He ever played upon the chords that would ring out the clarion notes of liberty.

He was the champion of the industrial development of the South. He was constantly calling the attention of his

---

[281]Rolf, Julian: The Making of a Journalist, p. 99.
[53]Editorial: Self-Made Men (d).
[282]Hillis, Newell D.: Great Books as Life Teachers—"Foreword."

own people to the possibilities of the South and at the same time he was influencing immigration to the South. While he knew that a lasting civilization must be based upon the material, he never lost sight of the spiritual values of life. And in his visions of the "New South" he always saw the two threads—the material and the spiritual—running in proper proportions in the fabric of our civilization.

CHAPTER III

HENRY W. GRADY AND OTHER JOURNALISTS

Mr. Grady and Henry Watterson

It is interesting to study the newspaper careers of Mr. Grady and Mr. Watterson, because they both had the same goal in view. Both were interested in the rehabilitation and development of the South. Both were loyal to the core to these United States, and both worked to bring about the reuniting of the South to the federal government in spirit as well as in name. In their purpose they were alike, but they differed as to methods. The South does not furnish two more interesting figures in the newspaper world. They were two great personalities which suggest many variations.

Mr. Watterson himself has this to say about the great service to the South Mr. Grady wrought in the days of reconstruction:

"Mr. Grady became a writer for the press when but little more than a boy, and during the darkest days of the Reconstruction period. There was in those days but a single political issue for the South. Our hand was in the lion's mouth, and we could do nothing, hope for nothing, until we got it out. The young Georgian was ardent, impetuous, the son of a father slain in battle, the offspring of a section, the child of a province; yet he rose to the situation with uncommon faculties of courage and perception; caught the struggle against reaction with perfect reach; and threw himself into the liberal and progressive movements of the time with the genius of a man born for both oratory and affairs."[283]

Of course, everyone knew there was but one great issue in the South after the war, and that was the rehabilitation of the South. The two were agreed upon the objectoinable element of the carpet-bag rule, and both claimed that there would be a solid South so long as the carpet-bagger made it a necessity, and both announced to the world that but for the policy of those in power the South would divide on many issues. I suppose it was because of this agreement and the fact that Mr. Watterson opened the columns of the *Courier Journal* to Mr. Grady soon after its establishment that caused him to, lay claim to Mr. Grady as one of his boys. According to Marse Henry's own statement they did not always agree. He says:

"We had broken a lance or two between us; but there had been no lick below the belt, and no hurt which was other than skin-deep,

[283]Harris, J. C.: H. W. G., His Life, Writings, and Speeches, p. 6 (b).

and during considerably more than a year before his death a most cordial and unreserved correspondence had passed between us."[284]

No doubt the "broken lance or two" was the occasion of Mr. Watterson's characterizing his combatant as "Henry Woodfire (Woodfin) Grady." That Mr. Grady recognized and admired Marse Henry's ability as an editorial writer is to be seen by what he has to say in "Southern Newspaper Writers,"[29] in which he comments favorably on his campaign editorials playing up Horace Greeley's presidential aspirations. He says this by way of conclusion on Mr. Watterson:

> "He is pert always, entertaining usually, and brilliant sometimes. But there is a slouchiness and slanginess about his editorials that even a perusal of his proof on his part would eliminate. He is not doing himself justice. With two-thirds of the work that he is doing taken off his shoulders he would be in two years at the head of his profession."[29]

While Marse Henry claimed the young Georgian as one of his boys, and while there was a mutual admiration, it is pretty safe to say Mr. Grady never copied anything from the *Courier-Journal*—either in method or style. Mr. Watterson in his political warfare used heavy artillery while Mr. Grady preferred the rapier; Mr. Watterson discussed expediencies while Mr. Grady stuck to principles; the one used the methods of the politician, while the other was more statesmanlike.

Since Mr. Watterson lived in Kentucky he was centrally located between the North and the South.[285] He, therefore, became a buffer in this great sectional fight. He wanted to see justice done to both sections, and he threw himself on the side of the weak and fought valiantly. He presented his views always from the logical standpoint. There was a pressing need for this argumentative type of patriot and Mr. Watterson fitted into the niche and performed his part well. But Mr. Grady was in the heart of the South and his position gave him a peculiar advantage to use his persuasive power in making an appeal to a people who responded more readily to his emotional writing, and because he was of necessity fighting fire with fire. There were many "fire-eaters" in the South, and especially there was one "unreconstructed rebel"[286] who was continually stirring the passions of the South against the North. Logic and argument were neces-

---

[284]Harris, J. C., H. W. G., His Life, Writings and Speeches, p. 7 (c).
[29]Editorial: Southern Newspaper Writers.
[285]Krock, A.: The Editorials of Henry Watterson, p. 17 (b).
[286]*Ibid.*, p. 39 (c).

sary, but the logic of events made it all the more necessary for such a type of journalist as Mr. Grady was. The only way to combat the appeals of the "fire-eaters" of both sections who were appealing to hate was to combat it by the emotional appeal of love and friendliness such as Mr. Grady practically always resorted to. Mr. Watterson was a master of sarcasm. Mr. Grady was a master of metaphor; Mr. Watterson was often vindictive; Mr. Grady, seldom. It is hard to say just which of these two peerless journalists accomplished the most. They were compeers, and there is good reason to believe the one was the complement of the other. The work of both was needed and the common goal of both, therefore, was reached much earlier than it would have been under different conditions.

If one will follow Mr. Watterson's editorials he will soon discover that he was dominated by politics. As he saw the situation in the South, governmental affairs must be kept before the people all the time. He thought it would be possible for the Democratic party to succeed in getting its desired ends by affiliating with certain liberal Republicans. Mr. Krock has this to say about his disposition to trade in politics in the campaign of 1872:

"The young editor's first adventures in national politics were in the campaign of 1872. In his autobiography he has given a great deal of space to the narration of how, with Halstead, Bowles and Horace White, he formed the 'Quadrilateral' of journalists at the Liberal Republican convention of that year in Cincinnati with the hope of nominating a Northern man other than Horace Greeley. Mr. Watterson's purpose being to urge the Democrats then to endorse the liberal Republican candidate and thereby 'get the South out of their irons' if their candidate won. The plan went through with the exception that Greeley, instead of Trumbull or Adams, was the Cincinnati nominee."[287]

This is one of the indications of Mr. Watterson's propensities of playing politics for the sake of expediency. This attitude of Marse Henry called down upon his head the disapproval of the leaders of the South. In his editorial on "I Told You So," in 1880, Mr. Grady discussed the actions of the Democrats in their willingness to accept any man, although such actions required the sacrificing of principles. It is very clear that he and Marse Henry did not agree upon this issue. This is what Mr. Grady has to say about the question:

"We have lost too much already by compromise. Point after point has been yielded, this man and that has been followed, until

[287]Krock, A.: The Editorial of Henry Watterson, p. 33 (a).

it has really looked as if we only wanted to get into power and did not care under what leadership or what platform."[54]

This idea of Mr. Grady is the same that called forth Marse Henry's invectives against Toombs and Stephens of Georgia when he said they were the "worst enemies the South had,"[288] during this Reconstruction period. Doubtless this and similar ideas of Mr. Grady's is what caused the "broken lance or two" between these journalists, and provoked Mr. Watterson's characterization, "Henry Woodfire (Woodfin) Grady."[289] This was one of the forms of sarcasm or caricature too often indulged in by Marse Henry.

Since Marse Henry says that Mr. Grady as a young man was impetuous and often not tactful in his manner of attack, it is interesting to review their reactions to what Mr. Watterson designates as the "Hayes Conspiracy"; that is, to the contested election returns in 1876. Both men did not hesitate to say that Hayes was placed in the presidential chair by fraud. Mr. Grady went to Florida as a special reporter for the *Constitution* and his reports were published also in the *New York Herald*. In his reports on the "election frauds" in Florida he went so far as to name men, who, he believed, had received money to cast their votes in favor of the republican contentions. He also suggested that Governor Hayes himself realized that these election returns were frauds and would be willing to drop the contest were he not in the hands of his party.[39] His write-up of the investigation of these frauds was considered the best of all the reporters on either side who were watching the proceedings. His impetuous nature did not cause any unfavorable criticism of his writings. But this cannot be said of Mr. Watterson, although he was a mature man at this juncture. Mr. Krock, in referring to Marse Henry's editorial of January 5, 1877, on "The Political Situation,"[290] in which he discussed the Hayes-Tilden contest, has this to say:

"It was this article which was responsible for the report around the United States that Henry Watterson proposed to lead an army of a hundred thousand men into Washington to prevent the certification of Hayes. While in this writing the editor counsels peace, there is a good deal of belligerency in his suggestion of massing the protestants in Washington. And what alarmed the Federal government most was the injunction to the Democrats of Kentucky to 'provide for the presence of at least ten thousand unarmed Kentuckians' in Washington a month later."[291]

---

[54]Editorial: I Told You So.
[288]Krock, A.: The Editorials of Henry Watterson, p. 41 (b).
[289]Watterson's: Marse Henry, p. 9.
[39]Editorial: Florida Frauds.
[290]Krock, A.: Editorial of Henry Watterson, p. 54 (a).
[291]*Ibid.*, p. 53 (d).

The fact is that Mr. Grady's writings at all times, though he did not fail to place the actions of men in their proper category, was done in such a spirit as to show his honesty of purpose. His writings were re-echoed in his pacificatory speeches in later years.

These two editors very often dealt in personalities. There were, of course, exceptions to the general practices of both of them, but for the most part each remained true to his type. Mr. Grady discussed his men in a genial and sympathetic manner, while Mr. Watterson wrote more from the standpoint of an unsympathetic critic.

In his character sketches, Mr. Grady was trying to influence the young men of his time. He wrote of John H. Inman[55] and Peter Cooper[58] as one would write of bosom friends who had turned adversity into success. Mr. Inman represented to him a type of man whose energy was put forth in the development of his country materially. Mr. Inman's life would count for more than the life of a politician in the young Georgian's eye, and why should he not write sympathetically about such a character? Peter Cooper was the type of the aged who had blessed his day and generation, and who was leaving a rich heritage of money, and, even more, a good name, to his children, and who was conscious in his last days of the blessing of the nation upon his head. Many were the men whose names and good deeds Mr. Grady held up to the rising generation. His optimistic outlook upon life ruled him, therefore he could not write in a vindictive spirit when he was living his truest life. There were two notable exceptions to this general practice; while a very young man ex-Governor Brown made a rather scathing arraignment of his paper which Mr. Grady felt he must defend, and in this defense he said some cutting things to ex-Governor Brown.[17] In later life he refers to this attack and makes amends for all he said. How sympathetically did he portray the great statesman in his editorial on the "Florida Frauds."[37] The other exception was his reply to General Toombs.[25] While he felt called upon to defend his paper against General Toombs, he expressed regret at having to mention his faults in old age. In this connection he says:

"It gives us real sorrow, when we read the grand speech which this old man made in the Senate of the United States in 1860, in

[55]Editorial: John H. Inman.
[58]Editorial: A Noble Life.
[17]Editorial: A Card.
[37]Editorial: Frauds in Florida.
[25]Editorial: Gen. Toombs and the Herald.

defense of his oppressed country that he did not die then. Let us remember him then and forget him now."[25]

And a few years later, when General Toombs died, Mr. Grady writes of him thus:

"The kingliest of Georgians is dead!"

.   .   .   .

"Bob Toombs is no more!
"Quenched is this imperious life. Stilled is the mighty heart! Gone the dauntless spirit! At rest the turbulent emotions. Pulseless, the splendid form."

.   .   .   .

"The unforgiven rebel awaits, in unbroken stillness, the final judgment of God. And death, touching the tranquil face with his unspeakable solemnity, revives therein something of the majesty and beauty of youth, that his people, gazing through the mist of tears, may see him last as they loved him best, when he stood among them in his kingly splendor."[292]

We are all inclined to say beautiful things in praise of the dead, but Mr. Grady could have said a great deal less and then have spoken in flattering terms of General Toombs.

Reviewing Mr. Watterson's editorials during the same time we reviewed Mr. Grady's—the Reconstruction period and the early eighties—we find that Mr. Watterson was more uniformly unkind in his attitude toward the men he wrote about. He was about ten years older than Mr. Grady and doubtless his experiences in the army had embittered him somewhat. In his early editorials, barring his personalities on his favorite politicians, one will scarcely find any personal editorial comments which are not rather abusive. He refers to ex-President Grant as a "voluptuary." Mr. Krock said on this subject:

"Mr. Watterson, like all of those who must write in the heat of the moment (1877), said harsher things than he intended. While he undoubtedly meant the bulk of the subjoined, he would have been shocked if, in 1923, he could have read his reference to General Grant as a "voluptuary."[293]

During the pre-election campaign of 1880, Mr. Watterson made a personal attack upon the character of General Garfield. This is the closing paragraph of his editorial, "Judge Black on Fraud":

"That 'omnipotent lie' was enthroned and Garfield fell down and worshiped it, offering incense along with such ruffians as J. Madison. Wells and his fellow-burglars with whom Garfield had held criminal intercourse in New Orleans. That 'omnipotent lie' Garfield worships today. He is stamped with the impress of the seal of the beast, and

[25]Editorial: Gen. Tooms and the Herald.
[292]Hudgins, H. C. & Co.: Life and Labors of H. W. G., pp. 39 (d) 40.
[293]Krock, A.: Editorials of Henry Watterson, p. 56 (a).

he has been chosen as the leader of the party which stands convicted before the Heaven, angels and men of the most infamous political crime of the century."[294]

Mr. Krock, in commenting upon the editorial from which the above-quoted paragraph is taken, said this:

"To a generation which remembers General Garfield the tradition of kindliness and culture and cherishes his memory as one who lost his life by assassination, this attack during the pre-election campaign of 1880, linking General Garfield with the Tilden affair, will light up some forgotten passages in American political history. In his auto-biography, Mr. Watterson forgot and forgave much of this sort of controversy."[295]

By way of contrast reread what Mr. Grady has to say about General Toombs,[296] and then consider the difference between his attitude and that of Mr. Watterson in the following paragraph:

"To be sure, Mr. Toombs has a certain power, limited indeed and applicable to a class that is passing away. Edwin Forrest, who was once a famous tragedian, can startle the cock-loft. There is a power in brazen impudence and abundant lungs; in a big belly; in coarse invectives; Mr. Toombs has this sort of power. It is the power of the mountebank who will roar you an' the groundlings shall cry 'let him roar again.' But it appeals to no intelligent, considerate feeling set of people; it promises nothing but destruction out of which Mr. Toombs will be pretty sure to profit, for he is, strange to say, a thrifty man, who, in spite of his political excesses, takes uncommon care of himself. But he is the very worse counsellor of others."[297]

It may be that Mr. Watterson has more nearly described General Toombs' character. He is evidently more vitriolic. The object here is to illustrate the two types of editors. Mr. Watterson started off in his early writings very much after the manner of the old-fashioned editorial writer who dealt too much in personalities instead of keeping closer to principles. Mr. Grady was among the very first of the new school of editors who laid aside the satirical type of editorial to "play up" principles and the virtues of men, rather than their vices.

But it is only fair to say that Mr. Watterson, after he reached middle age, mellowed quite a bit and left off to a great extent his bitter personal editorials. And by the time he had reached ripe old age he could write as sympathetically about "Blind Tom" as could Mr. Grady of his old black mammy. Witness here the human touch:

---

[294]Krock, A.: Editorials of Henry Watterson, p. 59 (b).
[295]Krock, A.: Editorials of Henry Watterson, p. 58 (a).
[296]See note 292.
[297]Krock, A.: Editorials of Henry Watterson, p. 39 (b).

"I cannot trust myself to write of him as I feel. It is as if some trusty, well-beloved mastiff—mute but affectionate—closely associated with the dead and gone—had been suddenly recalled to be as suddenly taken away. The wires that flash his death lighten a picture gallery for me of the old, familiar faces. What was he? Whence came he? Was he the Prince of the fairy tale held by wicked Enchantress; nor any Beauty—not even the Heaven-born Maid of Melody—to release him? Blind, deformed and black—as black even as Erebus— idiocy, idiocy of a mysterious, perpetual frenzy, the sole companion of his waking visions and his dreams—whence came he, and was he, and wherefore? That there was a soul there, be sure, imprisoned, chained, in that little black bosom, released at last; gone to the Angels, not to imitate the seraph-songs of Heaven, but to join the Choir Invisible for ever and for ever."[298]

As Mr. Krock suggests, Mr. Watterson in his Autobiography has laid aside his controversial style and has adopted the style of the familiar essay. Age has sweetened his disposition and he wrote with a genuinely human touch. The style in his Autobiography more nearly approached the inimitable style Mr. Grady used as a young man. Mr. Watterson developed his style; Mr. Grady was a born stylist.

During the Reconstruction period Mr. Watterson's style was not up to the standard set in later life. He was more interested in the thought and he hammered away with sledge-hammer blows. Mr. Krock said in this connection:

"Later in his editorial career, Mr. Watterson polished his phrases longer, but at this period he was writing in haste and at high temperature. Hence the bumpy construction."[299]

On the other hand, those connected with Mr. Grady during his early journalistic writing characterize it as the same style he used as a mature man. Mr. Avery, in speaking of his first contribution to the *Atlanta Constitution,* said:

"It had the marks that signalizes him today—sparkle, delicious humor, affluent diction, descriptive verity, luxuriance of imagination and the rarest vein of thought."[300]

Another associated with him on the *Atlanta Constitution* wrote this significant paragraph about Mr. Grady's style in general:

"Touching Grady's writings, I have no hesitation in declaring that they contain passages which worthily emulate the musical prose of Addison or the charming humor of Irving. 'H. W. G.'—the *nom de plume* of Henry W. Grady. How often have we for the time eschewed the plethoric press dispatches, the sage wisdom of the leader, the pointed pungency of the paragraph, and the lurid headlines of the last horrid sensation, to pounce with eager avidity on the *opima dapes* which

[298]Krock, A.: Editorials of Henry Watterson, p. 109 (c).
[299]*Ibid.*, p. 17 (c).
[300]Hudgins, H. C. & Co.: Life and Labors of Henry W. Grady, p. 41 (c).

is always served with the rarest juices of natural fatness, and the most piquant sauce of genuine humor, by this *chef de cusine* of the muses!"[301]

Mr. Krock, speaking of Mr. Watterson's style, later on said certain passages could be scanned, it is so poetical.[302] Let's compare passages from two editorials of each, written at Christmas time. The first quotations are from the last paragraphs of editorials written by Mr. Watterson, December 25, 1868, and December 25, 1869. In the last paragraph of the first editorial he is speaking of the pioneers of Kentucky, and he starts off thus:

"The canebrakes are all gone. The pioneers are all gone. Their graves are deep-sunken under the ploughshares, and are hid beneath the clover blooms. But the hardy manhood; the warm, impulsive love of freedom; the honest hatred of persecution; the keen sympathy with the weak and suffering, all these noble sentiments that honored the lives of the fathers remains and are illustrated by the children in the unanimity with which they resist the despotism, set up over their brothers at the South. Remove this despotism, and we may divide on a thousand issues; but as long as it continues we are one in opposing it as unnecessary, tyrannical, and cruel."[303]

"This Christmas essay," says Mr. Krock, "joined to the discussion of the state of public affairs, is companion to a second Christmas editorial which follows it. The date of the second was 1869, and in that article Mr. Watterson's aim was solely literary. As an example of the Victorian journalistic style, once so popular and now discarded, it has many points of interest."[304] This quotation is from the last paragraph referred to above:

"Out of the fallows which time plows up within us, out of the seams and scars of afflictions suffered and wretchedness nobly borne, spring up fresh violets. Bless God for them and Christmas, which is their ministering angel; and as we gather close together about the chimney, we shall none of us forget to bless the good Saint Nicholas, to whom thanks and praises and blessings be, so long as there is a peg in the mantelboard and a stocking to be hung, so long as there are little hearts to be glad and to glorify the morning that glorifies the Christmas year!"[305]

Let's compare extracts from two editorials written December 24 and 25, 1873, by Mr. Grady with the two quoted above. These are the most comparable of the writings of these men because of the season and the subjects discussed. Mr. Watterson discussed the state of affairs in the first edi-

[301]Hudgins, H. C. & Co.: Life and Labors of Henry W. Grady, p. 42 (d).
[302]Krock, A.: Editorials of Henry Watterson, p. 15 (d).
[303]*Ibid.*, p. 22 (c).
[304]*Ibid*, p. 25 (d).
[305]*Ibid.*, p. 25 (d).

torial, and alluded to the suffering on account of these conditions in his most delightful passage in his second editorial. The emotions of the two men are quite different, hence the difference in style. The quotation following is from Mr. Grady's Christmas editorial and the last paragraph:

"We know of a home, an humble one too; where tonight while the pillow of the cradle is being warmed, a darling little rascal, barely able to toddle, and with just four teeth in his busy mouth, will work his way up to the mantle piece, and hang Grandma's woolen stocking —too big by half for his meager gifts—on the nail therein embedded! And happy will he be! Noble will he be! Great will he be, if in all the life stretching out before him, his heart is filled, and his impulses started by no meaner motives, than the sturdy faith, the honest hope, the abiding confidence that inspires him, and as he pins the wrinkled old leggin to the chimneyboard tonight.
"God bless the children all—and fill their stockings full!"[20]

And on the next day Mr. Grady discoursed on "A Fat and Gentle Day," the last paragraph of which is as follows:

"Let all, be happy! Feel way down into the pocket, bring forth the surplus cent, and have one day of supreme enjoyment and rest. God knows we all need it, in this busy, restless, jostling world. In its humble way the *Herald* will celebrate the day, and with its mind's eye on one and all of its readers, it echoes that most eloquent of all Christmas speeches, 'Tiny Tim's Oration,' that came up in pure simpleness from his good little heart, and rested like a sunbeam, we know, on his quivering lips—'God bless us all, every one!'"[21]

One sees Mr. Watterson in these two editorials at his best, and Mr. Grady in his most natural atmosphere. Mr. Watterson in the first editorial was somewhat acrimonious in the statement of what might have been true, literally. He could not, even at Christmas time, leave off the discussion of politics. That he sympathized with the South cannot be doubted, but in expressing his sympathy he did it in a manner not exactly in keeping with the spirit of the season. In his second editorial he was more happy in his writing, but one cannot but feel that the sentiments expressed are more or less forced. At least his long, heavy sentences do not break up into rhythmic phrases as do Mr. Grady's sentences. His words are long and hard to pronounce, while Mr. Grady's words are, for the most part, monosyllabic and easy flowing. Mr. Watterson's sentences are studied; Mr. Grady's are spontaneous—flowing from a heart as unsophisticated as Tiny Tim's. Mr. Watterson is more interested in the thick of the political fight; Mr. Grady is more interested in the happiness of mankind, especially the happiness of little children. Mr. Watterson's feelings arise

[20]Editorial: The Little Ones and Their Stockings.
[21]Editorial: A Fat and Gentle Day.

from his antagonisms; Mr. Grady's sentiments flow from a heart that beats in unison with the truest impulses of human nature.

As has been suggested, Mr. Watterson's style and spirit in Marse Henry is more comparable with Mr. Grady's style and spirit.[306]   His writing is more in accord with the familiar essay type, in the conversational style.   Too, at this time he has lost interest in the controversial or disputatious forms of writing.   He looks at the mistakes of men more as foibles which make us all akin and call for our indulgence rather than our condemnation.   The humor in Marse Henry is more like the humor that characterizes Mr. Grady's whole newspaper career.

If it is true that the man is the style,[307] then we have a fairly good representation of these two journalists.   That they were both patriotic can readily be seen from their writings.   That they were both sincere in their efforts no one will deny, although they did not always agree in the methods to bring about the same goal or ideals.   If one examines their writings very closely he will find that Mr. Watterson indulged more in sarcasm and vitriolic writings than did Mr. Grady.   Mr. Grady mentions much more frequently his trust in his Heavenly Father, therefore it is safe to conclude that he was much more under the influence of religion than was Mr. Watterson.   All these things point to the fact that Mr. Watterson made his appeal, in his great work in helping to reconstruct the South, more to the intellect, and Mr. Grady in his appeals played more upon the emotions, therefore he was properly called the great peacemaker of the South.

MR. GRADY AND CHARLES A. DANA

Chas. A. Dana was a little over thirty years older than Mr. Grady.   He had almost as many years of experience in the newspaper work before Mr. Grady began to write, besides he had taken an active part in the Civil War as Assistant Secretary of War under Stanton.   However, it is interesting to compare his work during the Reconstruction Period with that of Mr. Grady's during the same period. While Mr. Watterson was the "buffer"[308] between the North and the South, Mr. Dana was the friend and advocate of the South at the North.   Mr. Dana, like Mr. Grady, was working in his own way in an effort to build up our common

[306]Watterson, Henry: Marse Henry, An Autobiography, Vol. I and II.
[307]Rhodes, Chas. E.: Effective Expression, p. 39ff.
[308]Krock: The Editorials of Henry Watterson, p. 42 (c).

country. But his work was more in the political arena and, true to his sense of justice and the principles of progress, he contended, as did Mr. Grady, for fair play and honest government. Wherever there was error or fraud in the government he was unrelenting in his attacks, and spared neither friend nor foe. He was a great admirer of General Grant and helped to elect him to the presidency, but he criticized and praised him alike when the occasion demanded. His work was, of course, more nationalistic than was Mr. Grady's, but in a very real sense he, too, was a complement of Mr. Grady in his work in the rehabilitation of the South. There was the need of an honest man to criticize national politics while the earnest workers of the South were trying to help recreate the material wealth of the South. This is the reason for comparing the writings of Mr. Dana to those of Mr. Grady. And, too, it will be an interesting study to compare the writings of these men from the literary standpoint. George H. Payne has said that successful newspaper writing is literary effort in a new field.[309] Is it not true that all the great editors have possessed the literary qualities in no small degree? Editors must be able to attract the attention of the reading public to their writings before they can hope to wield an influence, and this is best done by the use of literary qualities. If the editor would interest his readers he must appeal to the intelligence of his readers. When he appeals to them legitimately he is in the realm of the literary art.

Mr. Dana, in his prospectus in the *Sun*, January 27, 1868, expressed his policy which he ever afterward followed literally. The first paragraph reads as follows:

"In changing its proprietorship, The *Sun* will not in any respect change its principles or general line of conduct. It will continue to be an independent newspaper, wearing the livery of no party, and discussing public questions and the acts of public men on their merits alone. It will be guided, as it has been hitherto, by uncompromising loyalty to the Union, and will resist every attempt to weaken the bonds that unite the American people into one nation."[310]

During the campaign in 1886 he again expressed his independence and his sense of fairness and justice in the following:

. . . "In bestowing commendation upon him (General Grant) we reserve to ourselves the privilege of dealing as fairly and impartially by the nominee of the Democratic party as by him. The organ and champion of neither party, we shall speak freely of each accord-

[309]Payne, Geo. H.: Hist. of Journalism in U. S., p. 10, Intro.
[310]Wilson, Jas. H.: The Life of Chas. A. Dana, p. 381 (a).

ing to its merits, and hold the balance with even justice between the two, during the exciting canvass which the country is now entering."[311]

Mr. Dana was wedded to the newspaper work. In 1869 he was offered a position as customs collector in the city of New York. In declining the offer he makes a declaration of his estimate of his duty as an editor of an independent newspaper. The following is an excerpt from this statement:

"But I already hold an office of responsibility as a conductor of an independent newspaper, and I am persuaded that to abandon it or neglect it for the functions you offer me would be to leave a superior duty for one of much less importance. Nor is it certain that I can do more to help you in the pure and efficient administration of the Treasury Department by remaining here and denouncing and exposing political immorality than I could as appraisor by the most zealous effort to insure the faithful and honest collection of the customs."[312]

How similar is this statment to Mr. Grady's refusal to let his name be used in connection with the office of congressman a few years later. Both declared their purpose to stick to the duty as they saw it. While Mr. Dana saw his duty lying out before him in the political world, Mr. Grady saw his lying before him in helping to develop the material resources of his native state. As has been said before, Mr. Dana is nationalistic in his scope while Mr. Grady keeps his efforts confined for the most part to the development of the South. The following quotation from Mr. Grady's letter in which he declined to allow his name to be presented to the public as a candidate for congress will show the difference between these two journalists and at the same time show how each is wedded to his journalistic field.

"I shall be satisfied with the labors of my life, when those labors are over, 'if' my son, looking abroad upon a better and grander Georgia—a Georgia that has filled the destiny God intended for her—when her towns and cities are hives of industry and her country-side the exhaustless fields from which their stores are drawn—when every stream dances on its way to the music of spindles, and every forest echoes back the roar of the passing train—when her valleys smile with abundant harvest, and from her hill-sides come the tinkling bells as her herds and flocks go forth from their folds—when more than two million people proclaim her perfect independence, and bless her with their love—I shall be more than content, I say, if my son, looking upon such scenes as these, can stand up and say: 'My father bore a part in this work, and his name lives in the memory of his people.'"[213]

There is a very marked difference in the style of these two articles. Mr. Dana's style is best described by his own

---

[311]Wilson, Jas. H.: The Life of Chas. A. Dana, p. 395 (b).
[312]*Ibid.*, p. 415 (b).
[213]Harris, J. C.: Life of Henry W. Grady, p. 11 (d).

statement taken from his prospectus, in which he outlined the policy of the *Sun.* He said:

"It will study condensation, clearness, point, and will endeavor to present its daily photograph of the whole world's doings in the most luminous and lively manner."[314]

While Mr. Grady is clear and luminous, he is more profuse and lively. While he is setting forth what he conceives to be his duty, he allows his imagination to play in poetic flights as he gives us the picture of a "better and grander Georgia." He makes us see the prosperous towns and thriving industries, and he makes us hear the music of the stream as it goes dancing on its way to turn the wheels of industry, and he makes us listen to the tinkling cow-bells as the cattle feed upon a thousand hills wrapped in verdure, and he makes us wonder at the echoes of the roaring train in the beautiful valleys and, finally, he would have us see two or more million of happy Georgians as the result of his labors, while his son blesses and reveres his father's name as it lingers in the memories of his people.

Of course, Mr. Dana was too practical to allow himself to revel in such poetic flights. In fact, he was absorbed in exposing fraud and corruption of the political arena. He was not in the idealistic realm; he was down among the sordid affairs of this world and had to deal with the baser natures of mankind. He was not to blame. His was a glorious work if it did picture the dark side of human nature. Just what part he played in helping to reconstruct our whole social system in those dark days is hard to point out, but it remains a fact that he did perform a wholesome task assumed as the duty of his independence.

Mr. Dana did all in his power to elect General Grant to the presidency, but he did not make any effort to shield any of his weaknesses once in office. He did not like the official practices of President Grant in awarding, as he thought, official recognition for private gifts; neither did he like nor approve of the President's attitude toward the Mexican government, and in the early part of 1869 he spoke of his official practices as:

. . . "the corrupting and demoralizing practices of giving office in return for presents, his fatal disregard of law, his petty foreign policy, and his deplorable failure to represent the sentiment and to promote the manifest destiny of the country."[315]

But he as readily defends the President when the unscrupulous gold ring tries to connect the high office with an

[314]Wilson, Jas. H.: The Life of Chas. A. Dana, p. 381 (c).
[315]*Ibid.,* p. 116 (d).

attempted fraud.   This is Mr. Dana's comment upon the
situation:

> "He had no more to do with the gold speculation than any other
> innocent man, except that he ordered gold sold, and thus broke the
> ring.   The plans of the conspirators to involve General Grant, and
> thus make their own fortune or ruin his reputation, were very skil-
> ful and adroit, but his plain, straightforward letter scatters them all
> to the winds.   The whole country will believe General Grant, and will
> regard his letter with satisfaction."[316]

Mr. Dana was in favor of Congress instead of the President's prescribing the terms of Reconstruction, and he
thought the Southern people might expect some odious
terms, for he held they were deserving of some discipline;
however, he did not agree with unnecessary harsh terms on
the part of the government.   Mr. Dana's biographer, in
commenting upon this topic, has this to say:

> "His constant cry, so long as the Federal government undertook,
> under the authority of Congress, to control the provincial governments
> or to exercise any supervision whatever over State or federal elec-
> tions was: 'No force bill!   No negro domination!!' "[317]

Mr. Dana did not favor the Electoral Commission to settle the contest between Hayes and Tilden, and he claimed
that the Democrats in Congress committed "official suicide"
in agreeing to do it.   His reference to the decision of the
Commission is:

> "There is no process or method or invention or miracle by which
> a lie can be made truth or a fraud converted into an honest reality.
> . . .   No such settlement of the question can stand.   Nothing can
> stand but truth!"[318]

There were those who argued that it was necessary, if
possible, to keep the government out of the hands of the
Democrats at this time, because the election of the Democrats would put back in power the radical element of the
South.[319]   He had no fear of the South and wished everything to be settled at the ballot-box, and he was willing to
abide by the decision of the people, but he would not willing-
ly consent to the rule of the few or to a government of
fraud.   Listen to this statement in his early writings on
Reconstruction:

> "After twenty-five years of political strife, followed by four years
> of terrible war, the United States has destroyed slavery and its legiti-
> mate offspring, secession.   Our taste for fighting is satiated.   For

---

[316]Wilson, Jas. H.: The Life of Chas. A. Dana, p. 417 (c).
[317]*Ibid.*, p. 446 (a).
[318]*Ibid.*, p. 443 (d) f.
[319]Merriam, Geo. S.: The Life and Times of Samuel Bowles, p. 278 (d).

a century to come the American remedy for redress of grievances will be a peaceful resort to the ballot-box."[320]

Now when the party in power had, in his opinion, subverted the ballot-box, his righteous indignation was aroused and he did not fail ever afterward to condemn the proceedings of the Commission as a fraud perpetrated upon the American people. In January, 1881, Mr. Dana was asked to make a subscription to a fund to put President Hayes' portrait in the Hall of Fame. He declined after this manner:

"I decline to join in such subscription. I am not willing to do anything that may be designed or construed as a compliment to Mr. Hayes, or that may recognize his tenure of executive office at Washington, as anything other than an event of dishonor. He was not chosen president. . . .

"Sooner than honorably commemorate such an event or do public homage to such a man, I beg you, gentlemen, with your own hands first to destroy the portraits of John Adams and John Quincy Adams in Memorial Hall, and then to raze the ground of the hall itself."[321]

In his opinion of President Hayes' tenure of office he was in substantial agreement with Mr. Watterson and Mr. Grady. In fact, his principles were in agreement all the way with these men; however, his party alignments were not always the same as theirs. But he was in all respects a patriot rather than a partisan. He was for the United States and principles—not men.

Mr. Dana and Mr. Grady were agreed for the most part in the great task of building the nation and in their continual preaching of peace and fellowship. But Mr. Grady did not agree with Mr. Dana's selection of presidential candidates for the Democrats.[54] He did not believe in putting just any man on the ticket who might have some chance of winning, regardless of his political principles and former affiliations, although he did use his influence always for the Democratic nominees. They were complements of each other during this great Reconstruction period. Mr. Dana was continually fighting against the radical measures of Congress toward the South. He believed in a speedy restoration of the South for commercial as well as for other reasons. Mr. Dana was concerned with the political end of Reconstruction, while Mr. Grady was concerned more directly with the material rejuvenation of the South. He would have the North believe the South had buried the hatchet, and he would have his people know the blessings of

[320]Wilson, Jas. H.: The Life of Chas. A. Dana, p. 390 (c).
[321]*Ibid*, p. 457 (b).
[54]Editorial: I Told You So.

a re-united people. The patriotism of the one could not bear full fruition without the other. Both were opportunists—developing the work nearest at hand. Each was working accordnig to his highest ability.

Possibly the greatest contrast between these two men was in their religious views. Mr. Grady had the simple faith of a child. He believed that God had a hand in everything. Time and again in his editorials he expressed in no uncertain terms his faith in God. In 1881, he wrote a long communication to the *Atlanta Constitution,* in which he discussed the Atheistic Tide Sweeping over the Continent. This one sentence will show his belief:

"In the conflict that is coming, the church is impregnable, because the church is right; because it is founded on a rock."[323]

In another passage he says:

"I am not misled by the superb eloquence of Ingersoll nor the noisy blasphemy of his imitators."[323]

But it was otherwise with Mr. Dana. He was tolerant of all religious faiths or philosophies. In fact his religion seemed to be more of a philosophy than a religion. A friend of his asked him in his declining years if there were any evidence which would be received in a court of justice that there is any life hereafter. His reply was:

"Not a scintilla. It is all based on man's egotism and that hope which springs eternal in the human breast."[324]

No doubt this explains the strong optimistic spirit of Mr. Grady and the seeming lack of the same in Mr. Dana.

In the point of style, Mr. Grady and Mr. Dana were very different. Mr. Grady was more profuse and more poetical. Figures of speech were common. Nature and the world about him made an especial appeal to him. Mr. Grady's writings were prompted more from his broad human sympath:es. He saw life in the large. On the other hand, Mr. Dana was clear, direct, incisive, and possibly more logical. Mr. Dana was often moved by his strong dislikes. No man could write as many adverse criticisms as did Mr. Dana without developing a vindictive spirit. His keen analysis made him somewhat cynical at times. He seldom attempted to portray character—as a whole. When he did his sketches were of the stereotyped kind he sent back from the army front—mere catalogues of qualities.[325] No doubt his reports

[323]Harris, J. C.: Life of Henry W. Grady, p. 231.
[324]Wilson, Jas. H.: The Life of Chas. A. Dana, p. 451 (d).
[325]Dana, Chas. A.: Recollections of the Civil War, p. 63 (d) f.

from the front during the war materially affected his style in this respect. How different his characters were from Mr. Grady's sympathetic portrayal of his characters! Mr. Dana's writings were straightforward narrations or expositions. He never threw in any descriptive effects as did Mr. Grady. His style was elegance itself, but it had no interest for the reader aside from its content. It is true that what he wrote bristled with facts so incisive that they never missed their goal. His style was adapted to what he was doing. How well he would have succeeded in doing Mr. Grady's work is a conjecture, and vice versa.

MR. GRADY AND SAMUEL BOWLES, THE ELDER

Mr. Samuel Bowles, the Elder, is another one of those fearless men who dared to stand for what he thought was right. Were he living today he would be classed as a freelance in the newspaper world. He was a Republican, but he was not a "stand-patter," as the term is understood today. He was not a partisan in the sense that he put the party before his patriotism. He stood by his party when right, but he flayed it when wrong, and since he gave the last ounce of his life blood to his country during the stormy period of Reconstruction, a comparison of his editorial writings with those of Henry W. Grady is eminently proper. He is just another illustration of the power of the man uniting with the power of the moment to accomplish a great task. If education means the responding of the individual intelligently to his surroundings,[326] Mr. Bowles must have been an educated man in the true sense of the word, for in the light of history, barring a few personalities, his every act was honorable and justifiable. And his circumstances seemed to wield a powerful influence upon his character and the style of his writing. Living in Springfield, Massachusetts, and editing the *Republican*, surrounded by the New Englanders, he was a matter-of-fact writer. He had very little time for embellishment; he seldom, if ever, portrayed the beauties of nature in and around his native heath, although he did describe the beauties of nature on his travels when he was resting from his onerous labors. He worked at high tension and drew on his nervous energies too heavily. He, too, died, as did Mr. Grady, in the height of his powers. He lived long enough to see his labors in behalf of Reconstruction just beginning to bear fruitage, having died in 1877, in his early fifties.

---

[326]Adamson, J. E.: The Individual and the Environment, Intro., p. 3 (c).

Mr. Bowles was a controversialist in the newspaper world. He took issue with much that he considered wrong whenever he thought the wrong needed to be published to the reading public. He would not publish scandal for scandal's sake; it must be in his opinion something that would be best for society to know.[328] He refused to have the press limited to what the guilty would have published. This is what he said to a lawyer who was defending a questionable commercial concern:

"Of course, I cannot accept the limitations which you put upon journalism. The gathering and publication of *facts* is but one part of its vocation. To express *opinions* is a higher and larger share of its duties. The conduct of public men, before the public, is the legitimate subject of its discussion. The lawyer before the court, as the minister in his pulpit, the executive in his chair of state, and the legislator in his hall of assembly,—all these are alike public men, and their conduct in their public vocations is the proper theme of both journalistic report and discussion."[329]

Mr. Bowles not only asked independent action on the part of newspapers, but he considered independence of action on the part of public men the sign of ability and character. He asked no more for himself than he granted to others, but he reserved to journalism the right to praise the acts or condemn the acts of public men whenever he could justify such procedure on his part. In 1870 he advocated retrenchment in government expenditure, and when Congressman Dawes of his own district made a fight for this contention upon the floor of the House of Representatives, Mr. Bowles commented as follows:

"It is the boldest demonstration against narrow-minded partisanship almost ever made in Congress, and a token of the increasing independence of the man of real character and ability in public life. Anybody can denounce the sins of our enemies. There will be plenty of that done. It is more important that the offenses of our friends should be laid bare, than the dangers which they threaten should be exposed,—even that the capital should be furnished to our opponents to carry on the warfare against ourselves,—that we may be indicted and driven to purify our nation, reform our evils, and strengthen our souls."[330]

He believed that the Republicans needed to be saved from their own weaknesses rather than from the attacks of their enemies. This was always his attitude toward all organizations and toward every individual. It was a time that personal hatreds and personal aggrandizements should be held up to the public, and he considered it to be his duty to do his part of the publicity work.

---

[328]Merriam, Geo. S.: The Life and Times of Samuel Bowles, p. 90 (a).
[329]*Ibid.*, p. 99 (b).
[330]*Ibid.*, p. 118 (b).

His attitude toward Reconstruction was very sympathetic in reference to the South. While he was sympathetic, his argument was based upon justice and the psychology of the situation. Listen to the advice he gave to his party:

"The Republican party cannot long maintain its supremacy at the South by negro votes alone. The instincts of submission and dependence in them and of domination in the whites, are too strong to permit such a reversal of the familiar relations and the natural order. The slave-holding element has learned to combine, conspire, and command, in the best school on earth, and they will certainly come to the top. Nor is it desirable that such a state of things should be continued."

He continues his criticism of President Grant's administration when he attacks his Reconstruction policy. He never failed to criticize the "carpet-bag" government of the South. In 1871, he has this to say about the mistakes of the administration:

"Of all the mistakes—neither few nor small—of General Grant's Administration, the grand cardinal mistake, so far as the future of the country is concerned, has been his neglect to do anything important for the restoration of good feeling and loyalty at the South. He ought to have promoted amnesty; to have conciliated the majority while protecting the minority; to have had from the first a representative Southern man in the cabinet; and by personal visits to the South to have cultivated the acquaintance of the leaders and won their co-operation."[332]

Here we find Mr. Bowles preaching peace in what might have been a most effectual manner had his suggestion been followed literally. This critical tone of the *Republican* called forth adverse criticisms from the contemporary republican press. Mr. Bowles replied as follows:

"Very likely it is true, as a critical contemporary suggests, that the *Republican* is more apt to find fault with the Republican party than with the Democratic. The just parent is much more prone to discipline his own children than he is his neighbor's,—especially if there is reason for secret satisfaction in the improprieties of the latter. We confess to much more interest in the character and good conduct of the Republican party than in that of the Democratic. The Republican party is still worth saving, but it is almost hopeless and certainly discouraging work, reforming the Democrats. Our great anxiety is lest they should be so bad that they cannot longer be effectively used as a moral scarecrow to the Republican."[333]

And a short time after this he called upon the public to let their conscience take note of the trivial public affairs as well as the more important affairs. He was not in favor of the rule of the caucus, because it gave the perquisite office-seekers an opportunity to get hold of the reins of the

[332]Merriam, Geo. S.: The Life and Times of Samuel Bowles, p. 127 (b).
[333]*Ibid.*, p. 127 (b).

government. He appeals to the citizens to go to the polls and cast their votes for an honest government. This is his estimate of the caucus:

> "This whole caucus system, from the ward meeting up to the national convention, has been converted into a machine to relieve the people of the task of governing themselves. What is the result? That the whole framework of our government from top to bottom is being eaten out and worn away by a dry-rot; that we have almost come to look upon self-seeking and place-hunting and thieving the public money as a matter of course, disagreeable, to be sure, but inevitable; that in this free democratic country, 'politician' has become a term of reproach. How long can we go in this way?"[334]

Again in 1872, just before the Republican convention, Mr. Bowles made another plea for a government administered in the interest of all the people, and especially emphasized the importance of fair treatment of the South. When President Grant took the oath of office he said, "Let us have peace." But Mr. Bowles knew that his acts had not justified his platitudes. He again suggested the terms of a lasting peace when he wrote:

> "Shall the government be administered in the interest of the whole people, or, as in late years, in that of a party, a faction, or a person? Shall the people retain the right of local self-government, or shall they be governed more and more from Washington? Shall the memories and rancors of the war be perpetuated by a policy of proscription and hate, creating a disaffected and restless Poland in the Southern States, to be a constant source of uneasiness and peril; or shall the powerful instincts of patriotism and national unity, dormant for a season but never quite dead, be allowed full play under a policy of generous amnesty and reconciliation?"[335]

When President Grant sent an army to Louisiana during the contested elections of the Hayes-Tilden affair, Mr. Bowles characterized it as illegal, revolutionary, treasonable. He makes this argument:

> "Suppose that General Butler, defeated in a popular vote for governor of Massachusetts, had claimed the office under a strained construction of a doubtful statute, and the President had supported him by force of arms, and sent his soldiery to eject members from the State-house? If this sort of thing is lawful and right in Louisiana, it is lawful and right in Massachusetts."[336]

And when President Grant was pushing the force bill in the House, Mr. Bowles praised the moderation and self-control of the leaders of the South under the trying circumstances after he had condemned the lack of wisdom of those who were pushing this objectionable bill. He says:

---

[334]Merriam, Geo. S.: The Life and Times of Samuel Bowles. p. 137 (b).
[335]*Ibid.*, p. 179 (d).
[336]*Ibid.*, p. 236 (a).

"It is almost impossible to exaggerate the magnitude of the interest at stake, at this moment, between excitable neighbors. Never has a high-spirited people found itself in a case calling more urgently for the heroic virtues, justice, prudence, temperance, fortitude."[337]

It was through such writings that Mr. Bowles wielded a powerful influence in helping to knit the two sections together. The pacifying of the antagonistic sections of the United States was not a one-man job. Had there not been such men as Mr. Bowles and Mr. Dana at the North fighting for justice and fair play the Reconstruction days might have been continued indefinitely. The radical element at the North had to have some one of their own party to point out their faults, always holding up to their view the shoals toward which the ship of state was drifting, "precept upon precept, word upon word, here a little and there a little." Mr. Bowles did this as well, if not better, than any other Northern editor. His argument was put forth with cogent logic. His method was suited to the Northern temperament, as was the florid style of Mr. Grady suited to the excitable nature of the Southern people. Mr. Bowles, as well as others, was preparing his people for the universal appeal that came later from the eloquent tongue of Mr. Grady.[338] Mr. Grady did use at times very strong adjectives in describing the acts of the dominant party, but he could not and did not write in such terms so often as did Mr. Bowles. The Southern people were smarting under what they considered a tyrannical government and Mr. Grady's soft pedal was only the part of wisdom. His patriotic note and the portrayal of a new and better South materially was, indeed, proper under the circumstances. Since the great mass of people in the South had so little to do with politics it was best that their minds be turned to the beauties of nature and the blessing of a happy and contented people. This Mr. Grady did, while his Northern contemporary was fighting the battles for the bases of a sounder government for the nation, and especially for the Southern states.

When Mr. Bowles got away from the busy life of editing the political news and giving advice to his constituents, he often let his soul revel in the beauties of nature. While on a vacation in the West he writes some descriptive letters back to his paper. Here is his effort to describe the flowers he saw on this trip:

"I wish I could repeat the roll of their array of beauties, for the benefit of my flower-learned readers; I know most of them very well by sight, as the boy said of his unlearned alphabet, but cannot call

[337]Merriam, Geo. S.: The Life and Times of Samuel Bowles, p. 239 (d).
[338]New South: Harris, J. C., Life of H. W. G., p. 83 tf.

them by name. Blue and yellow are the dominating colors; of the former several varieties of little bell and trumpet shaped blossoms, pendant along stalwart stalks; again, a similar shaped flower, but more delicate, a little tube in pink and white, seem original here; and of the golden hues there babies and grand-babies of the sun-flower family in every shade and shape."[339]

Later he describes Grey's Peak as follows:

"It was the greatest sight in all our Colorado travel. In im-pressiveness, in overcomingness, it takes rank with the three or four great natural wonders of the world,—with Niagara Falls from the Tower, with the Yo-Semite Valley from Inspiration Point. No Swiss mountain view carries such majestic sweeps of distance, such sublime combinations of height and depth and breadth; such uplifting in the presence of God; such dwarfing of mortal sense, such welcome to the immortal thought."[340]

From these two quotations it is easily seen that his de-scriptions are detailed. One feels as if he were searching for the right word all the while to give adequate expression to his sense of the beautiful and the sublime. This is not strange when one recalls that for the most part his busy life had been given over to the affairs of politics, which re-quire incisive writings rather than detailed descriptions. While writing upon politics he was at home; not so in the world of beauty—at least he did not have the power of de-scription that Mr. Grady possessed. Compare Mr. Bowles' detailed description with the impressionistic writings of Mr. Grady in the following:

"Georgia is prolific of these balmy nooks, where the breezes play perpetually and the mosquito is unknown. There is New Holland Springs, a charming cut-off from the hot and striving world, where daisies and violets bloom spontaneous, where cool springs gush from under every hillside, and where the proprietors of the cottages hold out the savory inducement of a 'barbecue once a week.' " . . .
"Or further, we might find joy and repose in the shades of Yonah, that great mountain, rising fresh and splendid from the setting of brooks and groves, its sides spotted by never a dust-fleck, defiled by no man's hand—primeval and pure just as God fashioned it."[24]

Mr. Grady did not deal in detailed descriptions—he gave a broad view with a few bold sketches. Nor did he have to get outside his own state to find beauty. Wherever his eyes fell there was beauty. Mr. Bowles never took time to write about the beautiful things at home if he saw them; Mr. Grady wrote about them in his busiest days. The dif-ference, in a word, between these two great souls is this: The one was a matter-of-fact personage; the other was a poet unknown because he did not write verse.

[339]Merriam, Geo. S.: Life and Times of Samuel Bowles, p. 82 (b).
[340]*Ibid.*, p. 84 (b).
[24]Editorial: Where Shall We Spend the Summer?

SUMMARY

Henry W. Grady, Henry Watterson, Chas. A. Dana, Samuel Bowles, the Elder, were four great editors who wrote during the Reconstruction period. What the nation owes to these men for what they did during that trying period will never be fully known. General Lee had surrendered his sword to General Grant at Appomattox; there was peace only in name. The South had been conquered physically, but their pride was still unsubdued. Neither party in the great conflict could very readily forgive or forget the indignities of the other. The South cringed under the yoke placed upon it by the radical government of the North. Just how to put an end to this warfare of mind and heart was the great problem. Is not the patriotism of peace greater than the patriotism of war? Does it not take more courage and wisdom to settle the dispute after the conflict than it does to wield the battle-axe? The smouldering embers of the war were buried deep beneath the rubbish of the conflict. The nation was suffering commercially, spiritually, and morally, and still the radical elements on both sides of the Mason and Dixon Line were fanning the smouldering embers. Who shall lead the forces in this great spiritual conflict? There may have been others, and there were, who played a part in this great work, but the four men mentioned above were four great forces, each in his own way, and each complementing the remaining three.

Henry W. Grady, born in the South, the best product of the Old and the prophet of the New, gave his energies to the rehabilitating of the desolate South. He preached peace and patriotism to the nation, and loyalty to the South. He never ceased to call attention to the great natural resources of his own state and the South in general. He held up to the youth of his section the noble characters of our greatest and best men. He showed how grander it is to reconstruct the South upon proper material bases than to strive for political preferment. He showed to the world that there was naturally a very close fellow feeling between the freedman and his former master, and if certain meddlers would keep hands off the negro question, satisfactory and amicable relations would, in the due course of time, be established between the races.[27] His appeal was made more directly to the emotions of his readers, and since the Southern people responded more readily to such an appeal he was pre-eminently the man who should lead the South in this great spir-

---

[27]Editorial: The New Solution of the Negro Question.

itual rejuvenation. But fortunately his appeal was not to the baser emotions. He led his people along the side of the babbling brooks in paths strewn with violets, daisies and daffodils. He conversed with them in beautiful metaphors and laughed with them at the foibles of the great and the near great. He made them forget their troubles and see the bright side of life even amidst their desolations and sorrows. But this task was too great for any one mortal.

Mr. Watterson occupied a unique position. He lived in a state that was almost equally divided between the North and the South in the great conflict.[341] And as an editor his interests lay as much at the North as at the South. He therefore became a buffer between the two extremes. His part was more that of the politician than was Mr. Grady's. He emphasized the importance of the South's relegating its radical element to the rear and putting in the lead those who were willing to work for nationalization of the whole country.[342] Nor did he neglect to call attention to the North to its unfair treatment of the South. He pointed out the inconsistences of asking for peace and then taking pains to do the things that would stir up the animosities of the people whom they pretended to conciliate.[343] He was just as quick to place blame upon the leaders of the South when they did not conform to an honest intelligent course as he saw it.[344] It was true that Mr. Watterson was more interested in the politics of the nation than he was in the rehabilitation of the material welfare of the South. He was farther removed from the desolation of the South than was Mr. Grady and it was but natural that he saw the political trend of affairs more than he experienced the economic want at the South. And since he was more or less on intimate terms with both the North and the South it was proper that he devote his abilities to the political situation.

Mr. Dana was an independent in politics. His former relations to the government as Assistant Secretary of the Navy put him in close touch with governmental affairs. He was not interested in a political party *per se*. The party was a means to an end and when it failed to serve the great needs of the times he did not fail to criticize its shortcomings. He was a patriot first and a partisan afterwards. He wanted to see the nation restored to normalcy without unnecessary hardships being placed upon the de-

[341]Krock, A.: The Editorials of Henry Watterson, p. 15 (b).
[342]*Ibid*, p. 41 (c).
[343]*Ibid.*, p. 22 (c).
[344]*Ibid.*, p. 39 (d).

pleted South. All during the Reconstruction period he considered it his duty to point out the weaknesses in the administration. He criticized severely the habit of appointing to responsible positions in the administration of governmental affairs men more for personal reasons than for their insight into and efficiency in governmental administration.[345] Corruption was played up at every appearance.

Mr. Bowles was a Republican in party affiliations but he was an independent in his thinking. He, like Mr. Dana, wanted to see an honest administration. Corruption in government and in the economic world in general was condemned with all the power of his trenchant pen. He wished the Democratic party to be strong enough to keep continually before the nation the shortcomings of his own party.[346] The government must be administered, if honest, in the interest of the people as a whole. The policy of Reconstruction he condemned in vigorous terms. He objected to force bill or an army of occupation in the South to restore order. He believed in the supremacy of the white people of the South and censured the president for not inviting the confidence of the leaders of the South. He knew that the proper way to establish amicable relations between the sections was to co-operate with the leaders and relegate the carpet-bagger to his native state. He lived only to see his ideals for reconstruction merely started—the withdrawal of the army from the Southern states.

These men were literary men devoting their talents to the building of a better and grander nation by arguing for principles—the principles that would establish peace and prosperity in reality as well as in name. Each man had his part to play. Had these men in their several corners been heeded and had all the people known what they stood for, much misunderstanding between the sections would have long since been explained. Too often in the South the extremist was portrayed instead of such men as Dana and Bowles, and doubtless the same thing was true in the North. These men were men of destiny—destined to help clear up the misunderstandings between the sections and proclaim the principles of a permanent government. How far short of the realization of these things would Grady and Watterson have fallen had the job been left to them alone? Or how far short would Dana and Bowles have fallen had they been left alone to do the job? It was an impossibility

[345]Wilson, Jas. H.: The Life of Chas. A. Dana, p. 413 (d).
[346]Merriam, Geo. S.: The Life and Times of Samuel Bowles, p. 136 (c).

without the co-operation of these men, and others like them, in the various sections.

THE CONCLUSION

In the foregoing pages, Mr. Grady has been studied, first, as a stylist, and second, as an editorial writer, and third, in comparison with three of the leading editorial writers of his time, both in the South and in the North.

He had all those graces and qualities of style that make his writings enjoyable reading. He was noted for his descriptive verity, but he could as easily turn to that style known as impressionistic description. His humor bubbled up from the perennial flow of his broad human sympathies. He made his readers laugh with him; there was no sarcasm in his soul. He looked out upon nature and painted the beautiful pictures seen there only as a great personality can paint them. The good in his fellowmen he portrayed and held up their virtues as examples for youth to meditate upon. His poetic touches made all the world akin.

Nor was he less noted as an editorial writer. He handled the political questions with the insight of a statesman. In the building of the nation after the Civil War no other man discussed with so facile a pen the things that tended to the development of the South. His people owe to his memory a debt of gratitude for the unselfish efforts he put forth in the material development of the South. He was as truly interested in the development of the nation, and he lent the force of his pen in promoting peace between the sections. At all times, he called upon his people to co-operate for the good of all.

As an orator, the world recognizes Mr. Grady as the peer of the nation's greatest orators, but he is more than an orator: he is a man among men. As a man he compares favorably with the nation's greatest seers, and with the men who guided the nation's destiny through the power of their pens. With the growing power and favor of the press, Mr. Grady's name will continue to increase and finally when the history of his times is written, he will be classed among the great men and great editors of the last quarter of the nineteenth century.

PART TWO

The Material Studied:

THE EARLY JOURNALISTIC WRITINGS OF HENRY W. GRADY

Sources:

THE ATLANTA (GA.) CONSTITUTION

And

THE ATLANTA (GA.) HERALD

INDEX

THE EARLY JOURNALISTIC WRITINGS OF
HENRY W. GRADY.

1

Henry W. Grady,
Atlanta Constitution,
May 28, '69.

A PIQUANT LETTER WRITTEN WHILE AT THE UNIVERSITY OF VIRGINIA

Virginia women are glorious creatures—buxom, blushing, beautiful. There is a delightful vigor in their action, a luscious fulness in their forms, and a rosy glory in their complexion that we find nowhere else. They are all healthy and glowing—all frank and merry; as plump as partridges, and as pretty as Pearls. Could any man have witnessed the long procession that filed through the University grounds yesterday afternoon, and then fail to endorse the sentiment recorded above, he should be unanimously voted an ass.

The object of the procession alluded to, was the decoration of the soldiers' graves, and the destination of the procession was the soldiers' cemetery. We followed them (how could we help it?) up and down hill, till we stood among the graves of our hero dead. There was no lugubrious gloominess about the cemetery, but on the contrary, everybody was cheerful and happy, as this sincere tribute was paid to the memory of those immortal men who were buried in light and glory. Ere long every little mound had received its floral crown, and then a very squeaking-voiced man arose to address the crowd upon the "sad and solemn occasion which had called them together"; just then, by a most lucky dispensation of Providence, it began to rain. Squeaky had to suspend—the ladies became "frightened," you know—umbrellas were sought for and found—cloaks were jerked on, dresses looped up, ankles began to flash delightfully, and the whole thing grew exciting. Your correspondent having procured an umbrella, made advances to a delicious little bundle of curls, cloaks, and calico, that stood close by trembling prettily. The arrangement was consummated—curls cuddled up affectionately under our arm, and—this is the way they dressed the soldiers' graves at the University of Virginia.

The political world is becoming lively, by reason of the election on the 6th of July. The democrats have at length concluded their strength on Walker, and will vote for the constitution expurgated of test-oath and disfranchisement clause. The "Old Dominion" truly has to make a Hobson's choice. General Lee has spoken (in private) in terms of strong endorsement of Walker. There are very few democrats who will not vigorously support Walker against Wells— the Joe Brown of Virginia. Many prominent Radicals have declared in his favor and his election is very probable. Wells, poor dog, is squirming in agony of fear; Grant insists on expurgation of the test-oath and disfranchisement clause, and his carpet bag constituency will not submit to the proposed expurgation. Sharpe, of Washington, has helepd him out of this dilemma by the following scheme. He (Wells) was to remain in the position taken in the Gorland letter— viz.: acquiesce to the objections of Grant, and the party was to be instructed through the Leagues to vote in conflict with these objections. By this characteristic maneuver the rebellious Humphreys was hushed and there is harmony in their camp again.

The press is fighting actively for Walker; scathing leaders against

Wells and the unamended Constitution seem to be the leading features of the campaign. Very few attempts are made to eulogize our candidate, and most probably this is the wisest course; for Walker is not a political paragon, nor is the Constitution a model document, even when the two worst objectionable clauses are stricken out.

The leading politicians are waking up to the crises, buckling on their harness and preparing to strike for the "Old Dominion." Luks, Stewart, Johnston, McKenzie, Wingfield and a host of others are battling fiercely while Walker himself is to take the stump in a day or two, with appointments already to the 28th of June. Let us hope for the best and remember that God protects the right.

The University is doing bravely. The faculty and Board of Visitors are making improvements every day. Ex-governor Lowe of Maryland will deliver the Oration in place of Mr. O'Connor, who you will remember resigned some time since.

The Rev. Mr. Munsay will deliver an address to the Christian Association at the coming celebration. This address will probably be the most attractive feature of the final. As an orator Mr. Munsay is almost unequalled. The elections in College have just taken place, resulting as follows: Medalist, R. F. Smith, of Georgia vs. R. Morgan, Jr., of Georgia; Orator, W. Marshall, of Mississippi vs. H. W. Grady, of Georgia.

By the way, this system of College politics is a hard nut to crack. Boys, like apes, are imitative in their actions; hence you will find in every canvass within our college walls the same electioneering trickery, the same party combinations, and the same stump speaking which characterize the campaigns of older politicians. We have our caucuses—secret and open; we have our party issues and every candidate must define his platform and we have all the bluffings and villainies and chicanery that you will find in the outer world. And, in fact, so strongly are we tinctured with the mad spirit of the age that our elections are getting such affairs of importance, that an explosion is soon inevitable. And none of us would be surprised at the institution of a college "Imperialist," which should propose to give to the Faculty prerogatives in this department, and to utterly abolish our present republican form of College government.

(Signed) *King.*

The wheat is looking very well; in certain portions of the State, better than for ten years before. The fruit crop in and around Suffolk County was severely injured by the late frost. The complaints of the ravages of the fly on the tobacco plant are increasing as the planting season comes on, and many who contemplated raising tobacco will, in consequence of these complaints, plant corn instead.

2

Henry W. Grady (King Hans),
Atlanta Constitution,
August 17, 1869.

MARIETTA FAIR.

Your correspondent reached this place last night, and wrote to you shortly after arrival. At the time, he wrote to a lady friend. The letters were put into the wrong envelopes, and the young lady, bless her rosy lips (!) was regaled with a pondrous disquisition on fairs, etc., and such things, instead of the melting missive which she had a right to expect, while your editorial eyes were shocked at the sight of the ravings of a "spoon," and your dignity disturbed at the very flimsy way in which the document opened. You need not publish the letter that you received, as no matters of general interest are therein discussed. The lady is a cousin of mine, hence the little terms of endearment which you will notice scattered throughout the letter.

I was considerably disordered by my short ride from Atlanta. The train was very much crowded. I was forced, during the journey, to poise myself on a square inch of velvet cushion, and not being of that peculiar conical shape which alone would render the execution of this little gymnastic feat either practical or pleasant, and being surrounded, all the time, by two men, one of whom did not suggest "Eau de Cologne," you can imagine my agony. But when I had arrived at Marietta, and caught a glimpse of the bright halls and tempting supper table of that good hotel, the Kennesaw House, I was rendered very happy, and in a few moments I had completely forgotten my fragrant friend and my extempore gymnasium on the train.

You will pardon me for recording right here and now, the unqualified delight, the ecstatic gratification with which I devoured a dish of finely fixed up ham and eggs. Ham and eggs! ye delicious correlatives; ye savory soothers of stomichic cravings! ye Siamese twins of the edible world—how I love ye! (H & E every morning at the Kennesaw House.)

After supper, in loafing around, I found that a considerable crowd had already collected—besides the great number that came up with us, a good many had arrived in the afternoon on "The Pea-nut"; (Vulgarly called "The Goober"). The Kennesaw House was almost full before the Fair opened, by visitors from the country.

I was unable to find out anything at all concerning the schedule of pleasures for the week. Everybody with the smallest spark of intelligence, is busy, and have no time to talk. After peregrinating in frantic eagerness, the whole city, I gained only one item of information, viz.: the canine which resides in the hoop and barrel factory is of a very rapacious nature. I had a short and very rapid conversation with this horrid creature last night. Upon returning to my room, I beguiled my male chambermaid into a conversation, and determined to extort from him some facts concerning the mighty Fair which was to agitate this city for the coming week. The only item I could glean from him was, "Dey is goin' to have an animal show dis week; fur dey bring a leopard and a wild man and a parrot on de train today." That your correspondent will look eagerly for this incongruous menagerie on tomorrow, is an established fact.

The Fair is given for the purpose of raising funds for the establishment of a liberal school system in Marietta. It is endorsed by many leading men of the leading cities of the State.

There will be a good many dances, parties, concerts, exhibitions, etc., during the week, and, if I am correctly informed, one well assorted menagerie. A lively time is anticipated, especially at the menagerie. More anon.

3

Henry W. Grady (King Hans),
Atlanta Constitution,
August 19, 1869.

MARIETTA FAIR

This Fair, sir, is a lineal descendant of that one at which poor Moses, the Vicar's son, was emparadised out of his three years' earnings, and I confidently assent that it is a most hopeful scion of so hopeful stock. When a pinched up and ugly storekeeper asks you to buy an article, you can easily refuse him; but when a pair of deep blue eyes pleadingly glances into your face, when rosy-tipped fingers

piquantly push an article at you, and an arch, silvery voice coquettishly begs you "to buy"—why then, sir, I'll swear, you must buy even
this, the article in question be a little Noah's ark, filled with very
square animals. I bought one of these things which I hereby adver-
tise for sale, at a very liberal discount. All the articles in the grounds
are sold at their real value, but my goodness! they want to make a
Toodles of every man. I was offered, yesterday, the following articles
in about five minutes: a piano, a pair of baby shoes, a pound of
candy, a grist mill, a watermelon, a night-cap, a buggy (here I got a
little sulky), a whistle, a *thing*, a rooster, ice cream, two *things*, a
cradle and a bottle of Winslow's Soothing Syrup. And on each occasion, I was urged to buy, and am now happy in being unmolested, as
I have taken advantage of the Bankrupt law.

After supper we assembled at a tastefully decorated hall, for
the purpose of hearing a concert and witnessing an exhibition given
by the Free Schools. The programme consisted of songs by the
school and short farces acted by the few who had been selected as
best skilled in the histrionic art. Though the exhibition did not recall
Niblo's Garden, (for we've never been there), yet it was creditable
indeed. The pieces selected were simple, and the children, with not
much affectation and very much good taste, strutted their parts finely
over the ambitious boards. . . .

After the concert was over, everybody promenaded through the
park, and had a good time. The Marietta ladies, by their charming
manners and glowing beauty, as well as by their immense quantity
of goods which they sold, proved themselves most dam-sels (excuse
the hyphen).

We were introduced to one who bankrupted our purse during the
day, and now tried to get an unlimited draft on our affections. She
got it.

We can imagine nothing more delightful than promenading
through this beautiful park with a fine lady on your arm—no money
in your pocket to distract her attention from your discourse—the
band throwing out most melodious love notes—to catch the flash of
the bright eyes, as they peep, shyly at you, or the glitter of the pearly
teeth as they laugh love at your left shoulder; and not enough light
to let any one see what you are saying—just privacy enough to stir
up the passion in you, and just publicity enough to prevent your
getting spooney; in short, just joy enough to fill you with a glorious
happiness, and not enough to dissolve you in ecstacy. Plump perfection! Come up and try it. . . .

4

Henry W. Grady (King Hans),
Atlanta Constitution,
August 20, 1869.

MARIETTA FAIR

The Rev. Dr. Tucker did not speak, but (he not being here) his
place was filled by Col. David E. Butler of Morgan county. Col.
Butler made a very good speech. He possesses great fluency and a
captivating delivery. His views are intensely patriotic and practical.
He gave much good advice, and carried encouragement to the hearts
of all present by his sanguine sentiments. He held the crowd in
attention for about an hour. One idea I must be pardoned for alluding to. He says that he believes before the end of the world we
will have a regular telegraphic communication with Saturn, Jupiter,
etc. This is a beautiful theory, though slightly opposed to the teach-
ings of philosophy. I'd like to hear a man sing "Old Dog Tray"

after he had been planting telegraph poles about thirty miles beyond our atmosphere. He also believes that the stars are inhabited. This conclusion was arrived at by an argument of analogy. He thinks that the inhabitants of the stars never having sinned—this conclusion arrived at by a fancy flight—are as yet gifted with omniscience, etc., and hence can help run the telegraph wires. They had better run two-thirds of the way, as we have sinned and are not omniscient. I should like to suggest Atlanta a good terminus for this aerial cable. "Hole in the sky," Boutwell will represent "the management," on the part of the earth. Mr. Butler hopes for a universal language, for though the Babel music was pretty, yet the starites had no representation there and may now possess the tongue which will be spoken by all souls. The approaching comet will act as a kind of carrier dove between the worlds while the preliminaries are being arranged. Mr. Butler's speech was very well-timed and well received.

5

Henry W. Grady (King Hans),
The Press Excursion,
Atlanta Constitution,
August 26, 1869.

We started at the appointed time, and seldom have I seen a crowd in higher spirits. In spite of the dull reaction which inevitably follows such exciting sessions as the one we had last night, everybody is jolly. Yet this is not remarkable, when we consider the perfection which has been reached by Col. Hulbert in regard to the travelling arrangements. Your correspondent will venture to remark that things are "done up brown."

We are pulled by U. S. Grant, a powerful engine, which smokingly puffs along right merrily. Its fore-parts are radiant with the glories of a "star spangled banner," while over its latter end garlands are coquettishly thrown. A "festive cuss" of an engine it is. Next to the engine comes a condensed edition of the famous Delmonico attachment. Good cooks are now engaged in fixing up dinner which will make our hearts (?) glad, while in the corner great baskets of champagne are piled in regal profusion. (Now cut this last sentence out of Dr. Haygood's edition of the paper 'cause I don't want to have a fuss with nobody.) In the next car we have a barber shop, where skillful tonsors are in waiting. In the same car we have all the arrangements for fixing up and primping, and plenty of ice water to mix with the soap, and make good lather for the barbers.

The next car is the writing car. To each seat has been attached an elegant writing desk, with the usual appurtenances—at one of these your correspondent is now writing. The next is a superbly finished smoking car. After this comes the palace sleeping cars. I believe that few excursion parties have ever gone out more perfectly amazed.

Col. Hulbert is "a rattler." He is "Old King Cole" (not E. W. Cole, but the "jolly old soul.") The Press is finely represented on this excursion. I suppose already over forty papers have correspondents here. Prominent among the rest, we notice that old Nestor in the journalistic world, Col. Clisby, of Macon; the spirited and powerful chief of the *Chronicle* and *Sentinel* with his accomplished confrere, Moore; the venerable, yet sprightly, Maj. Martin, of the Columbus *Enquirer;* the intrepid and hard-working Willingham, and Christy, Atkinson, Brobston, Burke, Call and many others not less agreeable. With such an outfit and such a party, with representations from every city in the state save Savannah, how can the excursion be otherwise than pleasant and profitable?

Two or three ovations, I understand, have already been tendered the party, all of which we will of course accept.

Governor Bullock is on the train.

6

Henry W. Grady (King Hans),
Press Excursion,
Atlanta Constitution,
August 27, 1869.

Your correspondent has determined to write you short scrap letters by every mail, giving the largest amount of information in the smallest possible space.

The first halt made by the excursionists was near the Etowah river, to witness the working of the ballast machine. While there was nothing intricate or wonderful about this machine, except its enormous power, yet it was interesting as an evidence of the stable improvement now being worked out on the State Road; and in this connection we would suggest that one or two of these machines be bought by the city council of Atlanta for the purpose of breaking the rock used for grading the streets. One of these worked by an enterprising darkey or two, could do more work in an hour than a hundred would do from now till the comet comes. The one now working on the road cannot be procured, as Fitch is going to buy it to take to Griffin to grind rocks for the country fights which ever and anon enliven that little village.

The next stoppage was at the Howard Iron Works. These works are a mile and a half from Kingston, immediately upon the Western and Atlantic Railroad, and are the most complete of the kind in the South. Over 1,400 bushels of lime are sent from them per week—200 bushels per day. A force of over thirty-five men are regularly employed here. The quarry is inexhaustible. After being worked for twenty-five years, it is now just opened. Col. Howard informed us that after the quarry had been eight feet deeper, the hydraulic cement now being worked will be superseded by the pure, white, bird's-eye lime. The works are not making cement there now, as the machinery was destroyed during the war. Transportation can be had for the lime, on the Western Atlantic and Atlantic Railroad for two cents a mile per ton. . . .

The Cartersville band worked up a tune or two for us in a very creditable style, and then Mark A. Cooper addressed the Press Excursion in a chaste and sincere speech. He, after complimenting the liberal policy of the present administration, called attention to some specimens of mineral collected on the Van Wek Road, and from the Etowah Iron Works. Specimens of iron ore were shown containing at least 90 per cent of pure iron. Gold quartz, mineral paint, grindstone and hones, were shown in profusion. . . . While passing through the tunnel, many witticisms were perpetrated. Never did the Press shine with more brilliancy than during the transit, yet we can truthfully say, that we never saw as little ugliness in so large a crowd before, as was buried in the dark depths of that tremendous tunnel.

7

Henry W. Grady (King Hans),
The Press Excursion,
Atlanta Constitution,
August 29, 1869.

It was really amusing to see the fright under which the Press labored while wandering about under the earth. The main shaft of the mines runs an immense distance under the ground, and branches into numberless ramifications. About thirteen of us started at first, guided by imps of the mine—black, sooty little genii. After we had gone about one hundred yards, and the daylight was shut out, we were badly scared set of men. Some one asked the lamp-crested little scoundrel that was leading us, if there were any holes that we might step in. "Yes," says the young villian, "I soused up to my chin in one yesterday, and a fellow was drowned a day or two ago." The Press blanched, and Gen. Wright exclaimed, "I will give any amount of money to any man who will get me out of this place." A young Gnome took the offer, and the last we heard of them was a shivering sign from the Gen. as the guide told him that his light was nearly out, and he had no matches. About this time the mules and wagons commenced running to and fro. "Mule a-coming—scrouch to the wall," shrieked the guide. Looking up we saw a crowd of shouting fiends, with lamps blazing on their foreheads, and lighting up their eyes and teeth, come whirling down upon us, while along-side of them loomed the shadowy outlines of the mules. "Cou-ugh," shouted Wooten of the Newman *Herald*, and he turned, as did all of us, and spluttered along in the darkness at a tremendous rate. For about fifteen minutes, Wooten enjoyed the honor of being the leading editor of the *Georgia Press*. Your correspondent stumbled on a rock, and never did he hug a damsel with a more fervent grasp than the one with which he clapsed that rock. The mules passed in about three inches of me, which of course I enjoyed very much. We jumbled on after this for about half a mile, at a thousand risks, and at last my special guide informed us that a dark cavern was "Tom Smith's room." Anxious to meet anybody, we huddled in. Tom met us at the crack, and after welcoming us proceeded, with grim equanimity, to show us a place where the mountain had slipped the day before and nearly buried him alive. A perceptible shudder ran through the Press, and I turned my mournful thoughts to my wife and six children, whom I hoped to meet again. (Tom Smith, ye atrocious frightener of editors, I hereby hope that if you ever do this way again, that your wife won't love you, and that your children won't resemble you.) At this juncture, a car passed and offered to take us out for half a dollar. Gladly we crouched upon it, and at length reached the day-light. I will never go in another coal mine. Such had been the extreme fright endured by our party, that though we had been in about an hour, one man was found upon coming out to be *perfectly gray*. To save scientific men the trouble of making inquiries concerning this last assertion, I will state, the man alluded to was gray before he went into the cave.

8

Henry W. Grady (King Hans),
The Press Excursion,
Atlanta Constitution,
August 31, 1869.

The ghost of the old Rome—the seven-hilled Rome—is, I have no doubt at this very moment, rollicking most jollily among her phantom friends in the regions of the defunct, over the creditable manner in which her young Georgia namesake has located the "Press Gang" for the past few days. And not less jollily are the editors of the State rollicking for the same reason. And well might the venerable old spirit of departed Rome shake her shadowy sides with joy on this account, for the little "Mountain City" has crowned herself with glory.

On our arrival here, at 6 o'clock on Friday morning, we were met by the Mayor and his staff, who escorted us to the Choice House, where a sumptuous breakfast was prepared. We destroyed it. We spent the day in Rome, and had a splendid dinner, at which Mayor Hargrave, Governor Bullock, and Mr. Clisby, made little speeches. On these I shall not comment, as I shall probably report them in full. During the whole day fine carriages were in attendance at the hotel, and subject to the use of the Press, and a brass band discoursed good music the whilom. Every possible hospitality was shown us. In fact, only one thing can equal the extreme kindness shown us, and that is the intense surprise shown by the Southern editors, when they found so flourishing and beautiful a city, nestled among the mountains of Floyd. Many eminent men have said that the situation of Rome is second to none in the world—and it is generally believed that ere long, Atlanta will have her laurels rivalled by this, the most flourishing city of North Georgia.

9

Henry W. Grady (King Hans),
The Press Excursion,
Atlanta Constitution,
September 4, 1869.

We were opposed to the motion to thank Governor Bullock for many reasons. First the motion itself says, "We wish to ignore all political matters whatever, etc." Well, if you ignore politics altogether, Governor Bullock is thereby drawn from his political position, dwindles into the condition of a private citizen, and as such, deserves the thanks of nobody. Secondly, because the people of the State are beginning to look upon the Excursion with suspicion, and this official homage to Govenor Bullock will justly increase the suspicion. Thirdly, because we are opposed to tuckling to a tyrant, or licking the hand that lashes us—and lastly, because Governor Bullock knew he was looked upon as an interloper by most of the Press, from the very first; hence, should have had the good taste to have withdrawn, and because he did wrong and usurped Col. Hulbert's position, and placed the Press in a false position when he said at Cartersville, "I have invited several gentlemen to accompany me on this trip, etc." Still, we must make the best of it. This much we will say concerning the gentlemen who accompanied us on that trip. Every one of us will be watched with suspicious eyes for the next few months, and we must be careful to vindicate the Press against the insinuations which have been made against it.

Colonel Hulbert, we believe, was actuated by good motives, and of course, the Excursion will prove vastly beneficial to the State.

The Excursion is now over, and I will bid farewell to the pleasant rides, the sumptuous dinners, to the red hematite, and frown to the demons of the mines, and the baby of lies thereof; and retire to the manifold embraces of my wife and six children.

10

Henry W. Grady (King Hans),
Communication,
September 9, 1869.
Editor Constitution:

The *Intelligencer* of yesterday, very truculently comments upon a statement made by us in a letter published in your paper on the 4th inst. The statement was this: "We believe that bribery was attempted on the Press Excursion." The *Intelligencer* calls for facts or a withdrawal of the insinuation. We simply state that we are in possession of no facts which would directly prove that bribery was attempted. Had we been, we should have presented the facts and thus have made the assertion that bribery was attempted, rather than have said that "we believe bribery was attempted."

As to the withdrawal of the insinuation, we of course will do no such thing. We believe Governor Bullock accompanied the excursion with the intention of bartering executive patronage for the control, or partial control of the editorial columns of the Democratic newspapers. This belief is founded upon an opinion of Governor Bullock's policy in this direction as evidenced heretofore, and upon a number of little circumstances that we noted while upon the excursion. Without having time, space, or disposition to make these circumstances public, we will say that we are confident in asserting that in this belief expressed above, we are sustained by ever observant gentleman who was on the trip. You see, Mr. Intelligencer, facts are not always necessary to the creation of a belief. For instance: If a paper should condemn a certain political party very bitterly for a long time, and then suddenly turn and laud most profusely the leaders of the very party which it formerly condemned, and if this paper was to exhibit daily large sums of money (or the equivalent), that it had received from these party leaders, a belief would very naturally and very logically arise, to the effect that the said paper had sold its honor for patronage, or had been literally bought. This belief, I contend, would arise, although there might not have been any witnesses of the sale. Now, candidly and unprejudicedly, Mr. Intelligencer, don't you think this is so?

In conclusion, let us say, that if the *Intelligencer* needs any more information on this or any other points (as he doubtless will), we will be pleased to furnish it gratis.

11

Henry W. Grady (King Hans),
October 12, 1869.

REPLY TO S. A. E.

Mr. Constitution:

I have neither time nor desire to inflict your readers with painfully tiresome emanations from my pen; but I am imperatively called to this present writing. During the last two or three weeks I have noticed in your valuable paper insinuations from your correspondents that I had been saying things of love to various maidens and other girls. For on yesterday a conversation was pointed in which it was said openly that I made amatory remarks to a certain dam-sel in Marietta. Now it is to protest against these things I write. What, sir, must be the feelings of my wife when she reads in a public journal of my infidelity? What torrents of shame must rush into the hearts of my tender six when they are told of the treachery of their paternal head? Though you are neither woman, sir, or one of the half dozen, still you appreciate their truly awful emotions.

My heart bleeds and the tears flow from both of my eyes in simultaneous grief as I think how that estimable woman will be lacerated with agony, as away off in Constantinople where she is visiting her aunt's cousin, she sees the statement of my unfaithful infidelity. And how she will blush with shame as from the taunting looks of her neighbors, she knows they have found out the damnable secret. And they must all know, for next to the Rome *Courier*, the *Constitution* is more widely circulated in Constantinople than any Georgia paper. I can pursue this painful subject no farther, for torrents of tears blind me; but I will ask that you allow no more articles of the kind to enter the paper; if you have not sent out your Constantinople package that you suppress the present issue.

Alas! Alas! My poor wife and my unfortunate six.

Tell the miserable S. A. E. who caused all this that in my heart I forgive him. Oh! the lamentable half dozen and one over in Constantinople.

12

Henry W. Grady (King Hans),
November 23, 1869.

AT MACON FAIR

Dear Constitution:

Not a word about porcine monstrosities, about bovine busters, or equine wonders shall I tell you. Not a syllable shall I write about plows, thrashers, drills, gins, or anything smacking of agriculture, but to things lovelier and fancier by far shall I devote my "gray goose quill."

Ladies, my dear *Constitution*, ladies, and paintings, the fine arts shall give body to this document. Pigs you know, and horses and cows and even plows, may be useful and interesting in their way, but ladies, my dear fellow, are things after all. Were it not for ladies who would there be to eat pigs and run the plows? Ladies of all descriptions we have at the fair—from the most beautiful to the ugliest and scraggiest—from the most artless to the most artificial. We have never seen so many women (nor so much of them) in our lives before. Almost every city and hamlet in the State was represented; from almost every garden had fair flowers been plucked, bound in beautiful bouquets, with lively hued ribbons and sent to Macon to give delight to the eyes and olfactories of bewitched men. (Now, by Jove, I think that that sentence is a very creditable one—I feel quite comfortable about it.) I believe without fear of contradiction, I can assent that Athens was far ahead of all other cities, in respect to the exhibition of lovely and talented women. This is a monopoly that the "City of Colleges" has long enjoyed, and no one can claim that successful competition has yet been offered by any sister city. . . .

And when we assent (and we wot of what we speak) that the loveliest of all the Athens beauties did not attend the fair, and we promise that the fortune of that city is made.

Strangers of all grades and kinds from all lands and climes (tautological, but euphonic), agree in declaring that they have never seen a collection of fairer women anywhere, nor of handsome gentlemen either, though it behooves me not to speak of this. I cannot leave this branch of my subject without alluding to the superb style in which the Brown House, of Macon, is kept, to the great and successful efforts made by its proprietor to give pleasure and comfort to its guests. It was, by all odds, the most popular hotel, in the city during the fair, and I doubt not will be for all time. Prominent among its attractions is the courteous and accomplished clerk, Mr. S. W. Poole. By his kind and delicate attention—by his elegant and gentlemanly demeanor, he won the good will of all, and for some reason or other, particularly the ladies. We heard enough compliments and thanks expressed in regard to him, to have whelmed a man of ordinary capacity; but I suppose the surface of that Poole was scarcely ruffled, as he has become so used to it.

The exhibition of paintings was very fine. In my opinion the finest painting in the gallery was Pharaoh's horses, executed by Miss Franklin of Athens. The pictures represented the heads of the chariot horses of Pharaoh when the waters of the Dead Sea were closing upon them, and never have I seen the expression of fear so vividly set forth by any means. Even horror was expressed by certain contractions of nerve and muscle, and the eye fairly quivered with fright. I do not doubt that the picture will take a first-rate premium. . . By all odds the best fruit piece was by Mrs. Goodman, the excellent artist of your city. The picture is already famous, and I am confident will receive a distinguished premium. Its chief charm lies in the fact that it is so natural. I remember frequently, when a child, to have simply stood and looked at the picture, and to have completely satisfied my desire for fruit by merely eating through the eyes. It is perfect. The other departments of the fair—I am hungry and shall get something to eat.

13

Henry W. Grady,
The Atlanta Herald,
January 1, 1873.

"THE OLD YEAR IS DEAD—LONG LIVE THE NEW"

The same sad story!

"The old 'un is dead; the young 'un is doing as well as could be expected. Pass the snuff Sairey Gamp." . . . Well, the Old Year died full of honor and glory; rich with high achievements and star-reaching aspirations; full of tender, noble memories; fragrant with many a violet springing from the grave of many a buried hope.

The world has kept handsomely apace in the grand march of progress.

Every clime and country, and every interest, scientific, social, and religious has been bettered.

The Englishman has learnt that there is an "h" in the alphabet, a world across the waters, and a place where cockneys are not cultivated and "my Lord" does not polish his boots upon the basis of "my man." The Yankee has discovered that there is an increasing demand for wooden nutmegs and flannel sausages in the South; that dishonesty is not shrewdness, and that a carpet-bag, though a convenient, is not a safe piece of baggage to travel through Texas with. France has found freedom in a Republic, Spain has found trouble in Cuba, the "nigger" has found sorrow in freedom, and Stanley, of the New York *Herald*, has found Livingstone in a horn. The women have discovered India-rubber bustles, balloonatics have mastered the billowey air, and the preachers have about discovered how to get to Heaven without being religious; Boston has learnt how Columbia felt in '65, and a cow has taught Chicago in '72 what Sherman taught Atlanta in '64.

The Union Pacific railroad has been finished, and a credit moblier has finished the treasury; a canal has been built (somewhere near Suez) through whose accommodating waters the juices of one world is mixed with the juices of another; China has torn down her walls of selfishness, and having eaten up everything in the Celestial Kingdom, has got sociable enough to browse about on her neighbors; a bridge has been built across Behrings Strait, and the vivacious Kamschatkarians now step over to spend the evening with the Alaskarians; a pneumatic tube has been hoisted from Galveston to New York through which beef is easily "jerked," in six minutes. A submarine passage way has been built from Philadelphia to Havre, and so we Havre a new way across the ocean; it seems to us that something else has been built from somewhere or other to somewhere else, which unites something or other to something else; if not built, it soon will be. (There may be some romance in the above; but it's all right; we never let the matter of truth worry us when we get started on a matter of this sort. Liberal deductions will be made for all lies to those who never tell them.)

But seriously, we have much to be thankful for.

The cause of progress, and truth and enlightenment is advancing finely. The world is better, mellower, wealthier, wiser than ever before. The follies of an unripe age are exploding like bubbles as we get along down the vista.

All the voluptuous, sensuous dodges and pleas of the passion-wasted people have had their short, mad sway, and today at the pure shrine of hymen devouter worshippers kneel than ever knelt before; the cricket on the home hearth sings a cheerier song and pipes a blither lay than crickets ever sang or piped before. Free lovers who, twelve months ago, held high carnival in palaces now fester in prison houses; seducers who have been wont to carry their shame in brazen immunity, are now shot like dogs; society is safer, our system is purer than it has been in many a year, and profligacy which once ran riot, has now quieted down till its visciousness is satisfied by occasionally peeping through its fingers at a fine specimen of the leg drama.

The cause of science is not lagging. Clear-eyed, lofty-browed men are gazing deep into the mysteries of the universe, and daily unfolding volumes of new schemes, ideas and hopes. Step by step this noble band is conquering and advancing, going on, and ever on, even into the purplings of the glamour which hides the golden throne of God.

Over the world the causes of liberty are prospering. Theirs tells the story of French redemption, soft-muscled Italy is united and free, the Spanish bloodhound is brought to bay in Cuba, the English people are daily dropping the rusty relics of Feudal tyranny, the Knout is an impossibility in Russia, and even the sleepy Nemesis of Turkey's wrongs is writing a "Mene, mene" upon the silken walls of the Sultan's harem.

In our own Sunny South, only does liberty languish. Here only are honest men disfranchised, and the most despicable tortures put upon a proud people. And we are able to stand it!

Let the howling fanatics pile on their cowardly insults. Southern chivalry and pride is so omnipotent to all such attacks, that the snake-blooded Puritans will never extort even the luxury of a complaint from this people. To be chained down is the sign of greatness —cowards and weak men are never troubled this way.

Hence, all of us Georgians, Louisianians, Alabamians and Carolinians will meet the issue with heads up, and eyes to the sun, and the clanking of our chains shall be lost in the ringing of our welcome. "The old year is dead—long live the New Year!"

14

Henry W. Grady,
The Atlanta Herald,
January 10, 1873.

"Three Thousand Dollars"

Precisely!

That's just what it costs!

Three thousand dollars to run the legislature one day!

Think of it gentlemen! And for the Lord's sake be prompt, energetic and business-like in the dispatch of the business before you.

The State is poor; she is ridden down with debt; the taxes are grievous; the people are discouraged; hundreds of them are leaving her old hills; hence give us a short session, little legislation and light taxes.

Don't make long speeches.

It is probable that the most of you have especial sentiments that you must impress upon the House and Senate, and it may be that many of you have stored away in the old garret of your memory some gay, wordy, sophamoric. speech, from which you would fain shake the dust of years that are gone, and flash in pretty colors in the sunlight again.

If so, be brief.

The man must be of considerable consequence who can speak on any subject for three hours under the knowledge that his time is costing the State $500 an hour; yet such is the case.

There is no spectacle so sublime as to see two giant statesmen wrestling with the difference between "tweedle-dum and tweedle-dee" for four hours, while an admiring house claps its hands at seven dollars a day, and the people are bled to the tune of $2,000.

But we trust there will be none of this piruting during the session, and that most of the members will agree with Josh Billings, that "if a man don't strike ile in thirty minutes, he's either boring in the wrong place, or he's got a mighty dull augur."

Happy be the House that inaugurates the system of short speeches, that grapple the subject vividly and quickly, and either master it in a short, fierce struggle, or drop it and pass on to the next.

Life isn't near as long as it used to be, and if ever Demosthenes were to attempt to recount one of his six-hour philipics to an American audience of today, we believe in our soul that he would be embroidered with spoilt eggs and soft cabbage. Then, gentlemen, let us have a short, pleasant and lively session.

Go straight at your work and master it, then each and every one of you go home and commence teasing your wives for the next nomination to congress in your several districts.

That's a political business that will be cheaper to the state, if not more profitable to yourselves, than sitting here for the next sixty days, passing numerous laws to meet unnecessary crises.

You have made a good beginning; you have good materials; now go to work manfully, and let your watchword be "Economy."

15

Henry W. Grady,
The Atlanta Herald,
January 19, 1873.

"A Serious Social Evil"

The story of Mrs. Lydia Sherman whose recent conviction **for** poisoning the whole of her family has been published in New York

Herald, as told by the prisoner herself. We say story, although the papers call it a "confession" because it is a narrative of her whole life. Dispensing with all that is superfluous, and coming to the facts of her crime, we find that her first husband, who was a policeman, was dismissed from the service, which dismissal he took very much to heart and became sick. While in bed a stern police sergeant visited the house and serenely advised her to put her husband out of the way. The amiable wife reflected upon the advice for a day or two and then becoming "discouraged and down-hearted" decided that it would be a highly meritorious action on her part to send her sick spouse out of this world into the next. She accordingly purchased some arsenic, put it in his gruel and ushered him into eternity. All her other crimes—embracing the poisoning of two more husbands and several children, have no other explanation. Her victims took sick and she coolly dosed them arsenic the moment she became "discouraged and down-hearted."

The manner in which the wretch told her horrible story is the most remarkable of all. Her neck safe from the gallows rope, she confessed with unction of one who laid claim to many virtues and but few vices. She declared that she had "found Christ," and that she was now a Christian. So with placid and serene conscience, she unfolded her story for warning of other women, and went to the penitentiary, let us hope, never again to leave it, save in a coffin.

As this woman is just as sane as any person can be, it is impossible to read her narrative without protesting against the leniency which saved her from hanging. Upon what ground she escaped a verdict of murder in the first degree, we cannot imagine. Surely the jury and the court will not venture to assert that "down-heartedness and discouragement" arising from illness of husband and children, are sufficiently extenuating circumstances and are provocative to a dose of quieting arsenic! Heaven help us if our wives are to physic us with poison every time we become sick! If we concede that whenever one's wife gets "discouraged and down-hearted" she has a "terrible temptation" to put him out of the way, we most earnestly clamor for the speedy erection of a city hospital in Atlanta, so as to prevent the calamity of a town full of widows.

But after all Mrs. Lydia Sherman is only a strong-nerved specimen of a numerous class of her sex. There are, we fear, too many women who are not willing to endure the storms of life. Thank God! very few of them are plucky enough to administer arsenic to their husbands and children, but they certainly do make their own lives and the lives of all in their families very miserable. They demand never-ending sunshine. While their every whim is gratified, and while they are not troubled with cares incidental to most persons, they are kind and affectionate; but the moment sorrow crosses their threshold love and amiability retire through the back door. As we have said before, it is lucky that very few of them have the courage to commit murder, but the lives they lead those who are forced to endure their ill-temper, their complaints and their harsh language must be trying indeed.

That Mrs. Lydia Sherman's fate will be a warning to any of this class we have very little belief. If she had been hanged, even her end would not have affected them. They will go on scolding and quarreling with their husbands and children, until death, many of them, too, imagining that they are pious Christians.

Far be it from our purpose to arraign all women as social termigants. We believe—and have every reason to so believe—that a very large majority of the sex are kind, sweet and loving women who glory in sharing the adversities of their husbands, in ministering to them when sick and in devoting unremitting attention to their children. Our design has been merely to point out a very unamiable class—a class which we trust always "find Christ" in the end, but which without intending irreverence, we doubt very much if the Savior ever troubles himself to look for. Of course "while the lamp holds out the vilest sinner may return," and it is not impossible that Mrs. Sherman herself has really become a pious, contrite soul, rejoicing at her redemption; but we cannot say that the hope of final reformation would at all reconcile us to a life with one of them, even though we possessed every guarantee that she would not send us to the spirit land with arsenic. We greatly prefer the ordinarily sinful woman who is lovable always, who is strong when the clouds darken, and who will take us by the hand and follow us unmurmuringly through all the labyrinths of adversity, cheering us with her love, when we are weary, and disconsolate, and never harboring thoughts of cold poison, and never growing "discouraged and down-hearted" when afflictions of the body overtake us.

Life would be very insipid if it was nothing but sunshine. The sweetest things pall upon the taste if indulged in unceasingly. We prefer to see the clouds black sometimes, to hear the thunder peal and to see the lightning flash and the rain fall. While it lasts the storm may not be very pleasant, but it is certainly endurable, if one has not by his side a Lydia Sherman with an arsenic powder ready to administer in one's gruel, or a scolding tongue which seeks to make bad good by incessant grumblings and revilings. We say it is endurable because we know that the blue sky and the glorious sun are behind the blackness, and even if it be not ours to see them again, some happiness, at least, can be derived from knowing they are there, and expecting to greet us once more.

16

Henry W. Grady,
The Atlanta Herald,
March 23, 1873.

"IN A HUNDRED YEARS"

There is a sunrise, and a lark's song and an opening daisy to every night. We saw a man today whose life was a failure. He had worked and worked until the palms of his hands were worn to the bone; he had devised and planned, and continued till his head had almost burst with aching; he had agonized and wrestled with fate till his body was a ruin and his intellect wrecked; he had fought gamely, but the odds were piled against him, and cruel circumstances had dragged him to the dust. So there he lay, deserted by friends, bereft of fortune—a panting, gasping, fainting man. There officers of the law stood over him with the terrible instrument of their office; his wife, weak and sorrowful, and his hungry-eyed children were huddled around him, their eager pangs half dulled with wonder. The officer in the name of justice, and by the majesty of the law, laid his hand upon the door lock and declared that scanty furniture was seized in behalf of the state, and that the house must be vacated at once.

The poor man rises from the bed on which he is sitting; his children huddle around him and his wife leans weeping on his shoulder; he gazes around upon what has been his home; then upon the cold, cheerless snow; then upon his children. His lips quiver, a red flush shoots into his face, flashes there an instant, and dies out again. He strokes his wife's head softly with his hand, and murmurs tenderly into her ear: "Cheer up, Bessie, cheer up; it will be all right in a hundred years."

"It will be all right in a hundred years!"

Yes, Thank God, there is an end to all this striving, and end of all this yearning. Beyond the shores where Jordan lays the sands in golden heaps, beneath Jehovah's smile there's an "all right" for those who have missed it in this world. Where the shadows of the valley are chased back by the golden glimmers of Eden, there's the redemption for those who have slaved in the flesh; a reward for those who were marred on earth; a cross of honor for those who have died in harness.

Then let there be no faltering, no halting, no drooping. Be not turned aside by troubles, daunted by dangers or persuaded by the songs of sirens. Step up sharply. March on, and on, and on, through violet beds, and thorn clumps! Step brisk to music of eternity, and no matter what troubles lower over you, now, cheer your heart with the promise of "it's all coming right in a hundred years."

The poor wretch of yesterday couched the whole hope of life— the anchor of all our ventures in the few words of agony that faltered from his pale blue lips. And yet Christ died, and the hill of Calvary was rent, just to give one ray of comfort to that poor man that the law, in its majesty, had jumped in the jungle and wounded to death.

And he will go on, and on through many a dismal day, and through many a struggle, thinking that it will all be right in a hundred years. And his eyes grow brighter, and the blood will flush and die in the pale cheeks oftener, and the pinched features grow thinner, and the veil of flesh more and more threadbare, till he drops it altogether, and passing over the river lays him down on the golden banks and is baptized in immortal sunshine. And then, thank God, at last his "hundred years are out" and it's "all right" with him.

17

Henry W. Grady,
The Atlanta Herald,
May 20, 1873.

"A CARD"

I have just returned to the city, and find that ex-Governor Brown has accused me, as Business Manager of the *Herald*, of attempting to blackmail him out of $25. I shall not deem it necessary to denounce the assertion as falsehood, prefering rather by simple and concise recital of facts to prove it one.

On the occasion alluded to in an editorial in the *Herald* appeared two questions addressed to Governor Brown asking from him an answer to them. The questions were perspicuous and plain, and could have been intelligently and fully answered in twenty lines.

Shortly after the editorial appeared Governor Brown came to the *Herald* office, and stated that he had a reply written to our questions. We received him courteously and gladly, and told him we would publish them with pleasure. At the juncture we had no idea of charging anything for the answer, as we supposed he would, of course, confine himself to the legitimate discussion of the question propounded. When page after page in indeterminable succession, appeared, and the facile pen of the loquacious Governor slipped from the point at issue into violent attack on the Georgia Western Railway, into the persuasive puffing of certain coal deposits in North Georgia, and into the petition for a subsidy from the city for a little railway that the public had no interest in, and into the rapid expression of certain personal reflections neither pertinent nor edifying, I began to see that we had been imposed upon, and that on the little peg incautiously thrust through the *Herald* front door the willing Barkis was about to hand the tedious tale of a long and checkered life. Hence, without taking my bookkeeper into a back room and there persuading him with jingling gold and hissing argument up to the perpetrations of the damnable act, I instructed him to inform Governor Brown in a polite manner that as he had so grossly exceeded even the furtherest possibility of limit suggested by our modest questions, and had gone incontinently into the discussion of foreign and private matters, that we should be compelled to charge him for the extra space thus consumed, adding that we would simply charge him actual cost of composition. The bookkeeper did this. The Governor refused to submit to the charge. Right then and there I intended to cut off the prose epic that had been so profusely furnished, and publish only the four paragraphs bearing pertinently on the subject. My partners overruled this view of the subject, and I had to submit to the imposition. That it was an imposition no one can doubt, and it would find an apt parallel in the case of a merchant, who, on being asked whether or not he was guilty of some peculation, replied, "No, but I have a choice lot of hams, vegetables and canned goods," and then proceeded in a column of laudation to prove that he could outsell and out-satisfy any rival merchant in the city.

I do not regret the demand made upon Governor Brown. I should make it under the same circumstances, again and again. As Business Manager of the *Herald* office, I felt it my duty to protect the paper from this wanton use of its columns, and did the best I could to that end.

After this statement I feel that the use of epithets toward Governor Brown would be a waste of raw material, and in conclusion would merely try to remind him while so gratuitously accusing me of an attempt to blackmail, that the following sentence, yet wet with the juices of his eloquent pen, slightly paraphrased, develops strongly marked properties of the boomerang:

How natural it is for a man who knows that he would steal if he had the chance, to conclude that everybody does steal, who, he supposes, has the opportunity.

18

Alex St. Clair Abrams,
The Atlanta Herald,
July 4, 1873.

TODAY, VICKSBURG AND GETTYSBURG—1776 & 1863

Yielding to a custom many of our readers will regard "more honored in the breach than in the observance," we have decided to give our employees a holiday and suspend publication tomorrow.

This is the Fourth of July—the anniversary of the Declaration of American Independence, and the day on which Vicksburg surrendered and on which Lee was baffled at Gettysburg. Let those who can, rejoice on this anniversary of the day on which the death-knell of Southern Independence was sounded. For our part this "Glorious Fourth" is full of mournful recollections and bitterest regrets; for we feel once more the solemn stillness of the ramparts of Vicksburg, behind which so many had fought and starved for nearly fifty days— a stillness broken only after the sun had set, and the stars looked down upon the turbid waters of the Mississippi. It seemed then as the wail of the waters was for the young nation which had that day received her fatal stab, and lay weltering in her heart's blood, dying.

This day ninety-seven years ago a nation was born and a glorious impetus given to the cause of liberty throughout the world. For that, let us rejoice. This day ten years ago a nation was destroyed, and the South it was that fell. To us, then, the glories of 1776 were totally obscured by the disasters of 1863. If we are to look back upon the past for rejoicing let us be sure that no terrible calamity stands between us and joy. What interest has the South in this day as the anniversary of American Independence? Shall we make merry over the liberty it gave, when we do not enjoy that liberty? Shall we fire cannons in celebration of an independence we do not possess? Is it appropriate for us to thank God that on this day ninety-seven years ago, a people proclaimed their right to be governed by themselves, when that right is denied us? What a melancholy feast that must be which has the spectres of Vicksburg and of Gettysburg seated at the head of the table!

All this is sentiment, perhaps. So also is that overflowing patriotism which climbs over the mountain of disaster and humiliation, looking beyond a river of blood points to a happy, distant past, which can never come again; and asks us to renew associations on this day which are severed forever.

To the South of today the Fourth of July, 1776, is a tradition and a memory, while the Fourth of July, 1863, is a bitter reality and a confrontation. Let those who will it, seek the laurel of long ago; we sit beneath the cypress of yesterday and moan over unavailing sacrifices. Across ninety-seven years lie the shadows of liberty, and these alone remain to us. Shall we dance in the shadows when the substance has fled? There may be those as earnest, as honest and as sincere as we believe ourselves to be, who will; but they represent only success; ours are emblems of disaster.

The anniversary of American Independence, Vicksburg and Gettysburg! To disassociate them is impossible. A real glory, and a substantial cause of rejoicing for the North; a blurred picture and a frightful phantom for the South. Let us seek "a common brotherhood" and essay fraternization on such a day as this! It is noble, they say, for the injured to forgive. Let, then, the gushing orators of this day forgive Vicksburg; forgive oppression and humiliation; forgive overthrow and subjection; forgive desolation and poverty. Nay, let them also forget; and crossing that "bloody chasm," which is more a somber truth than a gloomy poetic fancy, join in the shouts of joy over Vicksburg and Gettysburg, and blend the glories of the Declaration of American Independence with the death scene of Southern liberty!

But for him who pens this, today is one of mournful reveries and solemn reflections. And to all Southern men, whose history dates from the Southern Declaration of Independence, 1776, is but half remembered story, and 1863 is the real drama. Thus, no matter how many cannons may be fired in the South; nor how many orations delivered, the phantom of the lost cause must confront us, and before we retire to rest tonight this Fourth of July will weigh upon our hearts as cold as the graves of Vicksburg and Gettysburg; whilst that anniversary we thought to make merry upon, will fade from our minds like the unreal thing it is, leaving in its stead only those sorrowful memories which cluster around the broken sword, the furled banner and the hecatomb of graves.

19

Henry W. Grady (King Hans),
The Atlanta Herald,
August 3, 1873.

DISMAL SWAMP, McBRIDE'S LITTLE STORY

"Is this Suffolk?" muttered McBride contemptuously, as he thrust his long neck out of the car window, and gazed at the sleepy looking town that lay blinking in the sunshine.

"Yes, massa; that is the name of dis place," answered a son of freedom that had the inevitable waiter of dirty lunch you always see at a Va. Ry. station, couched expectant on his left hand. "Won't you tek a nice piece of briled chicken?"

"Well, fellows, if this is Suffolk, and the Dismal Swamp ain't any bigger thing than the town, then I be hanged if I want to drive into it."

And, to be sure, the little town did present a poor appearance. It looked like a town in a trance—placid, easy and contented with only one man in sight on all its streets, and he stretched at full length on a pile of shingles, apparently trying to induce a drowsy dog to do some sort of trick, which the dog seems too lazy to attempt. The main street is very broad, and is ornamented with two rows of live oaks, which, by the way, seem to be the only live things in the place. It reminds me of a Georgia town in one respect; all chimneys are built on the outside of the houses. This barbarous habit prevails, as we have said, to an alarming extent, and each house looks as if it had an elongated wart on its back. The town has two thousand inhabitants. (This statement is sop to those who love statistics. I do not know whether it is correct or not. For their sakes I hope it is. I may throw out here that I am not to be depended upon at all in the figure line. I usually am at my statistics. In pure romance I consider myself reliable, and something of an authority.)

The Honeysuckles crawled out of their coat pockets, and started on a pilgrimage for lunch.

THE MAN WITH THE DOG

The man with the dog being the only human in sight, we drifted, as by a sort of destiny toward him. I do hope that man's dog was flattered by the fixed resolve with which his master confined his attentions to him to the utter exclusion of the Honeysuckles, although they had by this time approached within two feet of him.

"Hello, my friend!"

He looked up and we saw that he had only one eye. (From the devotion with which he had stuck to the training of his dog we had long since found out that he was a one-idea man.)

"How do you know I am your friend?" said he sternly, gazing at us out of his one orb reflectively.

Honeysuckle—taken aback—"Well, we didn't know it, but supposed it would be all right."

"Yes, maybe you did; but don't put on no airs with me; I'm a straight up and down white man, I am, I hope. Jump, pup, jump-ps-t-t-, jump!" He made a pantomime of "jumping" with his hands, while the dog gazed at him with a melancholy gaze, as one would gaze at a mad man.

Every Honeysuckle looked around the deserted village in hope of finding another man with whom to talk but failing, came back to our first love. "Well, my friend—that is, er-er—sir, we want to take a trip to the Dismal Swamp. We want to get some dinner and then we want to start. We want some active man (my Lord, where will we find him?) to take charge of the matter and make all the arrangements for us. We are willing to pay for it. I may say we are affluent. We are backed by capital, and to him"—getting airy and possessed as the man's face melts under these sentences—"who carries us in the inmost heart of that distinguished quagmire, and sets us by the side of Drummond Lake, where, sitting in the quiver of its ceaseless tide, we can, as it were, take Nature's wrists in our hands, and feel her pulse beat. To him I say we will scatter our ducats with a lavish hand."

"Well, I don't know about hearing no pulse beat for sich, but if you want to go down into the swamp in a rale style, I'm your man, and as straight up and down one as you ever seed. I hev a raft, and I kin git two likely niggers as runs, with me to pole you, and we kin mek it in cumf't'ble manner. You kin git a snack over that at the Hotel, and then you must hev some old suits of clothes, which the same I kin git fur you, as it is powerful spilin on good clothes in the swamp. I'll get all things ready while you eat your snack. Ps-s-t-t! Pup! Jump, sir; jump, jump, you son of a ———."

"Here, Cap," sung out McBride, "will we see any bears in the swamp?"

"Powerful apt; and wild cats too, and mebbe a painther."

"Then borrow us some good guns," quietly responded that truly martial man.

Why shall I describe the Hotel? Why the dinner? Why the negro wench that waited on the table barefooted, and whose feet made that peculiar scratching sound when she walks, as one would make who was shod with nutmeg graters? Why the long rows of paper strips suspended from the ceiling and swinging by perpetual motion nigger, apparently for the purpose of driving the flies off, but as the flies honestly believe, for the purpose of fanning the sweat off their brows while they prosecuted their work of punctuating everything on the table? Why shall I describe any feature of any village Hotel? They are all alike the world over.

But at dinner, between the cornbread and apple pie, McBride broke out in a new place, much to the gratification of his friends.

Says he, "The way that fellow with a dog snapped us up today gets me! It reminds me of a thing that happened to me at school once. I had just entered, and there was a boy named Bob, who was the bully of the school. It was generally understood, I being the only boy in school of his size, that I would be his rival. Now, on the very day I got there he took me to one side and commenced to tell me what a good fighter he was, how many boys he had whipped, and how dangerous he was. He was particularly careful to tell me what a bad boy he was with his teeth, and how he sunk them into a fellow's arms whenever he tackled them, and how he had two long ones just in front (showing them by a polite grin at this juncture) that would give him a good hold in the other boy's flesh! He showed me those teeth time and time again until he completely hacked me. I was on the point of collision with him several times, but the thought of those terrible front teeth cowed me every whack. Well, first thing I knew a little boy in the school jumped on the bully and whipped him in five minutes, and the rascal never thought of using his teeth anymore than if he didn't have any. It made me so mad when I saw how I had been fooled that I pitched in and whipped him three times that week. Now this rascal out here has been showing his teeth to us with a view of scaring us off; but I'll teach him a lesson—I'll bet I'll have to pitch him out of the boat in less than twenty-four hours. I've been there before; I know his sort. He thinks because we are rich, we are effeminate; but I'll show him—I'm not afraid of his front teeth."

The Preparation for the Start

By this time "Cap" had returned and announced ready. He looked like a porcupine, so did he bristle with guns, oars, axes, etc., and behind him came two negroes loaded down with bundles that he borrowed for the honeysuckles to array themselves in.

"Got me a gun?" says McBride.

"I consider as I'm a straight up and down man. When you told me to git a gun you might a consider it got. In course I've got it," and he handed McBride one of the most robust double-barrelled affairs that I ever saw, while Smith took an old flint and steel rifle that Cain and Abel must have shot robins with when they were boys.

"Come and git inter these clothes and lets travel; it's nigh midday, and I wants to strike Howell's by dark, and we must be jogging. Pat and Tom kin show you the way to the old ship, and if you could purvide me with a little of them duckets, I'll step around and buy some pervisions to take along wit us." Having furnished this haughty pauper with the requisite funds he departed, and the Honeysuckles commenced arraying themselves in the second-hand habiliments provided by "Cap," our selected guide. In the meantime, I will furnish some statistics that I hired a subordinate to collect for me. Young ladies can skip statistics if they so desire.

Statistics of Dismal Swamp

This Dismal Swamp is a vast body of half submerged land, fifty-three miles long, and about sixteen miles across. It has never been fully explored, and numbers of people have been lost in the attempt through it. No one lives in it except a few shingle cutters, who send their shingles to market by the Nansemond Canal, which penetrates its upper edge. This canal was built by a company, of which General George Washington was the first president, and he personally superintended the building of it. The shingles I am sorry to say (very sorry) are falling off. In the midst of the swamp there is a large lake of black inky water called Drummond's Lake, and it is on the edge of this lake that Dred the famous fugitive of Harriet Beecher Stowe hid himself from his owners. This is the only real objections I have to the swamp.

I have another dose of statistics which I will administer in my next (communication).

Into the Depths

It would have done you good to have seen this club when they were accoutered in their swamp clothes and announced ready to their cruel black guides who stood with perpetual lightning playing from ear to ear as they watched their proceedings. McBride had on a pair of white duck pants that barely covered his knee-caps, a Yankee summer overcoat, and a wool hat. Kimbal had a suit of ordinary jeans that was nearly big enough for McBride, and the others were attired not less ridiculously.

Under the guidance of the negro guides we struck out to the canal. Arrived there we found a regular built canal boat awaiting us, and "Cap" sitting near the locker packing in the "provisions" he had purchased, while the dog sat on the shore snapping at flies.

The club piled into the boat and made themselves as comfortable as possible. "Cap" called "Pup," and for the first time in the course of our acquaintance Pup "jumped." The two negroes took two long poles, fitted one end of them into a notch cut into the boat, and the other end under their armpits, one standing on each tow-path of the canal. They bent themselves down on the poles; the boat darted forward; the crew gave a cheer; the negroes struck a wild corn-song, and the honeysuckles were lost in the shade of the swamp.

Where for the present we will leave them.

20

Henry W. Grady,
The Atlanta Herald,
December 24, 1873.

"THE LITTLE ONES AND THEIR STOCKINGS"

We do sincerely hope that there is not a "little one" in all Atlanta who will not tonight be called by some loving voice to "hang up the stocking for Santa Claus to fill." Not that we would invoke to all of them the dainty luxuries of the rich, rare confections or costly toys! Not at all! For, to some of them, will come only the plebian peppermint, or the homely popcorn; the rugged top fashioned from the father's hands, or the whirligig pitched and twisted by the mother's fore fingers. But to all, poor and rich alike, do we pray may come the delicious pleasure of "hanging the stockings up"; the ecstacy of expectation and of faith; the exquisite pandering to the buoyant wonder, that uprising hope that makes the heart of a child so bright and so happy a thing.

God pity the boy, and God pity the girl whose sterile childhood has never been blessed with the legend of Santa Claus, and made joyous with a firm and unwavering belief in his power and ineffable justice.

Let the young ones "hang up their stockings." It does not matter that you are not able to fill them with rare and precious gifts. That is not what the children hang them up for. It is the expectation and the mystery of the thing that makes it so delightful. A rag doll, or a penny whistle that comes to them across the frosty roofs, through the silvery air, behind the dancing reindeer with their crystal bells, in Santa Claus' magical sleigh, and then down the sooty chimney, is consecrated with wonder, wrapt in a gorgeous glamour, that makes it better than silver and gold.

We know of a home, an humble one, too; where tonight while the pillow of a cradle is being warmed, a darling little rascal, barely able to toddle, and with just four teeth in his busy mouth, will work his way up to the mantle piece, and hang Grandma's woolen stocking —too big by half for his meager gifts—on the nail therein embedded! And happy will he be! Noble will he be! Great will he be, if in all the life stretching-out before him, his heart is filled and his impulses started by no meaner motives, than the sturdy faith, the honest hope, the abiding confidence that inspires him, as he pins the wrinkled old leggin to the chimney-board tonight.

God bless the children all and fill their stockings full!

21

Henry W. Grady,
The Atlanta Herald,
December 25, 1873.

"A Fat and Gentle Day"

If there is a time in all the year—and may the Temperance Societies forgive us for suggesting such a possibility—when it is pardonable to warm one's system with something a trifle spirituous, today is the day.

We do not mean to suggest the drinking of that sharp and fiercer whisky which nips the nerves and twists them in its merciless fingers, sets the blood on fire and blears the eyes! Not at all. Rather that better article, drawn by deft machinery from the russet apple!—the liquid sunniness of a whole summer's shining, as it were, given up by the fruit as the swan pours out her dying song! This elixir, over which centuries have smacked their raptured lips, subjected into sugar, mellowed into marriage with fumy egg-foam, and spiced into nog; this is what we mean! O, nog! thou creamy golden joy! robbed of all the fierceness of intoxication, gently insinuating thy delicious aroma even into the exclusive marrow of the bones; warming up, enfragranting, mellowing the whole corpus from top into toe, sending the rose into the lips, dimples into the cheeks, lazy sparkles into the eyes, and putting Christmas fairies to painting sunset pictures upon the summit of the enchanted nose! Surely there can be no sin in bending at thy gentle shrine! Nothing illicit in supping thy aroma! nothing in all thy concoction, O, famous nog, that should forbid the faithful!

Today is a day of carousal anyhow, both by precedent and principle. Not a debasing carousal which commences in brandy straight and climaxes in a gin-sling and a gutter. But of the innocent carousal which commences on roast turkey with wine sauce, climbs up to a crowning nog, then beams around the hearthstone, dipping itself through the family circle, and at last dozes off beautified between snowy sheets on a comely couch.

Of a certainty there can be nothing to condemn, on this day of universal joy, in a feast to which the whole family drawn together in sympathy and love may come, and of which a bowl of nog is the crowning feature.

It sets the thing off aptly, and completes the circle of all the felicities. But "nog" or no "nog," our readers must celebrate today, and be merry, happy, and hospitable.

The soul of all Christendom, softens on this blessed day. England lights her Yule log, hangs the magic mistletoe over the parlor door, and gives herself up to robust enjoyment; France, the mother of Christmas elegancies will open her choicest flagon, crack her finest confections and go mad with raptures; Germany, best fed and happiest of all nations, will today deck the streets of quaint old Berlin for the Christ Child; Russia turning her back upon her Khirvan wars, will luxuriate in grotesque ceremonies of the Greek Church, while Austria will give herself up to the Holy Catholic festivities.

Here in America, too, let us be happy. Here where the heartiness of the Englishman whose emblem is his wassail cup, is joined with the simplicity and cordial joy of the German, where Protestants, Catholics, and all join one happy whole, let us have rare and bounteous festivities.

Let all be happy! Feel way down into the pocket; bring forth the last surplus cent, and have one day of supreme enjoyment and of rest. God knows we all need it, in this busy, restless, jostling world. In its humble way the *Herald* will celebrate the day, and with its mind's eye on one and all of its readers, it echoes that most eloquent of all Christmas speeches, "Tiny Tim's Oration," that came up in pure simpleness from his good little heart, and rested like a sunbeam, we know, on his quivering lips—"God bless us all, every one!"

22

Henry W. Grady,
The Atlanta Herald,
April 26, 1874.

"Shall We Burn or Bury?"

"Under the daisies" has always seemed to us a proper place to put our corpses. To lay them amid the waving elms 'longside the winding river has seemed to be the correct thing and Hamlet, saying to Ophelia's attendants,

"Go lay her in the grateful ground
Where sweet violets may spring,"

has been accounted quite a proper speaking person. Now, however, the order of things has changed. Your corpse, dear reader, is no longer to be comfortably tucked under the moss of some leafy hillside, but you are to be burned; put in a furnace, subjected to a fire like that through which the Hebrew children trod, and the volatile parts of you sent whizzing up the flue while the solid flesh is to be reduced to ashes; in short you are to undergo the elegant process of cremation.

Cremation societies are forming all over the North, whose object is to prove the cremation is the thing. They argue that the population is becoming so dense, and deaths so numerous, corpses so plentiful, and burials so consequently frequent, the soil of new large cities is noxious and tainted, and is infecting water veins. They argue that cremation is much cheaper, it being impossible for a genteel corpse to get buried in a satisfactory manner for less than a hundred dollars, while it might be shot up through a furnace chimney with becoming pomp and ceremony for a fifth of that sum. They argue again, that it is less awful to send the essence of your friend gracefully wafting through a flue, on its way to the home of the sunbeams and cloudlets, than to put it into the clamy, cold ground, where it will mould and mildew, or be despoiled by the worms—those audacious bandits of the grave.

Those arguments are telling. There are clubs already formed, and numbering hundreds, who have sworn that when any one of their number dies he shall be burned; so that if Providence is propitious we may look for a practical example of the theory very soon.

But here is one argument upon the subject advanced by Sir. Henry Thomson, that strikes us with peculiar force. This gentleman, who has evidently figured things down to a notch, tells us that the gallons of ashes left in the furnaces as the last analysis of the gentleman, is of inestimable value as a fertilizer. With a mournfulness born of his infinite research, he deplores the amount of fatness that has been lost to the sons of man by the burying away of three hundred generations of approved guano, and calls upon the world to stop the wastage at once.

If it be any consolation to Sir Henry, we desire to waft across the seas at once, the information that there is one editor at least in America who fully grasps his idea and embraces his doctrine.

It is sweet to think that one can be of some use after he is dead, and in many cases be worth more when dead than he was worth while living. It is comfortable, too, to get the essence of corpses placed in your hand that you may dispose of them as you please. What a comfort one could take in tenderly stowing the ashes of his pretty young wife in the orchard or garden and know that she would fling him kisses through the dancing peach blossoms of the ensuing spring, or laugh him a greeting from the petals of a fresh blown morning glory! With that solid smack of joy, too, could he get even with his high-nosed mother-in-law, by planting her aristocratic ashes in a vegetable bed and forcing her to reproduce herself in the plebian potato or the unassuming squash. With what a tender delicacy could he compliment even the ashes of his good old mother by mingling her deftly with the stately cabbage, to the worship of which her life had been devoted.

The adoption of this theory would admit of the bringing of aesthetics into gardening, with the resultant of immense improvement. Certain sort of men would, of course, produce only certain sorts of fruits or vegetables; an astute gardener would be that one who studied the habits of the one and the demands of the other, and adjusted the two with skill. What, for instance, would give a tone and richness to a bed of garlic like bespreading it with the ashes of a dozen or so pronounced Italians? Where could flowers be found equal in brilliancy of color, sweetness of perfume, and gracefulness of carriage, to those springing in sweet resurrection from the remains of a well-ordered belle? From what could come a fairer crop of "beets" than the ashes of a score of loafers captured in the free lunch saloons or slain upon the curb-stones? Who doubts but that the essence of an old smoker would give additional greenness to the nicotinous plant? or that the remains of a toper would give renewed pungency to the inspiring mint?

This thought, as there were no neat theory without its dangers, suggests a doubt that the gardeners must weigh well before they go fully into the business. If the habits of the man can be transmitted to its vegetable sequence, cannot also his diseases? May not the miserable dyspeptic die happy in the hope that he will send his indigestible infirmities through at least one generation of potatoes to the man who incautiously eats them? May not each corpse that is hacked with disease carry some subtle contagion into the juices of its particular plant? In short, may it not become necessary for a vegetable vender to guarantee that his wares were "all raised from ashes warranted sound in mind and body?"

However, without pursuing this interesting subject further, we announce that, taking this view of the case, we are a pronounced crematist.

23

Henry W. Grady,
The Atlanta Herald,
May 12, 1874.

"HAPPY, HONEST ENGLAND"

"What shall I do with all this money?"

This was the breezy salutation of the English Chancellor of the Exchequer to the British Parliament, as he brought in his budget the other day with a surplus of six millions over the estimates.

Free sugar, a penny off the income tax, and six millions surplus. With this triune of glories, Johnny Bull can well afford to sit down

in his solid comfortable sort of way, and laugh at perspiring, push-ahead, enterprising, but always poor America. Ease and wealth across there—shoddy and sham over here. Honesty and prudence at helm over there; rings and cliques wrecking the government over here. High salaries and good men in office there; low salaries and perquisite hunting bummers in office here. An oak tree the emblem of the kingdom over there; a mushroom the pride of our nation over here.

With all of America's boasted progress in the sciences of govern-ing, she might find something of practical profit in the study of that government, where defalcations is the exception and not the rule; with all her boundless resources, and her remorseless income, she might find something new in the theory of taxation in that country where each class yields its equitable proportion to the general ex-chequer; in the study of English politics she might at least see the propriety of eliminating Butlerism from her own governmental affairs.

But America, great in her own concert, wise in her own genera-tion, is slow to learn. It will be many a day, we fear, before an American Secretary of the Treasury will tickle an American Congress with the putting of that delicious conundrum: "What shall I do with all this money?"

24

Henry W. Grady,
The Atlanta Herald,
May 24, 1874.

"WHERE SHALL WE SPEND THE SUMMER?"

Despite the general poverty which followed that war, in which says the author of Ca Ira, "The South lost her negroes and jewelry" a sense of returning riches is moving our people to inquire in a luxurious sort of way, "Where shall we spend the summer?"

The characteristics of these queries, if such soft yearnings can be presumed to harden into any characteristics, is a decided aversion to the high prices and terrible jams of the Northern Saratogas, and a prediliction, as strong as it is sensible, in favor of quieter nooks, and cooler retreats of our own and neighboring states.

Premising all remarks by the assertion that Atlanta and its su-burbs are not excelled anywhere as summer resorts, we proceed to advise the unwary and inform the ignorant. What a man wants when he flees the vexations of his city home, is a total escape from dust and swelter, where he can catch the fragrance of the growing grass and the budding trees; hear the songs of birds and babble of brooks; see the sun rise over a dewy meadow and the stars shine upon a fringed lake, where he can shed the offensive dress-coat, tear off the cravat which suffocates while it decorates; and in collar-less comfort and abandon of a duster, roam the clover fields, fish, shoot, eat or read, and snooze at his absolute pleasure. The stately dinners, the dusty drives, the full dress balls, the sardine-box bed-rooms, and iniquitous mosquitoes; and the jam, the mash, and the perspiration of a fashionable resort will not suit them. They are annoyances of home aggravated by the fact of "having company to dinner" every day.

We cannot reach the pitch of heroism attained by Sydney Smith, when he declared that rather than sweat through another season in the city he would fly from the haunts of men until he was "twelve miles from a lemon," but we do advise a careful survey of the at-tractions of the quiet and simple retreats, before one plunges into the reeking dissipations of Saratoga, Newport or White Sulphur.

Georgia is prolific of these balmy nooks, where the breezes play perpetual and the mosquito is unknown. There is New Holland Springs, a charming cut off from the hot and striving world, where daisies and violets bloom spontaneous, where cool springs gush from under every hillside, and where the proprietors of the cottages hold out the savory inducement of a "barbecue once a week." There is Catoosa, with its matchless scenery, its silvery stream and grand old groves, where the jealous leaves, so green and cool, let in just enough of the sun's golden fretwork to enliven the scene, sweeter than a painted landscape. Or that magic vale, erst, the home of the wild-eyed Indian-Maiden-sweet, Nacooche. Or Tallulah, with its hundreds of spray-falls, filling the air with a delicious freshness, and the ear with a lullaby softer than mother ever sang to sleeping babe. Or further, we might find joy and repose in the shades of Yonah, that great mountain, rising fresh and splendid from a setting of brooks and groves, its sides spotted by never a dust-fleck, defiled by no man's hand—primeval and pure just as God fashioned it.

Then there is Marietta, Stone Mountain, or any of a score of villages which dot Atlanta's railroad lines—all fat and fit places for an August loitering.

There is still another resource to the man who really seeks rest for the summer, and respite from its troubles. To strike a bargain with some study old farmer, who has a spare room, and "will board a couple for a while at $12.50 a month." If you select the right sort of a farmer you are sure to find his house a roomy, drowsy nest, perched on the shady side of the hill filled with marmalade, pickles, cordials, preserves, etc., which with supplements of chicken knocked from the trees, butter yet trembling from the agitation of the churn-handle, lambs killed at yester sunset, milk poured from jugs that live in the spring branch, are all yours to eat and revel in, for the modicum mentioned above. The family you will find affable and pleasant—capital listeners, and yet full of information that strikes you like a revelation. The beds are downy, and all the surroundings full of pleasantness and peace. This we prefer to any other style of summer resort. It is worth a hundred dollars to lie on the hay stack every evening in the balm of the falling dew, and watch the daughter, always a buxom and comely lass, milk the cows and feed the calves.

Still another plan is proposed by some of our citizens, who propose to buy twenty or thirty acres of picturesque land at Toccoa City, and put up cottages after the manner of the gentlemen mentioned by a writer from Macon. . .

At all events, the crowded and fashionable resorts will get but few of our people. And those who patronize them will, before the season is over, feel like Jerrold when he said, "Faith, I feel like stripping off my flesh and sitting down in my skeleton to cool."

25

Henry W. Grady,
The Atlanta Herald,
January 17, 1875.

"GENERAL TOOMBS AND THE HERALD"

As General Toombs continues to talk disgracefully about the press of the state, and the *Herald* in particular, we feel it our duty to make a brief statement of the facts connected with the loan by General Toombs to the *Herald*. In Georgia, where General Toombs' habits are well known, and the propensity which these habits produce, it is hardly necessary to correct any statement which the poor old man may make. In fact the connection which he has had in days gone by with the history of Georgia makes it very painful to characterize his conduct as it deserves.

We understand from several gentlemen that on Thursday evening at the Kimball House, while surrounded by a large crowd, General Toombs, after denouncing the Georgia Senate as a set of thieves and robbers, stated that he regarded the whole press of the state as venal and corrupt. He further said that he had been "feeding the d—d *Herald* while it had been fighting him, and that he had loaned the paper five thousand dollars, and they had robbed him of every cent of it." We have no doubt General Toombs said all these things. He is in the habit of talking just in this manner on any occasion when he can find listeners. We are also convinced that if we were to go to General Toombs and charge him with such language, he would deny ever having used it. It gives us real sorrow, when we read the grand speech which this old man made in the Senate of the United States in 1860, in defense of his oppressed country that he did not die then. How sad the contrast then and now! Let us remember him then and forget him now.

It gives us real pain to make the following statement. It is made in sorrow, not anger, and solely to vindicate ourselves from the charges of rascality and ingratitude.

Early in 1873, General Toombs met Col. Alston at the Kimball House and asked him how he was getting on with the *Herald*. Col. Alston replied, "Very well, indeed, except that we are pressed heavily by old debts." General Toombs said quickly, "Why didn't you apply to me, you know I have always had thirty or forty thousand on hand. I will give you a check now if you want it." Col. A—, of course declined such impulsive generosity, for fear that later deliberations might produce regret. Subsequently, when the paper was in temporary trouble, he wrote General Toombs, recounting his generous offer and requesting the loan of four or five thousand dollars, stating, at the same time, that as he was a public man, the paper might frequently be called on to differ with him. This letter was sent by one of the firm to a letter of credit for five thousand dollars, which was used by the *Herald Publishing Company* for four thousand during Col. A's absence at the North.

It was unfortunate for our relations that on nearly every public question which arose, the *Herald* took ground against General Toombs. This provoked his anger, and when Col. A returned from the North he heard of the unkind manner in which General Toombs was in the habit of speaking about the *Herald*. Col. A called on him at the Kimball House, and told him he was pained to hear of his remarks, but he had made it a rule through life never to quarrel with a creditor for pressing his claim. Up to this time General Toombs did not even have the acknowledgment, from Col. A of the debt, but only a quasimortgage drawn by the members of the firm, accompanied with the assurance that Col. A would sign the mortgage and give real estate security on his return from the North. This Col. A readily agreed to do at once, whereupon another of General Toombs' generous fits came over him, and he rang the bell for another bottle and said, "G—d d—n it, Bob, you and I are no plebians—we are gentlemen! Here; take the papers and tear them up, and pay the money to my grandchildren. Those fellows have offered to pay 12 per cent; 7 per cent is all I want. I am no d—d broker, but a Southern gentleman like yourself." Col. A refused to take the papers, but informed General Toombs that he was just on the eve of going to

Griffin, to be absent about a week, but immediately on his return would call on Colonel Bleckley and fix it up in accordance with his wishes. He left absolutely overwhelmed with General Toombs' generosity. This was on Friday; Col. A becoming unwell returned to Atlanta on Tuesday, and met a gentleman in the train, who asked, in anxiety: "What has happened between you and Toombs?" "Nothing; why do you ask?" He replied: "Toombs says he came here to get you to sign some papers, and you ran away, after making a positive agreement with him." Col. A was astonished, and hearing that Toombs had ordered the sheriff to close up the paper by Saturday night, Col. A took the train and went at once to Washington. He called on his arrival to see General Toombs, who was quite embarrassed at seeing him. Col. A entered immediately upon the subject of his mission, when General Toombs interrupted him by asking him where he was stopping. He replied, "At the hotel." At this the General made the remark, "Why did you not come to my house? To stop at the hotel in Washington is to argue that you don't know anybody." He then invited Col. A in his office, and said to him, "You need not refer to the business between us. I telegraphed Bleckley as soon as I got your letter." Col. A. said, "General, write him at once and give instructions." He agreed to do it. Col. A was entertained hospitably, and returned to Atlanta again impressed with the grandeur of the old man's generosity. When he reached the *Herald* office he found the sheriff in the office with orders to levy and sell without delay. Col. A told him that he had just returned from seeing General Toombs, but this did not avail, whereupon Col. A. called on Col. N. J. Hammond, who represented Col. Bleckley. Col. A. informed him that Toombs had telegraphed and written to Col. Bleckley to stay proceedings. Mr. Hammond sent for Col. B's mail, but so far from the telegrams and the letters being of that tenor which Col. A supposed, they contained positive instructions to proceed without further delay. Here was conduct bordering on infamy. So Col. A turned to Col. Hammond and said to him, "You are bound to make your client's money. This is your duty, but you have no right to oppress me. Give me 15 days and I will pay you." After more than two hours' painful hesitation Col. Hammond yielded. Col. A raised the money and paid General Toombs every dollar, with 12 per cent interest, and he delivered up the execution, and the mortgage on which it was founded.

The foregoing statement is absolutely correct and founded on record, so that the *Herald* has robbed him of five thousand dollars, he is simply laboring under a delusion.

He loaned the money like a prince and collected like a Shylock.

26

Henry W. Grady,
The Atlanta Herald,
April 10, 1875.

"A Platform of Peace and Good Will"

We are just now seeing belied a hoary tradition of this government. The assertion accredited for a century that the South was the home of the fire-eaters, and that the conservatists dwelt in the calm and frosty North is just now being put to denial. Gordon and Lamar ask for peace and concord and are willing to buy it by an acquiescence in the results of the war. Eaton, of Connecticut and Allen, of Ohio, insist that the old Bourbon flag shall again be raised even at the cost of perpetuation of strife between the sections. Almost every Southern man we have talked to confesses that the negro is free, and that he must remain free. They acknowledge that he has the right of suffrage, and propose to guarantee him the enjoyment of that right; and yet we hear of an absolute certainty that the two newly elected Congressmen in New Hampshire deny the validity of the amendments, and propose to open the very dead question again. We predict that at the National Democratic Convention of '76 the Southern delegates will advocate the adoption of a platform upon which the sections can be reconciled and the country rehabilitated, and that the Northern delegates will insist upon disintering the issues which were settled at Appomattox, and have been since a dozen times buried.

The truth is the Southern people want peace and quiet. They are tired of this miserable sectional strife which is checking the growth of either section, and paralyzing the energies of both. We respectfully request that we be allowed to "rally around the flag." This Republic is of our own making. It was our Jefferson that framed its declaration; our Washington that led its young armies to a victorious independence; our Patrick Henry that stirred the colonies to resistance; our Madison that led it through its second war; our Andrew Jackson that saved it at New Orleans; our Clay and Calhoun that made it illustrious; our section that gave its most illustrious Presidents; our cotton that enriched it; our civilization that clarified it, and as the Centennial anniversary of our liberties approaches, we begin to feel something of the old-time thrill of pride and love, and to feel like edging in across the threshold once more.

We want to see the Centennial Canvass fought upon a platform that is in harmony with the year and its suggestions and memories. We want to see the Democrats calling for peace and reconciliations, where the Radicals insist upon keeping alive the passions and prejudices of the war; pledging the negro his rights, while the Radicals insist that we do not intend to give them to him; offering the people honesty, purity and fidelity in the Government, while the Radicals defend their record of crime and corruption; demanding a return to the constitutional methods of Government, while the Radical party insists on concentrating a power at Washington which shall strangle the states; and on this platform build broad enough for all America to stand upon, we want to see Thurman or Hendricks, or Tilden placed, and nominated as the Centennial President of the Republic. We are anxious to see the best Government the world ever saw enter its second century under the right sort of auspices.

27

Henry W. Grady,
The Atlanta Herald,
May 5, 1875.

"THE NEW SOLUTION OF THE NEGRO QUESTION"

It pleases us to see our Northern friends take such a vivid interest in the future of the negro, we are grieved to see them waste so much valuable time and space in the discussion of the subject. The best way to solve the question, is to let it quietly solve itself. The only effect of discussion, is to irritate. The Northern people and more especially the Northern journalists, utterly misunderstand the premises, and hence cannot expect to stumble upon other than false conclusions.

The first error that they make, is in regard to the feeling that the whites entertain toward the negro. They assume, by an extension of that false logic of that extremely unfair book, "Uncle Tom's Cabin," that the relations existing between the negro slave and his owner was harsh, antagonizing and oppressive; that the white man, having held his slave in subjection, by the bloodhound, and the lash, finds his hatred of the unfortunate darkey redoubled, now that he is rendered unable to vent it freely. This is altogether wrong. In ninety cases out of a hundred, an extremely tender feeling went out from the master to his slave. He was proud of him, attached to him, careful of his wants. On festal days, he was always remembered at the feast; and when Christmas came he always shared with "Massa's family" the delights of that blissful season. His interests and his master's were identical, and we affirm without the fear of challenge, that in no country and in no time, did a more intimate, a more pleasant and more sympathetic relation exist between capitalist and the laborer than in our old-time Dixie; never or nowhere did master's heart go out so fully and so quickly to laborer; never or nowhere was laborer better cared for or happier. Added to this feeling of sympathy with, and the kindness for, the black man which survived the change of relations, there is another reason why the intelligent white man must and does feel kindly towards the negro. This is his commendable course during the war. While our whole forces of old and young men were in Virginia or Tennessee confronting the Northern armies our homes were left defenseless— our women and children unprotected.

Now altogether there were thousands of negroes surrounding these defenseless homes, and in charge of these unprotected women; although they were told day after day that the war then progressing involved their freedom, and was being waged in their interest; and although they knew that the whole face of the land, with its tempting treasures lay open to their rapine and plunder, yet they remained faithful to the trust confided by their masters, and guarded the interests of the home folks with an unwavering fidelity. We doubt if history will furnish a parallel of such absolute faith on the one hand, and such superb loyalty on the other, as was furnished in those terrible days, when the mother of the household in Dixie, with her little children, huddling around her, and her husband and sons on the battlefield, would place her only gun in the hands of the very men they were fighting to enslave, and bid him sleep on her doormat and guard the house through the night. For his fidelity and forbearance then, and by the memories of the long gone peaceful and harmonious years, which later differences have not effaced, the white man of the South is today ready to unite with the black man in an honest attempt to build up his fortunes and to work out for himself a future.

An error even more egregious than the one above corrected is the assumption that the negro cherishes a natural animosity to his former owner. Every single interest that the negro has, and every attachment that he ever had is with the men in whose midst he lives today, and whose slave he formerly was. He gets his living from them; they rent him lands; they give him work; they assist him when he is in distress; they advise him when he is in dilemma. In them his whole world is centered. Beyond them, and outside of them he has but little knowledge of men or things; and does not care to learn more. His only practical acquaintance with the Yankee is through the Freedman's Bureau, which swindled him out of about three millions of dollars of his first precious earning, and this acquaintance, it is safe to say, he doesn't care to extend.

It may be asked now if the feelings of the two races are so reciprocally kind, why it is that they have been so bitterly estranged, and engaged in so deadly a war upon each other. The answer to this natural, though not profound question, lies in the nature of the political issues which have been presented to us since the war. The amendments which guaranteed freedom and political rights to the negro, and the bill which gives him social rights, were naturally opposed solidly and bitterly by the white race, and just as strenuously supported by the negroes. These were class issues which inevitably arrayed the classes against each other. The contests over these amendments, in which the one class sought to repress what the other felt bound to assert and establish, have produced all the trouble, and engendered all the bitterness. Two races voting en masse against each other, must, at last become involved in a struggle in which the weaker race must suffer.

The true solution of the negro problem is to eliminate from our politics all questions on which he can be massed against the whites. He must divide his vote. He may vote freely and openly, but he must take himself out of the hands of the foolish and wicked leaders who use him for the purpose of corruption. He must watch the drift of public affairs, and judge for himself as to what principles or what candidate he shall support with his ballot. Instead of letting others, who have proved themselves incapable and treacherous, think for him, he must think for himself. He must not follow the whispered command of some midnight league, but he must hear the truth spoken openly and bravely in the sunlight, and become its champion. When this is done, all the prejudices that have taken possession of either class will melt away; a perfect comity and sympathy will be established, and the white man taking the negro by the hand will lead him out of his miserable condition.

Even as it has been; with an eternal clash and contest between the races and with an insidious enemy at the negro's back, we see from the last Comptroller's report that the negroes of Georgia own over six million of dollars' worth of property, all of which has been acquired in the past five or six years. With the obstacles removed—with a full and absolute concord existing—with the "war of races" an impossibility, the "color line," a myth, and the "carpet-bagger" a refugee from the land of adoption, the negro problem will be solved; solved with a rapidity and completeness that will be astonishing. With the last piece of class legislation an accomplished fact, with all amendments, and Civil Right bill operative and binding with the white man willing and the negro anxious; why cannot these differences pass away, and this miserable struggle end forever? There is only one thing to prevent. The Northern people. And they cannot prevent it if they will only take a piece of advice that we can utter in two words. That advice is, "Hands off!"

28

R. A. Alston,
The Atlanta Herald,
May 6, 1875.

"A Brace of Incidents"

Apropos of the editorial in the *Herald* of yesterday, affirming that there was an intimate and sympathetic relationship existing between the Southern negro and his old master, we publish two incidents that happened in South Carolina, before the war.

Illustrative of the jealousy with which masters guard the rights of their slaves, we will relate an incident which came under our personal observation. There lived in Charleston, a very wealthy planter

who was regarded as rather surly in temper, and harsh in his treatment of his slaves. A little negro belonging to one of the aristocracy,
persisted in playing tag in front of this gentleman's house. One
day he was driven home in his carriage, and seeing this negro en-
gaged in his usual evening pastime, he ordered his coachman to
catch him up and carry him in the coach-house and thrash him
soundly. His master hearing it prosecuted the master of the coachman, and he was found guilty, of course. Sentence day arrived and
Mr. Petigru, the most eminent lawyer of South Carolina, rising in
his seat, said, "May it please your honor, I would be glad if you
would give my client a sealed sentence." That stern old Roman,
Judge Withers, quietly remarked: "Mr. Petigru, I must decline to give
your client a sealed sentence. He is a man of prominence, and his
standing here in the presence of this large audience and receiving
lecture which I propose to give him, is no small share of his punish-
ment. A pecuniary fine will not meet the case. Mr. Sheriff, bring
in the prisoner." In a few moments this rich and powerful man
was marched before the judge, puffing with important rage. For half
an hour Judge Withers gave him a lecture which those who heard it
long remembered, and closed it with these words, "The sentence of the
court is, that you pay five hundred dollars, and go to jail for six
weeks." The writer saw him marched to jail, where, he no doubt,
meditated upon the majesty of South Carolina's law, and the duty
of respecting the rights of humblest of her citizens.

Another fact known to the writer: A few days since a
prominent jurist remarked that he could not remember a case
in Georgia where a white man had been hanged for killing a
negro. We replied that we were not sufficiently acquainted with
the history of the judicial proceedings of Georgia to deny the
statement but one thing I could testify to, and that was, that
white men had been hanged in South Carolina for killing negroes, and then related the following: A man whose business consisted in catching runaway slaves, borrowed some dogs from a prominent and wealthy young man living in one of the upper districts of
South Carolina for the purpose of catching a notorious runaway.
The young man accompanied him in the search. The negro was
tracked and the dogs tore his flesh so badly that he died. The negro
catcher was tried for murder, and the young man as an accessory.
Both were found guilty. There was a tremendous effort made to
screen them during the trial, but without avail. The next step was
to procure a pardon. Failing in this, it was decided to rescue them.
The young man's strong family connections and wealth, threatened
but law in this glorious little commonwealth was supreme, and the
governor ordered two military companies from Charleston to carry
out the sentence. One of these companies was the Marion Artillery,
Capt. J. Gadsden King, to which the writer belonged. This stern
array of authority prevented the slightest demonstration at the gallows, and the men expiated their crime with their lives.

The more we consider this negro question, the more we are impressed with the injustice which the Southern people have suffered
for nearly fifty years, for simply maintaining in its integrity an
institution of domestic servitude which time can never improve for
the benefit of the laborer.

We are amazed at the indifference with which we regarded all
the lies that were circulated in the pictorial histories and periodicals.
Feeling conscious of our own rectitude, we never supposed that they
referred to us. When we saw the pictures of a half-naked negro
working on a West India plantation, and a broad-brimmed, high-

booted individual with a pistol buckled on him, standing over him with a lash, our childish sympathies went out to the poor negro and we shuddered at such slavery, and yet the whole world was pointing to us as that man. These were the books out of which our children learned their geography, and still we never dreamed that if such pictures made this kind of impression on us, what must have been their influence upon the rest of the world who pointed to us as the very barbarians.

This was the mistake we made during the war, in allowing slavery to be elevated into being regarded as the cause of our strife, when it was merely one of the incidents. Let the status of the negro regulate itself, and so identical are the interests of the two races living in an agricultural community like the South that strife will cease and prosperity once more bless our law-cursed country.

29

Henry W. Grady,
The Atlanta Herald,
September 14, 1875.

"SOUTHERN NEWSPAPER WRITERS"

It has been said that there is not a first-class journalist in the South. While this remark is untrue and unjustified, the writer would have come nearer the truth had he said that there is not a first-class editorial writer in the South. We have a score of men, who, with imperfect news facilities, untrained assistants and slender resources, nevertheless manage to present newspapers that would not discredit the populous North with its network of telegraph wires and its lightning mail trains. Our journalists make up better newspapers than Northern journalists could make under the same circumstances. They have become wide-awake and shifty through necessity, and the general knack of making a great deal out of a little, comes natural to them.

But the great fault of Southern journalism is its lack of first-class editorial writers. This lack is the result of poverty. The publishers are too poor, or their income is too circumscribed to allow of their employing a sufficient number of writers to do the work properly. Southern newspapers generally have one editorial writer. He is relied on to fill an average of three columns a day. He must fill these columns whether he be inclined to write or not—whether he be sick or in health. Even if he has an assistant, the assistant cannot carry his responsibility. He is looked upon as the editor, and the publishers look to him, at least, to write the leading editorials. The result of this overwork is, very legitimately, to depreciate the quality of the work done. The editor being required to furnish editorials upon at least two, and frequently half a dozen dissimilar topics daily, of necessity, hardly reaches the bottom of either one of his subjects. No editor who hopes to make an impression upon his age, should write more than one leader a day, and he should not write more than three a week. None of the editorial workers upon the New York papers do more than this, and most of them do less. As a consequence, the editorials of the New York papers, and particularly the *World* and *Tribune* are models of style and power. The drudgery that the Southern editor is forced to do is telling upon Southern journalism. It is hard to put the finger on any man this side the line who is a first-class editorial writer. We have fine correspondents, racy reporters, good paragraphists, but few fine writers. The most noticeable effect of the hurry and embarrassment under

which our Southern journalists are forced to write is that it affords
them no leisure in which to look over their work, to spy out its defects, and determine upon the points at which it should be corrected.
As a consequence, the defects become fixtures, the mannerisms are
confirmed, and the style becomes more and more fixed and monotonous
day after day.   The peculiarities of the writer are sprinkled
through his writings with no attempt at repression, and the editorials
all read alike, though one may treat of a grave and the other of a
gay subject.   Now there is Mr. Watterson, of the *Courier Journal*,
who is perhaps the smartest writer on the Southern press.   He did
some very brilliant and earnest work in the Greeley campaign, doing
the best writing that was done in that desperate and sentimental
campaign.   But he has not written a dozen great editorials since.
His work is all flippant, thinnish, and without any sturdy backbone
of purpose.   He is pert always, entertaining usually, and brilliant
sometimes.   But there is a slouchiness and slanginess about his
editorial that even a perusal of his proof on his part would eliminate.
He is not doing himself justice.   With two-thirds of the work that
he is doing taken off his shoulders he would be in two years at
the head of his profession.   In our opinion there is no writer in
the South equal to Col. John Forsyth, of the *Mobile Register*.   His
editorials, which are ornate beyond the fancy of some persons,
are never overloaded with words, and are always firm, pointed and
elegant.   There is a delicate classical flavor about Mr. Forsyth's
work, coupled with an elegance of diction, that we find in hardly
another Southern paper.   Next to Mr. Forsyth, Mr. Albert Roberts
of the old *Nashville Banner*, is the best writer on our press.   His
fight against the contraction of the currency made in the last issue
of the *Banner*, was the most effective and notable business that we
have seen in a newspaper in many a day.   Mr. Roberts showed signs
of overwork before his paper consolidated with the *American*, but
we hope that under the new arrangement he will find sufficient
leisure to devote himself strictly to editorial writing, and throw off
the drudgery of the profession.   If he can do so, he will make the
American a power in the opening campaign.

In Georgia we have a great many good newspaper men, one
"trained journalist," but very few finished editorial writers.   We
have six or seven creditable newspapers, but hardly a single one in
which the editorial page is not the weakest part of the paper.   It
will be almost impossible for any man who reads them all daily, to
recall a half dozen notable editorials that have appeared in any of
them during the present year.   Since Col. Albert Lamar left the
Sanctum, Col. John H. Martin, of the *Columbus Enquirer*, is the best
editorial writer on the Georgia press.   The secret of his power is
earnestness and purpose.   His editorials are put in the sweet and
strong old Anglo-Saxon, and are full of conviction.   He never writes
unless he has something to write about, a good but neglected rule.
Next to Col. Martin, we should put an editorial writer on the *Chronicle
and Sentinel*, whether Mr. Walsh or Mr. Wright we are unable to
say.   This writer, whoever he is, stands alongside of Col. Martin,
and displays a pleasant versatility and wonderful strength.   Col.
Styles, of the *Albany News*, is the best Campaign writer in Georgia,
or in the South.   To handle a paper for three months ahead of the
election—when "lightning is playing along the line"—he hasn't an
equal in the range of our knowledge.   Col. Randall, of the *Augusta
Constitutionalist*, is the most brilliant worker that we have, but his
editorials lack the grip that they should have.   They do not take
hold of the public mind as they ought to.   Mr. Willingham, of the

9

Rome Courier, is as good a worker as there is on the press, and supports one of the very best editorial broadsides that we have. He is ungrammatical once in awhile, and ungraceful very often. And yet of all these editors and their daily work, who is there that can remember half dozen notable editorials that either of them, or all of them have given to the public in the last six months?

The reason for this is apparent, has been stated above. It is over-work. There is not one of the editors that we have mentioned who is not daily concerned as much about the general make-up of the paper, its locals, its telegrams and its correspondence, as he is about his own legitimate work. Indeed, we believe some of them set up their own editorials, and Mr. Willingham, we are certain, carries on a flourishing line of job work. Until through some means or other our editors shall be able to make their sanctum their castle, and devote themselves strictly to their work, we shall not reach a high pitch of excellence. For all of this, though, we are proud of Georgia journalism. There are reputations to be made and lost in the coming campaign. It will be a grand battle, and every soldier may wear his spurs. We shall expect our Georgia brothers to be foremost in the fight, and we are certain that some of them, at least, will emerge from the affray knighted in honor.

30

Henry W. Grady.

"A PATCHWORK PALACE—THE STORY OF A HOME"
(A set lecture)

The Kindling of the Spark.

Mr. Mortimer Pitts was a chiffonier. Ah! I will translate and confess. He was a rag-picker.

After a patient study of the responsibility that the statement carries, I do not hesitate to say that he was the poorest man that ever existed. He lived literally "from hand to mouth." His breakfast was a crust; his dinner a question; his supper a regret. His earthly wealth, beyond the rags that covered him was—a cow, that I believe gave both butter-milk and sweet-milk—a dog, that gave neither—and a hand-cart in which he wheeled his wares about. His wife had a wash-tub that she held in her own title, a scrubbing board similarly possessed, and two chairs that came to her as a dowry.

In opposition to this poverty, my poor hero had—First, a name (Mortimer Pitts, Esqr.) that his parents whose noses were in the air when they christened him, had saddled upon him aspiringly, but that followed him through life, his condition being put in contrast with its rich syllables as a sort of standing sarcasm—and second, a perfect wealth of tow-headed children with shallow-blue eyes. These blonde brats came tumbling like April showers from the perennial Mrs. Pitts, who, withal she was a deprecating woman, responded to her lord, with a enthusiasm that nothing could dampen, and a promptness at delivery that nothing could check. Mr. Pitts giving his wife, on the arrival of "her ships from the sea" a look in which pride wrestled bitterly with judgment, took the little ones to his arms loyally and tenderly, giving them plenty of kisses, when there were no crusts, and all in all, the days—hard days though they were—passed happily enough. The rag-picker never looked above the tow-heads of his bairns, or beyond his wife's shallow-blue eyes. His world was very small. The chirping of the cricket that lived beneath the hearth-stone filled it with music, and the sunbeams that crept through the cracks of the hovel, filled it with light.

Troubles only strengthened bonds of love and sympathy that held the brood together; and when once in awhile the wolf showed his gaunt form at the door, the white faces, and the blue eyes, and the tow-heads, only huddled the closer to each other, until in very shame, the intruder would take himself off.

Mr. Pitts had no home. With the restlessness of an Arab, he flitted from one part of the city to another, hardly becoming notable as the ragged phenomenon of the neighborhood before he left it. He was famous as the early market-maids, by pushing his white, rounded face usually set in a circle of smaller faces, through the windows of long deserted hovels—whether these were miserable shells of houses that whistled when the wind blew and cried when the rain fell, and had their cheeks pinched as if they had lost their teeth, you might be sure of finding Mr. Pitts at one time or another. I do not care to state how many times, my poor hero with a uncertain step and a pitifully wandering look—his fertile wife usually in remote or imminent process of fruitage of his wan and sedate brood of bairns—his cow a thoroughly conscientious creature, who passed her scanty diet to milk, to the woeful neglect of tissue—and his dog, too honest for any foolish pride ambling along in an unpretending bench-legged sort of a way—how many times I say, this melancholy white procession passed through the streets, seeking for shelter in which it might hide its wretchedness, and ward off the storm, I do not care to state.

During these periods of transition, Mr. Pitts was wonderfully low spirited. "Even a bird has its nest; and the poorest animal has some sort of a hole or a roost whar it can go when it is wory," he said to me once, when I caught him fluttering aimlessly out of a house that under the influence of a storm had spit out its western wall, and dropped its upper jaw rather dangerously on the back of the cow. And from that time forth, I fancied I had noticed my poor friend's face growing whiter, and the blue in his eyes deepening, and his lips becoming more tremulous and uncertain. The shuffling figure, begirt with chiffonier's bells and dragging the wobbling cart, gradually bended forward, and the look of sweet childish content was gone from his brow, and a great dark wrinkle had knotted itself there.

And now let me tell you about the starting of the palace.

One day in the spring time, when uprising sap ran through every fiber of the forest, and made the trees as drunk as lords—when the birds were full-throated and the air was woven thick with their songs of love and praise—when the brooks kissed their uttermost banks, and the earth gave birth to flowers, and all nature was elastic and alert, and thrilled to the core with the ecstacy of the sun's new courtship—a divine passion fell like a spark into Mr. Mortimer Pitts' heart. How it ever broke through the hideous crust of poverty that cased the man about, I do not know, aught but that God put it there in his own sweet way. But there it was. It dropped into the great cold, dead heart like a spark—and there it grasped and trembled, and grew into a blaze, and swept through his soul, and fed upon its bitterness, until the scales fell off, and the eyes flashed and sparkled, and the old man was illumined with splendid glow like that which hurries youth to its love, or a soldier to his charge. You would not have believed it to have seen him. You would have laughed had you been told that the old fellow sweltering in the dust, harnessed like a dog to a cart, and plying his pick into the garbage-heaps like a man worn down to the stupidity of a machine, was burning and bursting with a great ambition—that a passion as pure and as strong as ever kindled blue blood or steeled gruttle nerves, was tugging at his heart strings. And yet so it was. The rag-picker was filled with a consuming fire—and as he worked and toiled and starved, his soul sobbed and laughed, and cursed and prayed. Mr. Pitts wanted a home. A man named Napoleon once wanted Universal Empire—Mr. Pitts was vastly the more daring dreamer of the two.

I do not think he ever had a home. Possibly, away back beyond the years, a dim sweet memory of a hearth-stone, and a gable roof with the rain pattering on it, and a cupboard, and a clock, and a deep, still well, came to him like an echo or a dream. Be this as it may, our hero, crushed into the very mud by poverty—upon knees and hands beneath his burden—fighting like a beast for his daily bread— shut out irrevocably from all suggestions of home, embittered by starvation—with his faculties chained down apparently to the dreary problem of today—nevertheless did lift his eyes into the gray future and set his soul upon a home!

31

Henry W. Grady,
The Atlanta Herald,
September 22, 1875.

"THAT JONES"

It will be remembered that some months ago we explained that the appearance of certain ungrammatical phrases in the *Herald* by laying them to eccentricities of a reporter named Jones. This reporter has absolutely no idea of tense or mood; and very little of orthography. And yet he was so ubiquitous, his legs were so prompt and so cheerful, he collected news in such a delicious hurry-skurry, that we winked at his grammar, while we commended his general get-up-and-get. He kept his place and roamed through our establishment with the ease and irregularity of an untamed omnibus horse.

We have trouble with Jones, and as the public was kind enough to betray an interest in the recital of our early struggles with this unlicensed roust-about, we recur to the subject this morning. One morning we were shocked to find the following sentence in the *Herald*, "Wiley Redding is the man who *done* the deed," and a little further on, "He spread out his shawl and told her to walk over it and she *done* it." We summoned Jones, who flew up the steps, and lit, as it were, for an instant on the door-sill. We commenced a spirited remonstrance, but Jones cut us short, "Whazze-matter with the sentence?" asked he. We began to explain, but he stopped us again, "You object to word *done* do you? All right," and in a jiffy he was gone, having explained that he had heard that "a wood car had threw a girl up, down town," and he was going "to see into it." Things ran smoothly for a few days, and we were congratulating ourselves that Jones was cured. One Friday morning—we can never forget it—we ran upon the following sentence: "The city assessors have did their work, and have did it in a shorter time than was ever did before."

We walked into Jones' room, and found that young man beguiling his stomach with a bit of Bologna and a pretzel. We presented, in as mild a manner as possible, our grievance. A look of incredulity passed over his face, and he asked in a dazed sort of way, "You object to that sentence?" We repeated our objections. Then Jones' despair was magnificent. He tossed his pretzel out of the window, with an air of a man who had nothing to live for, and exclaimed, "Now what can I do! A few days ago you objected to the use of 'done'—I at once stopped using it altogether. Now you object to using 'did.' Now, when you have gave me, the word you want used in these cases, I'll know what to do."

That very day we smote him. We relieved him from active duty, and sent him to the springs with orders to brush up on his grammar. He came back the other day. We rejoice that we are able to say that he has conquered the troubles that have heretofore embarrassed him, and now saunters down the by-ways of speech, with the easy air of a slippered grammarian. It is true that he still uses the word "blowed," instead of "blew," but we really can't find it in our heart to object to this small license. In fact, we are not certain but that we prefer the first word of the two. There's a wild air of scope, expanse, and power, about "blowed," that we look for in vain in the prim, tame word, "blew." The one has luxuriant stretch over it; a kind of teasing of the mane to the heavens, and neighing to the desert winds. The other smacks of the martingale, and calls up a suspicion of red-morocco nostrils, and haughty glass eyes.

So we have no objections to Jones on this score. But he has contracted a habit that is just as bad as the other. While at the springs he met a reporter of the *New York Sun*, who kindly consented, while helping spend his loose cash, to instruct him in the tricks of sentimental journalism. He gave him especially some rules for getting up head-lines of the latest style. You can't imagine how the "Gerraceous Hevings" method of journalism seized upon Jones' mind. It became his night-mare. It followed him throughout the day and made him moody. He put on standing collars, and bought a pair of velveteen pantaloons. The first morning after he came back to work the local page was sprinkled about with head-lines until it looked as if the advertisement had gotten drunk and jumped over the column-rules. A little girl was bitten by a dog, near Mr. Castleberry's. Jones worked it up into a column article, and started it out with the harrowing title—"The Fatal Fangs; or the Sleuth-Hound of Castleberry's Hill." A negro man tickled another's ribs with a pen-knife. Jones regaled us the next morning with, "A Bucket of Blood; or Carnage in the Glare of the Gas Lamps." A gentleman fell off of the curb-stone and sprained his ankle—Jones had it, "Into the Abyss; A Terrific Tumble from a Curb-Stone." Two newsboys had a fight, and Jones wiping the tears from his blood-shot eyes, indited a column about "The Demon Newsboys; or War Among the Arabs."

It is very trying to us. We aim to publish a decorous paper. There is nothing of the gasp or spasm, or Boston dip, about us. And yet Jones lifts us up to heights and plunges us into depths that we know not of. He is regarded in our office as a sort of journalistic maniac. He is looked at with suspicion by the whole force, except the "devil" and press-boy, who look up to him with an admiration hardly short of worship. We have a man of lymphatic temperament, who sleeps in the ice house and feeds on cold potatoes, whose duty is to follow this blazing fiend of a reporter, and crush the fire and passion out of Jones' head-lines, just as tradition tells us there are old women who ride across the sky on broom-sticks and sweep up the sparks from the tracks of the comets. This man is a sort of Babcock fire extinguisher, and he plays a perpetual stream on Jones.

And yet, why should we complain? The "perfect reporter" has not yet been evolved.

He may lie hidden—a precious gem—in the folds of a great future; but we have not heard from him yet. He is possibly coming along with the "trained journalist." If so, until this couple shall reach the earth, and revive the memory of Cervantes' famous pair, we shall be content with Jones. We shall try to keep his fiery shape, in the shadow of the fish-blooded phantom that plies in his wake; and if he at times flashes before the public we beg them to close their eyes until he is again put in eclipse.

32

Henry W. Grady,
The Atlanta Herald,
October 1, 1875.

"How Atlanta is Fed"

The arrival of the oyster always inspires us.

The coming of the noisiest creature on earth does not gladden things up so much as does the entry of this unobtrusive traveler, that slips in on the half-shell and drops into the ice barrel like a sigh or an exhalation, and is heard of no more until he reappears in the cheerful fricassee or the mild mannered stew. He comes attended with clouds of savory suggestions, that pile themselves in sweet, dim masses on the epicure's horizon. He is the pioneer of roasts unnumbered—of soups and sturdy pies; of steaming dishes, and smoking bowls, before which the perishable trumptery of summer fades like a dream. Great fat turkeys spitted to the point of perfection, and bursting with dressing that embodies the suggestions of nineteen centuries; partridges, that incomparable game-bird, enthroned upon toast; shad, trout, perch, and the baked black bass, that blessed ornament of December dinner-tables; devilled crabs, those funny fellows that walk backwards all through life, but gloriously retrieve their reputation in death; shrimp-pies, the very crisis of things savory and rich; the traditional roast pig, with the apple trembling in his fixed lips; rice-birds, celery, lobster-croquets, pickles, jellies, shadines, bananas, hares, venison, nuts, and all the tribe of canned delights—these and this, the melange, appetizing and ravishing, that comes with that season, of which the oyster is at once the token and the crown. This immaculate bivalve—the best pearl ever found within shell—is here. His enchanting fragrance hangs around the restaurants like a cloud, and the rich brown shells rise in monumental grandeur before their doors. And as we put behind us the fragile trash with which we have beguiled the summer, and whet our appetites for the work of the ripe winter season, it may be well for the readers of the *Herald* to know what the outlook for the winter is, what the grocers and the marketers will have, what they will ask for, and when they will have it.

33

Henry W. Grady,
The Atlanta Herald,
November 24, 1875.

"The War Between the States"

Last night, at seven o'clock exactly, was begun in this city, the second war between the States of this Union.

Not a war similar to that one which, born in sectional hate, begun at Fort Sumter, desolated the South, wasted a generation of men, put the Republic to mourning, and ended beneath the Apple Tree of Appomattox. Not such a war, with its desolating savagery, but a war of friendliest emulation—a war in which "the old thirteen" states are rivals in generosity, each striving to outdo the other in good; each rallying with a splendid energy around the standard of Atlanta's pet institution—the Young Men's Library!

It is the old fight over again—though for new gauges of battle and on new bloodless battle-field—South Carolina with her impulsive packet—emptying prodigality, challenges the deliberate and strenuous liberality of Massachusetts; Georgia, with the old open-handed extravagance that has distinguished her sons from time immemorial calls New York, with her superb resources and her great metropolitan heart, to the scratch; Virginia, the mother of States and the world's pattern of hospitality, puts herself against Pennsylvania, which boasts the model city of America, and is imbued with the kindly Quakerish spirit; Maryland defies Connecticut; and Delaware and Rhode Island, the bantams of the two sections, are dropped in the ring together, both gaffed by careful hands, their neck-feathers up, and their wings akimbo.

Markham's new hotel is the scene of the conflict, and it is waged fiercely every night. The representatives of each State rally manfully around their new methods of war. We see much that is auspicious in the present occasion with its rival of old memories, its renewal of old associations, and its reawakening of old revolutionary traditions. It is a fit opening to a great Centennial of next year, and the pervading interest taken in our little side-show gives a token that the old sectional partisan hate is dying out, if indeed, it is not already dead. Our people cannot find anything better to do than going down to Markham's to watch the tournament of states.

34

Henry W. Grady,
The Atlanta Herald,
November 25, 1875.

"The Okeefenokee Swamp Expedition"

We fear—very much fear—that the world does not properly appreciate the discoveries being daily made and reported by the *Constitution* explorers in the Okeefenokee Swamp.

Stanley traveling in Africa, receives his meed of praise—those amorous young rascals on board the *Dandora*, won the applause of a world for simply sailing up to Disco and kissing and squeezing the pretty Disco girls; "Jones," pushing, in his own sweet way, through Ponce de Leon's trackless wilds, has achieved a reputation that may make his grandchildren haughty; but Clark, plodding along with the heroism of a martyr, through the mush-bottomed Okeefenokee, now up to his neck in water, and now shinning along a log, with alligators at his side, snakes in his boots, and bugs in his hair—beyond the reach of woman's smiles, or the "smiles" of that more exhilarating sort—Clark, we very much fear, is not agitating the continent in precisely the manner he would like.

The contemporary press, with a forgetfulness perfectly inexplicable, fail to copy the glowing letters he has written; and their readers will never get (unless indeed these letters should be published in book form) the benefit of these discoveries that are therein detailed. In his first letter, we notice a piece of information that would have been full compensation for the whole trip, if not another discovery had been made. We allude, of course, to the fact announced in display type, that the expedition found a persimmon tree growing upon Billy's Island. As is well known, it has been rumored for many years that there was a persimmon tree growing on William's Isle; but this is the first authoritative statement ever issued upon the subject. We suppose that appreciating the importance of the statement, Col. Clark did not promulgate it until he had ascertained beyond a doubt, that it was a persimmon tree. He doubtless went to the root of the matter, rummaged through its trunk, examined its bark, discussed it in all its branches, and hacked it with his hatchet! Indeed the remark casually dropped, that "it was full of ripe fruit," justifies the belief that he twined his adventuresome legs around its body, and shinning his way to the top, ate some of the persimmons. Under these circumstances, we cannot doubt that it is a persimmon tree, and the fact may be telegraphed at once to Persimmonville.

There is only one thing lacking in the report of this wonderful expedition, and that is the failure on its part to meet any wild animals. This lack is supplied, as best it can be, by frequent references to the trace of wild beasts. The public blood is frozen at the frequent intervals with such expressions as this, "In the morning we went out to where we heard the noise, and found where an American panther had left his footprints." And if the American panther had passed that way the next day, he would doubtless have found where an American exploring expedition "had left its footprints." We are promised "a picture of the scene from Mr. Hyde." We shall expect the foreground of this picture to be two sets of footprints leading in opposite directions; the footprints of an American panther, and the footprints of an American expedition—"led by Col. C."

Another thrilling incident is related in the following burning words: "Hearing the dog give a significant growl, we called him back. A few steps further ahead, we saw where a very large bear had just passed along into the island. We immediately 'deployed' out, but he undoubtedly winded us and made his escape." If there is anything to equal in adventure of meeting a bear face to face it is to find a place where a bear has just passed along. There is a charm in looking at his tracks, and calculating how far off he is, and wondering whether or not he has any notion of coming back. It is quite fortunate that the bear "winded" the party and "made his escape." Had he not "deployed out," Col. Clark being up a tree (where, like the Quaker in the play, "he had climbed to see the scenery") friend Willingham would have had him at fearful disadvantage.

It must not be imagined though, that the expedition has not yet encountered a single wild beast. It has met and conquered one. We say "one" because we do not yet credit the story of the fight with the polecat, published in the *Commonwealth*. The encounter we refer to although it must have been a terrific one, is told with a charming air of modesty in the following words: "We killed an Opossum." Had a writer not repressed by personal feeling, been a witness of this thing, he would have written something like this: "The Opossum then gave forth a terrific roar that set wild echoes flying over the swamp, and with one bound was almost upon Col. C.— That gentleman met him gallantly with the left-hand barrel of his revolver, and tore away his fore shoulder. The wounded beast rolled backward in agony for an instant and then, rearing upon hind legs, rushed upon the gifted Colonel and folded him in his embrace. It was a fearful moment. The Colonel's ribs were snapping beneath the horrible pressure, and his eyeballs were forced almost out of his head. Just at this instant the State Geologist ran forward and thrust his theodolite 80 or 90 degrees into the monster's most vital part, and Colonel C. commenced carving his giblets with his paper cutter. The negro cook walked in with his frying pan, and the driver poured two broadsides from a shotgun in his head, dropped. The monster seized Col. C.'s left ear in his enormous jaws, and wrenching it clear off his head, dropped a bloody corpse. The gallant Colonel was not at all daunted, but at once raised himself on his left arm, waved his paper cutter above his head, and shouted defiantly, 'Now bring in another alligator!' "

35

Henry W. Grady,
Constitution,
December 3, 1876.

FLORIDA

The last of the evidence is now before the canvassing board and we may look for a decision of this knotty case, about next Tuesday evening. The democrats will submit their general argument, covering all the contested counties on Monday, at ten o'clock, in writing. It is quite elaborate, and is drawn with utmost care, and is said to be a literally irresistable argument. All the mass of facts presented have been sifted down and reduced to generalties and the most positive principles of law brought to bear on each case. Ex-Governor Brown, who had with Colonel Biddle, of Philadelphia, the direction of it, says he is perfectly satisfied with the basis on which it rests much more so than he expected he could be. Says he, "We have the state fairly, and I think we shall be able to hold it. If we do not, we will show the American people very plainly that it does belong to us."

The sensation of today is that the second negro candidate for elector, Humphreys, received the appointment of shipping master at Pensacola some months ago, and it is said only resigned a few days since. Is this another crooked hairpin?

36

Henry W. Grady, .
Constitution,
December 5, 1876.

FLORIDA

The democrats have surely won the fight, if there is one spark of honesty of fairness in any member of the board beyond Cocke. They presented an argument today that was simply irresistable. It reviewed the forgery and bribery that the radicals have used to get up their testimony and made a showing that will shock the American people. I have just left a consultation in Governor Brown's room where the prevailing opinion was that the democrats would get the verdict of the board on tomorrow. If any of the usual signs can be relied upon this opinion will be verified. Of course, Cowgill can vote square against all facts and evidence and this will upset all calculations that are based on this presumed honesty. It is believed he will not be brave enough to voluntarily take upon himself the infamy that will follow upon his sustaining the republicans in their corrupt and reckless scheme. The republicans announced after the democrats' argument was concluded that they would offer no general argument but piled in another lot of negro affidavits. They had about one hundred negroes brought last night and they spent the night in making affidavits. The democrats have closed their evidence and argument and will await the result patiently and calmly. If they are cheated out of Florida, then Sam Randall is the right man for speaker. His nerve and grit will stand the test to which they will be put when the counting of the vote is commenced.

37

Henry W. Grady,
Constitution,
December 8, 1876.

FLORIDA

The great case on which the electoral vote of this state hangs and the presidential problem depends for solution is all made up and before the board. The arguments are all prepared and your correspondent has been permitted to make a brief of each of them.

And tonight with a dispatch from St. Paul, Minnesota, asking the probable result, I am utterly unable to even guess at it.

The democrats have made a plain and convincing case. They have proved the most of the frauds upon the republicans, in which bribery, forgery and perjury have a conspicuous definite point. They have proved beyond the shadow of a doubt that 219 votes from Alachua, 346 votes from Duval, 129 votes from Jefferson, 138 votes proved to have been cast in other counties by jail-birds, should be thrown out.

I sat and looked at the man (Dr. Cowgill) yesterday during the session of the board and wondered if he appreciated, as he sat there perking his head about like a drunken woodpecker, that he was the most potential man in America.

And yet so it is! He holds more power between his flippant fingers today than has ever been vouchsafed to any one man since Washington died. He has the absolute making of a president. By simply voting "yes" four times tomorrow, he will settle the problem that has pitched the nation to a tip-toe, and make Samuel Tilden the next president beyond dispute or peradventure, of this republic.

No man has ever had this opportunity before. It is to be hoped that he will be wise enough to use this enormous responsibility that the accident of politics has put upon him, fairly and justly.

You have learned by the time this reaches you that Governor Brown has been quite ill. I did not wire you, because of his request that it should not be done. I may say now though, that for two days there was very serious fear that his sickness might terminate fatally. He had pneumonia which is especially fatal in this changeable climate.

You may imagine that the democrats were very blue, when he was at his worst. Although I have a great deal to do with the Ex-Governor —although he took occasion once to rise up and "sit down" on an enterprise with which I was connected with a vigor and emphasis only equaled by that with which Humpty Dumpty sits down on the inflated baby in the play, I never knew until he was sick what mental power the man had. He lay there in the bed, with two fly-blisters pulling torture out of his breast, and every breath he drew cutting his lungs like a knife, and surrounded by a pile of law books, which were being read to him, made up the skeleton of a legal argument on which the democrats will rest their case tomorrow. On Thursday night there was a ball in the dining room which is separated by a single wall from his room. The clamor was fearful. A brass band was blowing its brains out through some exceedingly noisy horns. A half dozen greased elbows were sawing across as many resonant fiddles, and the shouts and laughter were literally ear-splitting. I expressed the fear that it might make him worse by keeping him awake.

"Oh, no!" said he, "I can will myself to sleep at any time I want to."

And almost straightway he shut his eyes and did so. I arose and looked at him with wonder in my eyes. A sort of smile came to the sleeping face, and I have no doubt he was dreaming that he was snoozing away after a hard day's work in the old log cabin at Canton, winter's air pattering drowsily on the shelving house-top, and the wind sobbing huskily against the stout oaken door.

I started out of the room on tip-toe foolishly thinking of waking the sleeper. Jeff, his faithful attendant, laughed at my caution and said:

"You might shoot your pistol off right in the Governor's ear, and he wouldn't wake less he wanted to."

I solemnly believe that Jeff was right.

38

Henry W. Grady,
Constitution,
December 9, 1876.

FLORIDA

It is charming to sit down now after the struggle in Florida, so full of subtlety and strenuous endeavor, is over, and reflect that the matter was all settled beyond revision before the fight was opened, and that McLin and Cowgill were both predetermined, through either gall or greenbacks, on robbing the people of their choice for the presidency. There was never a moment when proof as strong as holy writ would have prevailed for one moment against the stupid and venal purpose of these men. They had made up their minds weeks ago to throw out enough democratic counties or force enough republican returns to give the republicans the electors, the Governor, the congressmen, and the legislature. Despite the overwhelming and crushing proof, they did this thing. Had it been necessary in doing this that a dozen more counties should have been thrown out then out they would have gone. It was a simple question of "yea or nay." I will refer to simply four counties that will serve as a sample of the action in the whole canvass.

But this unparalleled rascality will avail literally nothing. Arrangements were made immediately upon its consummation to check it. The democratic electors met and, backed with the certificate of the attorney general cast their votes for Tilden. They then issued a protest to the radical electors, and put them under notice of contest. Then, after preparing an address to Hon. Sam J. Randall, speaker of the house, they adjourned.

The congressional committee will arrive on tomorrow, and will go to work. This committee, I promise you, will develop a story of fraud that will sicken public sentiment.

The developments made before the board amount to comparatively nothing. The deliberate purpose of this board was to suppress the truth. Witness after witness, laden with important testimony—testimony known to be vital to democratic cause—were shut out from the board by a rule, as fiickle as it was infamous. What patches of truth the democrats did manage to work out, were elicited from witnesses accidentally or slyly brought before the board. They were disheartened day after day, when they went to the door of the canvassing room with essential witnesses, by having them turned back, before they had opened their mouths.

The value of the Oregon matter is just this: There has not been a moment in the last three weeks when the democrats did not know they could throw out Florida, Louisiana, and Carolina, and be sustained by public sentiment in so doing. They knew that the states were not only fairly democratic, but could be proven to be so. The only trouble in the way was a technical one. There was some doubt as to whether the house or the senate had the right to go behind the certificate of the Governor, as to whether either house could break under the *prima facie* votes or question or overturn the great and sovereign seal of the state. The radicals having in their hands all the machinery of the three contested states, having republican governors, and returning boards in three democratic states, determined through these two willing instruments of fraud to steal the states bodily and reverse their legal votes. In order that this miserable plan might stand they commenced crying out that the certificates of a Governor was final and ultimate—that, backed by the great seal of the state, it could not be contested.

39

Henry W. Grady,
Constitution,
December 9, 1876.

FORGERIES IN FLORIDA

An interview that I consider very important, in several respects, has just taken place.

Ex-Governor Brown is here en route homeward. Ex-Governor Noyes and Attorney General Little, of Ohio, who were in Florida as The Special Reporters of Mr. Hayes were on the same train. To-day they received a dispatch from Ohio that was believed to be from Governor Hayes. They approached Governor Brown after the reception of the dispatch, and asked if he would give them his candid and unpartisan view of the election in Florida, and the status of politics in the South. They invoked his candor with earnestness that impressed your correspondent with the idea that they were inspired from some higher source than their own curiosity.

The Ex-Governor, thoroughly impressed with the true history of the election, gave these gentlemen a long talk, showing up the history of the fraud in Florida in exhaustive and decisive manner that left them no room for doubt. He said to them he was morally certain that the state had given Tilden a clear majority, and that the Hayes majority had been builded up through direct and simple fraud; that the majority had been put at the absurd figures of 923, simply because that much was required to elect their state and congressional ticket as well as the electoral—that if more had been required the board would have unhesitatingly voted it.

If, as we suspected, the gentlemen sought the ex-Governor's opinion at the suggestion of Governor Hayes, he left no room for doubt as to the message that they should carry back to him. Governor Brown stated to them in as plain terms as polite language could put them, that no man who had a regard for the good opinion of his fellow-people could take the presidential chair on such a title as was furnished by Florida.

That Governor Hayes has exhibited severe doubts of late as to whether or not as an honorable citizen, with a regard for his reputation, he could afford to take the presidential chair now even if it were offered him there is no doubt. There is not a man in the South whose opinion is more valuable in the North or more prized by the masses than Governor Brown's, I consider it quite probable that Governor Hayes desired to get it, and if so, he may certainly "get it." The ex-Governor has never had but one opinion about Florida since the exhaustive and elaborate inspection he gave the election returns during the first week of his visit there.

It was quite a noticeable fact that the crowd who boarded the special train bearing "the visiting statesmen" home, nine-tenths of them asked for Governor Brown first. He was the hero at the homeward march.

40

Henry W. Grady,
Constitution,
December 21, 1876.

GLOBES OF GOLD

You can hardly appreciate the reluctance with which I begin a
letter on oranges. With a reputation for veracity already shattered,
because of the tales I have been compelled to tell during six years of
journalistic work, I naturally shrink from a story that must exceed in
wonder and marvel those glittering romances with which an ingenious
copper-colored liar beguiled the fancy of the Princess Scherezerade for
a thousand and one nights.

I shall go in bodily, however, and shall not be disappointed if those
very people who swallowed the fish and hen stories that have made
my name notorious shall rebel at the orange stories about to follow;
just as the old lady who gave great belief to her grandson when he
spun yarns about the mermaids, but belabored him with a broom who
tried to make her believe in flying fish!

As the profit is so enormous, the labor so light and the reward so
certain in orange planting, it may be asked why Florida is not "one
solid orange grove"? I reply that it is fast becoming so. The number of new trees set out in the last ten years is simply incredible.
The new trees have hardly begun to bear as yet; when their fruit
does come on, the world will be astonished at the amazing fertility
of our "American Italy." Some idea of the extent of the new groves
may be had when I call to mind that within a radius of ten miles of
Leesburg in Sumpter County, there are 52,000 trees that will be
bearing full fruitage in three or four years. At 800 oranges to the
tree, a very low estimate, there will be furnished annually, three years
from now, from this half a county forty million oranges.

41

Henry W. Grady,
Constitution,
December 27, 1876.

FLORIDA

Rapidly and yet none the less surely do the frauds in the Florida
election turn up to the daylight. It was thought by some that the
infamy developed by the returning board was the end of the chapter.
Your correspondent always contended that the thorough investigation
made by the congressional committee would develop newer and higher
frauds.

I have not been disappointed. The investigations of the frauds
at Richardson's precinct in Leon county, has brought to light the
most infamous and shameful fraud I have ever met in political history. . . .

Some one has asked me "What sort of a looking man is Pasco?"

Pasco is a ridiculuosly yellow man of medium height. He has
black whiskers that glisten, but do not grow thick. His eyes are
lustrous jet, and he has the dreamy, far-away, listening-to-an-echo
look, that I have heretofore supposed to be peculiar to husheesh eaters.
His voice is soft and toned down, until it sounds something like a
banana tastes. His hands are warm and feel like velvet. He is careful of his dress, wearing rich snuff color, reaching up to a modest maroon in the cravat, and dropping into a retiring drab in the pantaloons. He carries his head well forward, his legs moving in short,
quick steps, as if they were trying to catch up. I should say his

favorite perfume is musk—his favorite cigar a cigarette—his favorite wine, Sillery; his favorite musical instrument, a flute. The idea he gives an observer is one of repression. He does not carry his claws peeled, to scratch himself with, as some bantish beasts do; but keeps them snugly sheathed, until he is ready to spring on the enemy. And then they flash out, cold and clean, like stillettoes in moonlight.

Samuel is the very devil in a political fight. He throws his dainty hands about freely, and every time he hits he lacerates. He is the coming democrat of Florida, if I am any judge of what constitutes the thing to come with. He made most of the brilliant moves that were made by the local people in the late tussle, and stood higher in the confidence of the visiting consultants than any other Florida man. Withal he is a warm friend, a pleasant companion and a fine lawyer.

Altogether he is a tawny little hero; a hero in a campaign that is lost for the present—but none the less a hero!

42

Henry W. Grady,
Constitution,
December 29, 1876.

FAIR FLORIDA

I went up the famous St. John's yesterday—the handsomest river in America—and over to St. Augustine—the oldest city in America. The St. John's is really a series of lovely lakes! The water is of a smart lavender color, and trims out yellow. In repose it is a translucent maroon—when severely ruffled it breaks into bright amber. In some places a rich warm tropical color that had better be called "tawny" enlivened here and there with green groves, that had all the delicious freshness of spring about them. here were fine houses at frequent intervals, in the most cases having boat awnings at the river side, in which jaunty yachts were lazily swinging.

I saw "Mandrin," the home of Harriet Beecher Stowe, and was rejoiced to find that it was no great "shakes" after all. I am disposed to think that Harriet blows an exaggerated bugle, and that her "fine place" is mostly on paper. At any rate, I revenge myself on her by turning up my nose at it as we passed.

The boats that ply the river are very fine. There are three or four of the best Hudson river boats here, and two of the "Old Dominion" line. The boat we were on was perfect in its way. It was a real floating palace. There was only one bar to bliss on the boat—a little beast of a child—a true enfant terrible. Such a child it was I imagine that evoked Charles Lamb's natty toast at a dinner table. Glancing sternly across dishes at a pest of a child that had been making the occasion intolerable, this genial humorist arose and said: "I propose a toast to the memory of that much-abused man—Herod!" Our child, the bother of boat, late in the day developed a desire to jump overboard which desire the mother, much to the disappointment of the passengers, and with a shameful sacrifice of the public weal to private affection, refused to humor it in.

There was only one other point of discomfort, which the reader will pardon me for touching on, to-wit: the withering respectability of the head waiter who hovered near during the dining hour. I am peculiarly suscepible to scorn of hotel waiters. I have rarely seen one of these austere creatures so urbane and affable that I could really unbosom myself to him and with a free hand pour the desires of my soul at his feet. Many a time have I been checked suddenly half way down a bill of fare by one glance of contempt from the glittering eye of the waiter. I have had them to fasten their hasilisk orbs on my face, and glue me with the gaze of scorn, until every mouthful I took would nearly choke me, and when in pure desperation I would send my particular waiter to the kitchen for something I did not want, he would call up a new one with a fresh eye, and get him to watch me while he was gone. Ah! many's the time I have sacrificed my stomach to my pride, and fled hungry before the dumb bull-dozing of the hotel waiter!

This head waiter was the most respectable person I have ever seen or heard of. He was a leisurely creature in lavender pants and side whiskers. As we entered the dining-room a cold chill ran down my back as I felt that the head waiter had singled me out as one to make an example of. I felt him fix his eyes on a little double-chin that Florida tit-bits have added to my face. Then I saw a sneer hovering between hatred and contempt, curl his upper lip, and I felt that my doom was sealed.

As I seated myself, I found that he had retired to the staircase and was resting his head languidly on his hand, as if the daily contemplations of gluttons had well-nigh finished him. I supposed he noticed that I was taking rather too discursive a glance down the bill of fare. Anyhow, he glided over to me, placing his hand on the back of my chair, said with an air of mock politeness, "Will you have some of the shad, or the venison, or turkey?" I should have liked to have had all three of them, but was no accent on the fatal conjunction, and I took some shad. He returned to his stand by the stairs, and leaning his head on his hand to take a rest, as it were, shot baleful glances at me, as if he should say, "Young man, I *do* hope, for decency's sake, you won't eat yourself into a sweat." I could not stand it longer. I arose from a half-eaten shad, and leading my wife, who is a heroine spirit of culinary investigation, makes it a point to eat every "a la" on the bill of fare, from the table I withdrew.

At Tocci, a little station on the river, we left the boat to take a ridiculous little railroad out to St. Augustine. The railroad was formerly a horse-car road. A little engine has supplied the place of the mule, but the street cars still remain. It has been felicitously said of this road that it was "two streaks of rush and the right way." But the little engine, giving a snort that would have done credit to a larger machine, dashed into the heart of the woods, and in two hours we were in St. Augustine.

This city was the first one built by white people in America. It was founded in 1527—long before I was born. There are houses in its limits that are three hundred years old. Houses beneath where roof men may have sat, who knew Columbus personally and have shaken hands with Ponce de Leon. The oldest cathedral stands in St. Augustine. It is pre-Napoleon, pre-Washington, back of everything we really know of or care about. It is a shaking sign-post, behind which lies history. My baby toddled up to its hoary sides and pecked them with a stick. I drew him back reverently. I could not bear to see an infant slapping eternity in the face!

In these two the ages salute each other. Here one century speaks to another. Here the past gossips with the present. An old adobe house that might have been ancient when Washington was born, sits next to a pert Yankee cottage on which the paint is hardly dry. Never were the years so tumbled up before. Here Ichabod Slick of Vermont whistles Yankee Doodle in the back yard of Senor Yelazoma of Castile.

There are some wonderful old forts in this city. They were built by the Spaniards some time before the war—say in 1560. They are built of coquina and stone, and were probably big things in those days, but an iron-clad would pulverize one of them in forty minutes. One of these forts was built by contractors—doubtless carpet-baggers who came down with the Freedman's bureau, and it cost $14,000,000. This in 1560 was a big pile of money. When they reported the cost to King Philip in Spain, that monarch shaded his eyes with his hands and gazed intently over the ocean. "What are you looking at?" asked one of the carpet-baggers. "I am trying to see that fort. If it cost $14,000,000, it should be high enough to be visible from here." The carpet-baggers blushed and applied for another contract. They got it and built a fort further up the street. The bill for it was $20,-000,000. When they presented it to King Philip he said, in evident astonishment, "Why, there must be some mistake here, I didn't order you to build it of gold!"

But old buildings are dangerous things for a man with an imagination to fool with. You remember that fellow who told such big tales that his wife notified him that she would watch him, and when she found him running beyond the limits of credulity, she would press his foot. Shortly afterwards said he, "I saw a house in Italy 2,500 feet long, 2,000 feet high"—here his wife's feet came down on his like a trip hammer, and he concluded, "and a foot and a half wide." I shall drop the old forts.

The Indians in the fort are great features of interest. These stolid fellows came of a lineage that antedates even the oldest houses here. Their fathers had lived for centuries in quiet possession of the country before the new-fashioned white folks came. I blush to confess that I spent most of my time in this ancient city with the Indians. I saw a very pretty squaw leading a handsome, athletic child.

"Yours?" I asked.

"Ye-es, he mine," she said.

"Not full blood Indian?" I asked.

"No," she replied proudly, "him part Injun—part Inguneer!"

They are taking great pains to civilize the sons of the forest. They have taught them to wear coats, hats, boots, and breeches, the only trouble being that they will only consent to wear one of these useful articles at a time. I was so much interested in the advances they were making that I determined to do something to hurry their civilization. A tourist ahead of me gave them a long lecture on the advantages of civilized life. I laughed at this. I would be practical. I would not advise them to civilize. I would help them civilize. I stepped forward and gave one of them a plug of tobacco, and to another a pack of cards. Deeds, not words for me! I remember Mark Twain's noble letter in reply to a committee of ladies: "You ask me," he wrote, "to assist you in establishing an orphanage asylum. I might write you a long letter in reply. I prefer something practical, however. As evidence of my earnest sympathy, I will be one of one hundred men to contribute five babies each, toward starting this noble charity."

In the evening we took the train back to Tocci, and then the boat back to Jacksonville. We swept past the score of little villages with abnormal hotel developments, until at last the light of the city gleamed through the hazy night and the deadened clamor of the town floated over the water to our boat. I do not think there is any sight on earth—except possibly looking into the heart of a great, still forest from some hilltop—that is lovelier than that which is furnished to the passenger in a steamer, as he sweeps up in early night-time to a city that looks down with its myriad of twinkling eyes, in the translucent waters of the river.

43

Henry W. Grady,
Constitution,
March 8, 1877.

COMMENT ON SENATOR BENJ. H. HILL

I am inclined to think that some of this dangerous prominence is due to Mr. Hill's foolhardy frankness, and his absurd disregard of all proprieties of politics. In moments of which he is not even an approximate leader, he manages to draw the fire from every bush and emerge from the fracas the one banged-up man of the party.

The worst of it is, that no reformation can be hoped from Mr. Hill in the matter of detail. He will continue to cut across fields to the goal he is striving for. Instead of sauntering along the road with the party, he will scrub his buttons off in scrambling over fences, and manage to step on every vicious thistle in his ill-advised route.

The comfort of it all lives in the fact that the abuse does not hurt Mr. Hill. It falls like rain drops from a duck's back. There is a greatness of brain and soul about the man that has drawn the people about him.

Mr. Hill must not rest upon his oars, however. His future is yet a problem. His entrance into the senate will open a career that is utterly new and different from what he has yet had. Taken from the body of the house, where he was a hardly distinguishable atom in a mass. In the calm critical senate, with its few members, he will have an individuality to sustain, that will command not only the highest ability but the utmost decorum and observance of small proprieties. He will be thrown among thinkers and profound statesmen, and will find that the alert skirmisher and parliamentary brawler, that was his chief foe in the house, has already proved a cipher in the senate.

Mr. Hill must become the representation of some great policy, some statesmanlike method in the senate if he wishes to have an illustrious career. He cannot trust to the exigencies of amnesty debates, or sentimental defenses of the South. If he does this he will become a notoriety, and miss being a statesman.

It will hardly do for him to risk his future upon the idea of becoming the champion of states rights, and checking hideous progress of civilization. He must define a policy, marked and positive, and link it to his name, as Calhoun, Clay, Webster and Benton did.

The sentimental is passing out of our politics—sectional prejudices are about to die a death from which there will be no resurrection. The great men of the future must become the authors of and champions of some intelligent and reformatory or progressive movements.

I have little doubt that Mr. Hill will find the true way, and imbed his name and fame in the very heart of the time in which he lives. He will remember that the leadership he acquired in the Confederate senate was won by the readiness and ability with which he improved a hundred opportunities which came unsolicited to his hands, and will appreciate the fact that he must now make his opportunity, as well as learn how to improve it.

How will it do for him to open his senatorial work by tackling the Pacific Railroad bill in which one hundred and fifty million dollars of governmental money are at stake? or putting himself upon the question of a thorough and permanent civil service reform?

44

Henry W. Grady,
Constitution,
July 6, 1878.

"Dick Dawson's Dangle"

A Curious Case of Superstition

In his detailed confession Dawson makes some very queer state-
ments. The confession is now in possession of your reporter, and is
a strange document. I am convinced from a careful reading of it
that Dawson killed his brother-in-law through the influence of a superstitious fear. He says in his confession that Lucinda (wife of the
murdered man, Frank Cunningham, Col.) asked him to kill her husband, but that he refused to do it, and told her she was foolish to
think of such a thing, and that she must not talk to him about it any
more.

It seemed that the determined woman then shifted the pivot of
her plans, and began to play on Dick's superstitious fears. She told
him that her husband had gone to an old fortune teller who lived
near by and had paid him to conjure him. She found that this
startled her paramour, and she continued to play on this string. Every
accident or misfortune that happened Dick was laid by this artful
woman to the effect of the "spell," until at last the poor devil was
thoroughly frightened. She persuaded him that his garden spot, his
fish lines and all were conjured and at last she played the desperate
card that resulted in her husband's death.

One evening she was romping with Dick in the back yard of his
home. During her frolic she pulled some hair out of the top of his
head. Dick thought nothing serious of this but attributed it to her
playful disposition. That evening, however, she sought Dick in the
field where he was at work, and told him she had an important confession to make. She then told that her husband had sent her to see
him, and had told her that she must get him nine hairs out of his
head—to be sure and get them out of the "mole" of the head. When
Dick asked her what she wanted with them she said that it was to
finish conjuring him with. She said the fortune-teller had told
Cunningham to get these hairs and wrapt them around a rusty nail
he had furnished him with; then go and stick this nail in a certain
tree in the woods and hit it once a day for nine days. At the end of
the nine days the nail would be driven in and at that time Dawson
would die. As soon as Dawson heard this he was very much excited
and alarmed. In his confession, he says that from this time forward
he did not hesitate about killing Cunningham. He felt that he must
put him out of the way. He very soon arranged a plan by which
the bloody work could be done—being still assisted and urged on by
Lucinda. He invited Frank to come down to his house on Saturday,
stating that he was going to kill a hog, and he would give him half
of it. Frank went without suspecting anything. The two men played
marbles for a while. At last Dick proposed that they should go out
and get the meat. He carried his gun, and a hoe with him. When
they reached a quiet place, Dick told him to go to a gully near by and
he would find the meat. Frank went to look for it. As he bended
forward, Dick levelled the gun and shot him in the back. Frank fell
forward into the gully. He recovered, however, scrambled out and
hurried toward Dick. Dick says, "He rose straight up and looked
at me without saying a word." He then advanced towards Dick,
clutching a stick as he went. Dick met him with the uplifted bar,
and drove it full into his face. He fell again, groaning so fearfully

that Dick says to put him out of his misery he shot the remaining load of his gun into the breast of the prostrate man. He died instantly.

45

Henry W. Grady,
Constitution,
July 12, 1876.

LESTER AND FELTON

And here, ahead of all the rest, the bloody old seventh opens the political ball!

While the other districts are as cool as cucumbers, the old seventh is ablaze. The fires are lit on the hilltops of Bartow, Whitfield and Cobb; old Floyd is in a redhot condition and the sparks are kindling in all the other counties.

I never saw in my life such excitement as has already been created in this campaign. I predict that the fight between Lester and Felton will be the most heated and fiery Georgia has seen since the war. Felton's canvass has already been full of enthuiasm and glow. He has ridden upon a ground-swell into office both times. He has been opposed heretofore by arguments and methods.

But John Lester's fight promises to be as brilliant and electric as Felton's ever was. He goes in with his hat off, his eyes flashing, his empty sleeve dangling in the breeze, surrounded by a whooping host. The old style canting, deprecating way of meeting Felton and his impetuous followers has been done away with, and hereafter we shall have hurrah against hurrah, sentiment against sentiment, gush against gush. The Lester men, like the Feltonites of old, will wear smiles on their faces, ringing shouts on their lips, and will carry flags by day and torches by night! We are going to have music and uproar and glare in the seventh until the night of the 5th of November, and after that crepe, black eyes and calm.

The mettle of both the men in the race can be adjudged when we note how quickly they have locked arms in a deadly struggle. The ink is hardly dry on Lester's acceptance. He has made a phenomenal speech or two in Rome and today, in response to a challenge, accepted before it got cold, he is in Cartersville to meet Felton on his own ground among his own friends.

The meeting between these champions, while it was only announced yesterday, brought a large crowd to a pleasant little city. On the up train this morning squads of anxious patriots, a crowd of probably fifty getting on at Marietta. They were friends of each candidate, Lester's friends being probably in excess.

Dr. Felton was in the city early jogging around among his friends. Lester came down on the Rome train accompanied by about one hundred and fifty people—the majority of them his friends. The town was full by the time the hour for the speaking had arrived, and the court house being unable to hold the vast crowd, an adjournment was had to a pleasant grove. The arrangements for the speaking were very soon made, Lester to open in a two hours' speech, Felton to follow in a two hours' speech, Lester to rejoin in 15 minutes, and Felton to close in 15 minutes. It will be seen that Lester went in under disadvantages. The crowd gathered leisurely in the grove, and was scattered in groups chatting pleasantly, when Dr. Felton, wearing a loose alpaca coat, a broad straw hat and brown linen pants, came to Judge Lester and said:

"It is already five minutes after the time, Judge."

And at this Lester smiling stepped gallantly on the platform. He was greeted with an unexpectedly liberal round of applause, and settled down like a man to his work. It was very soon perceived that he was fighting around loose, just humming around until he could see Felton's hand. He soon wound up, however, and got the crowd well waked up. He threw in a lot of anecdotes, frequent bursts of eloquence, and at last got down to discussion of what he had heard Felton intended to attack him on. The first point was that he had supported Coles (republican) against Pierce Young, in the campaign of '68. He denied this. He explained that owing to an agreement reached by friends of General Gordon, who was running for Governor, and was being supported by Coles, it was arranged that the canvassers should take no part in the congressional race—especially as it was thought Young could not take his seat, if he was elected. "But," said he, "I declare in this open sunshine, by the God who hears me and will judge me, that I never made any speeches in that canvass."

He had heard that it would be charged that he had received $10,-000 from Governor Brown for lobbying for the lease. He explained that he received a retainer of $1,000 from Governor Brown to defend the integrity of the lease in case it became a matter of judicial inquiry, but that he did not lobby the case at all—did not ask a single member to vote for it and did not agree or expect to do so; that he took the fee as a lawyer and in consideration of legal services. He then got a telling shot by recalling a speech made by Felton at Marietta in the Trammel fight, when Felton eulogized him (Lester) very highly, and said, "Why did not the conspirators nominate a man like Lester, your honored fellow-citizen? Because he is too pure for their purposes. If he were nominated, I would at once ground my arms and support him!" Judge Lester then said if he was worthy of Felton's support then he was worthy of it now.

He then told an anecdote of a very wicked man, who suddenly reformed and joined the church. He was shortly afterwards seized with the most tormenting pains, and at last exclaimed in his agony, "Oh, Lord! What have I done lately to merit all this?"

46

Henry W. Grady,
Constitution,
July 13, 1878.

The Saucy Seventh

Looking over my hastily written special yesterday—indited in the heart of the howling multitude, and with the heat of the conflict still in my veins, there is but one modification that suggests itself in my cooler moments. I doubt if I expressed in quite strong enough terms, the dauntlessness and pluck of George Lester's fight, or suggested quite plain enough the good results that will flow from it.

I have heard every man of note in Georgia speak, and I believe that the two men who met on Thursday are the best "stump" speakers in the state, excepting Dr. Miller, and do not believe either of them could be matched.

Felton is the most finished orator, and has the most commanding presence and the highest culture. Lester is the most genial talker and the most versatile. His speech is all tears and smiles. It is a delightful mixture of fun and eloquence—of humor and passion. Both are alert, quick as a flash and full of nerve. Both are well poised, adroit and imperturbable. Either catches the humor of the crowd on the instant and rides it snugly. Both are impassioned, or pretend to be. Either can dash his voice with tears or stiffen it with the ring of the clarion. Lester is inimitable on anecdotes, Felton is matchless in certain kind of raillery. I don't know which is the best "stump-speaker." If I were forced to give an opinion I should say both.

47

Henry W. Grady,
Constitution,
August 10, 1878.

UNIVERSITY OF GEORGIA

At last the trustees of the university have given us a positive and decided change in the administration of its affairs.

To start with, the knife of retrenchment has been put sharply to the body of the college. Two professorships have been abolished and the chancellorship has been given to a professor. There has been effected a saving of $6,000 per annum, and the educative power of the faculty has not been impaired. The present administration may be considered permanent, if we accept the chair now held by General William M. Browne. This gentleman has already resigned his position, the resignation (now in the hands of the trustees) to take effect from the close of the present college year. With this exception the chairs as now filled will stand. There is no abler faculty in any college in the South.

The election of Dr. Mell to the chancellorship is universally confessed a rare stroke of policy. It may be said that this venerable man has already declined the office he has now accepted, a half dozen times. He has repeatedly refused to let his name go before the trustees when he was assured that his consent would result in his election. He refused, notably, to antagonize Dr. Lipscomb when he left the college.

Dr. Mell's election was received with an enthusiasm almost unprecedented. Among the post-bellum alumni the election is especially popular. The new chancellor held a sort of reception in the morning after his election, and hundreds of graduates and friends crowded in to shake his hand and pledge their enthusiastic support to the new regime. The doctor was at first very much disinclined to accept the office. After the ovation that he received at the hands of those interested, he could no longer hesitate, and he wrote his letter of acceptance and pledged his life to the sacred work of rebuilding the fortunes of the old university. A careful survey of all the departments of the university fail to discover a single element that is not enrapport with the chancellor. The Phi Kappa society passed resolutions of congratulations and support. The class of '68 did the same thing, as did the class of '75.

So that to an almost unequalled mental and physical equipment for performing the duties of the chancellorship, Dr. Mell enters upon his work backed by the hearty, unreserved and cordial support of every element of the university.

Indeed the whole commencement season was marked by unmistakable and plentiful signs of a hearty and positive re-awakening among the friends of the old college. Professor Wilcox truly remarked that the lack of strength in the Southern college was due, as much as to anything else, to the fact that the alumni never revisited their alma maters, and consequently never found themselves aroused in her behalf. The return of an unprecedented number of alumni to the present commencement provoked a hearty interest and awakened a fine enthusiasm. The election of Davenport Jackson, Esq., as trustee was a capital move. He was unanimous choice of his classmates of '68, who put him forward as their candidate. His almost unanimous election was a deserved tribute to one of the foremost young men of the

South, and an appreciated compliment to his class. The members of the class pledged themselves to support his trusteeship with earnest, undivided effort; and to supplement the rare good sense and brave impartial judgment that he will take the board by an enthusiastic work in behalf of the university. An agreement was made that each member of the class would strive to secure the matriculation of two new students, at the opening session. Their efforts will certainly be productive of good.

Altogether, it may be fairly expected that the old university will show decided signs of improvement upon the opening next October and its growth during the coming year will be decided and positive. There are forces at work upon its regeneration that cannot fail to produce decided results. The trustees have closed a laborious, painstaking, and well-directed session, and the work will tell upon the future of the college. With less than one hundred students in attendance now, I predict that one hundred and fifty or more will greet the visitors at the next commencement. And this prediction will do to close with.

48

Henry W. Grady,
Constitution,
August 13, 1878.

'VERSITY TOPICS

The present commencement season at Athens inaugurated a practice that is bound to become popular, and that will give much strength to the university. I allude to the matter of class reunions. Nothing so strengthens a university as to have her alumni come back to her classic shades after busy years of absence and renew their pledges to their alma mater and warm up their enthusiasm in her behalf.

A leading feature of the late commencement was the decennial reunion of the class of 1868.

Ten years ago thirty-two young men just starting life, sat around a giant oak in the campus at Athens smoking a calumet, after an ancient and respectable custom. Before the parting words were uttered, they clasped hands and pledged each other that in ten years from that day every living member of the class would meet again on that spot.

On last Wednesday afternoon twenty-one members of the class, responding to a tender sense of comradeship, were present at the old oak. Three of those who sat about it in '68 were dead. The remaining few were debarred from being present. At 7 o'clock at night the class met to enjoy a superb banquet which had been prepared by the ladies of Athens. The banquet was elegant. Turkey, ham, roast pig, barbecued lamb, chicken croquets, salads, etc., made up the solids, while cakes, creams, jellies, fruits, etc., made the desserts. The wines—claret, sherry, madeira, Rhine wines and champagne—were exquisite, having been ordered specially from Schneider's.

There never was an occasion fuller of more tender and sweeter joys. The speeches were all short, gossipy and full of reminiscences. There was not a speaker who took the floor that did not falter before he finished recalling the old memories—many of them broke down with emotion while talking of the dead members of the class.

A decided stir was created by the announcement made by Mr. W. W. Thomas, that according to the best vital statistics, five members of the class should have been dead before this reunion took place and that two members of the class are now living who should have died—that in the next ten years five members went dead—and in the next ten about ten members. Upon this alarming presentation of facts, several members arose and offered their resignation from the class, asserting that they could not remain in so deadly an organization. They were prevailed upon, however, to withdraw their resignations and agree to "stick it out" with the boys, as a committee was appointed to revise the insurance statistics.

The sketches of the various members as written by Mr. W. W. Thomas, of Athens, the class historian, was the most admirable piece of work. It is witty, pathetic, humorous, and touching. No similar work was ever done so well, and none will ever surpass it. We insert the closing remarks of this exquisite production.

49

Henry W. Grady,
Constitution,
September 26, 1878

The Ride to the Sea

It is impossible to conceive of a more positive contrast, in contiguous cities, than exists between Atlanta and Savannah.

Atlanta is smart and restless—Savannah slow and steadfast. Atlanta's characteristic is a certain sort of brawling progress, while Savannah has a heavy but uneventful growth that would wear out the patience of her more active sister. Atlanta has scanty capital but turns it rapidly and gives it no rest, while Savannah, with massive wealth, hoards it continuously, or permits it to run in sluggish currents. In social aspects, Savannah is reserved and undemonstrative, believing more in a pedigree than in a bank account. Its good society is bunched together, and hedged about by a platoon of social police against which adventurers may charge in vain, and from which many good people are turned away. Once inside the charmed circle, however, no braver or better company can be found. Sympathetic, earnest, hospitable and cultured, they soon satisfy the guest that most newcomers are intruders, and many of them worse. Atlanta is just the opposite. She is open, chatty and cosmopolitan. In love with excitement and novelty, a stranger has a sort of game flavor about him, and is at once introduced with some pride and a great deal of earnestness into the best society. Of course, once in a while an adventurer is admitted, but then the good people rise up, mash his head and put him out the back door; and then hurry with a smile to the front door to meet the next fellow. She has welcome for every decent man that seeks a home within her gates, and meets him with an enthusiasm and warmth that is a revelation to a Savannah man but that, I know from experience, is mighty toothsome to a stranger.

In appearance Savannah is the handsomest city in the South. It has a certain leisurely beauty that Atlanta can never aspire to. It appears to have been placed originally by wealthy settlers with whom comfort and culture were more than money. The streets are wide and straight, and shaded with trees on each side and in the center—a long swath of grass usually occupying more space in the middle of the street than we give in Atlanta to a whole thoroughfare. Every square or two there is a beautiful well kept park, in which the sparrows and children play, and which lead up to the great park itself—an enclosure of rare beauty. This roominess gives an indescribable impression, especially to the residents of crowded cities. What strikes the Atlanta man most forcibly, however, is the deep sense of quiet that pervades everything. The people move along the streets in a leisurely decorous way—the carriages move easily through tne sand, the horse's hoofs dropping with muffled sound. The residence lots are all enclosed with high brick walls, and all domestic clamor is thus shut in—and it is said that the policemen instead of using shrill whistles or rattles breathe their alarm through flutes, and let it steal in restful soprano toward the station house.

The most of the houses are of brick or stone, and most of them gray with age—the very picture of solid long enduring comfort. One of the neat modern houses that make up Atlanta's gay picturesque system, would be sadly out of place among these severely respectable old veterans. To plant one of our pretty wooden cottages, born in all the newness of white, green and pink, amid these massive houses, would be to reach the height of incongruity.

An air of snugness and home-likeness is given to the city by the habit of enclosing the whole of the premises in a solid wall of masonry. This wall is usually 10 to 12 feet high, and encloses the whole of the lot just as closely as a house would do it. Over the wall the laughter of children comes occasionally, and banana trees, magnolias, etc., lift their heads above it. The yards are just as private as the houses. It must strike a Savannah man with a sort of horror to look at our bare yards all exposed to the gaze of neighbors and shown off with a simple picket fence. No idea can be formed of the well-ordered air of solidity and steadfastness it gives the city to have these whole blocks of residences closed in.

One of the most notable sights of the South is the cemetery at Savannah. It is known as Bonaventure and is owned by a private corporation. It is said that the owners have adopted the idea—a piece of aesthetic economy—never putting any improvement in the cemetery, or arresting by artificial means the progress of decay. They hold, and with reason, too, that a graveyard should not have smooth-trimmed pastures, close clipped hedges, and tended flower beds, cut into all sorts of unnatural shapes but rather that it should have broad paths, littered with fallen leaves, old oaks draped with funeral moss, with their dead limbs still hanging to their trunks, where for years they had looked down on the silent city of the dead. The effect is grand. Bonaventure is an ideal graveyard—a sort of open Westminster Abbey. The tombs are massive, ancient and venerable, the grass is luxuriant and creeps over the graves. There the gray moss winds its arms about the limbs of the lusty oaks, and in a silent, eternal pressure chokes down the rising life of the tree, and represses the throbbings that else would burst into gay irreverent foliage—a solemn stillness holds all the scene, and so far away from the bustling world is the scene and its suggestions that one almost looks to see a hare leap adown the vast silence of the forest. Here in this deep solitude, the eternal past salutes the eternal future—and the present oppressed with cares and emotions, and the pains and ecstacies of the world and wooed by the infinite peace and restfulness of the scene, feels like falling down and praying that "this fever called living may be conquered at last!" Really, one could find a pleasure in fleeing the maddening crowd, and lying down to dreamless and endless sleep in that placid city. Probably the managers feared the strength of this longing, as they have posted a placard—"No interments allowed here without written permits!" I never see anything without comparing it to the same thing in Atlanta—and standing in Bonaventure I must confess that I was shocked at the intolerable newness of the Atlanta cemetery. It is so red and green and bright, that one can hardly get his consent to die and be buried there. There are no primeval trees—no endless avenues on which checkered lights and shadows fall—but only a few impertinent saplings, that look sprightly and irreverent, and I believe are whitewashed. Oakland is as good as it can be—it is sacred, with a thousand hallowed memories—but it will hold the bodies of all of us, and our children's children before it can approach the simple grandeur of Bonaventure.

50

Henry W. Grady,
Constitution,
November 2, 1878.

"CLOSE UP BOYS"

About ninety days ago—to be exact, on the 12th of August—the campaign was opened in this district at this city. I witnessed that first meeting between Lester and Felton, those two incomparable pleaders, and saw their bright swords play in deadly fence as they tried each other's temper. It was mid-summer then, and I sat in the broiling sun jotting down my impressions, while the candidates perspired through their linen breeches. Today muffled in an overcoat, with withering leaves of winter dropping all around me, I come to witness the closing scenes of the campaign. What storms have raged in this blessed district since that warm August day! How the masses have been changed and rallied, and been forced back and urged forward! How the lines have wavered and broken, and formed again! With what desperate graveness has the parson struggled, and with what heroic enthusiasm has "our George" lifted the old flag from the dust and unfurled it to the sunlight! How the people have hurrahed and cursed, and begged and laughed and cursed, prayed and fought over this stubborn issue! The like of this campaign has not been seen since the mad days of Troup and Clark.

The crowd that gathered today to hear Gordon and Lester was simply immense. I doubt if North Georgia ever before saw such an assemblage—I am certain I never did outside of Atlanta. Your correspondent came on the five o'clock passenger train. Although this was before day, every little station on the road was packed with people waiting to get to the speaking. They swarmed on our train, heedless of the protests of the conductor, and the only way he could keep them from loading the train down was to hurry out. From each station we left them stringing after the train for full fifty yards. The regular excursion train which followed, was packed to its utmost capacity, on top and inside, and still hundreds were left on the sides of the track.

At 9:30 the train from the upper end arrived. It halted at the upper end of the village, and the vast crowd went out to meet it shouting for Lester, and hurrahing for newcomers. The train—a longer one of twenty-three cars—was literally packed. The cars were crowded to suffocation, and on the top of every car, and on the platforms, there were thick clusters of men, waving Lester flags, yelling like the devil, and gesticulating like mad men. Even the tender and the foot-boards were filled. As the enormous crowd poured from the cars, the large area between the St. James and the track was one solid mass of people, alive with enthusiasm, and hoarse with hurrahs for Lester.

The excitement was thrilling and unprecedented. The exultation was contagious, and the most obtuse spectators were kindled as they looked upon the surging people below. An occasional glimpse of Lester or Gordon on the high piazza would touch the mass off in a roar of rapturous applause.

51

Henry W. Grady,
Constitution,
August 21, 1879.

GEORGIA FORTUNES

Georgia is a state of decorous ways and marginal opportunity. An income of $10,000 is first class for a lawyer, and $5,000 is not to be sneezed at. In fact, there are many lawyers who would eagerly sneeze at $3,000. The biggest fees ever made in Georgia, that I can hear of, were made by Ben Hill. He got $60,000 in cash in the Metcalf case, and was entitled to more than double that much. He got a cost fee of $65,000 in '62 when it was worth in gold about $50,000. He made $25,000 in the Kimball House litigation. But these were phenomenal fees. Wright Alexander in Rome got a cash fee of $10,000 in one enclosure, and I suppose several fees of this size have been paid.

The fortunes of the future in Georgia are to be made in the manufacturing enterprises—in the handling of cotton, and in railroad stocks. There was a time, and that only eight years ago when everybody was crazy over iron furnaces. There were furnaces near Rome that made 70 to 80 per cent in one year. But the bottom fell out of iron in no time. I am not sure but that some men will make fortunes in gold-mining in the next ten years.

Georgia was knocked stone-blind during the war. She was ripped up, set on fire, gored and hamstrung. Her recuperation is simply a miracle. She lost millions upon millions of slave property alone. And yet the union cannot show a state more prosperous. There are thousands of private fortunes today being builded up into the quarter-million and half-million, and they would pass the six-figure mark if it were not for one thing. They are scattered at the death of their originators. Every fortune that we have discussed will be split into several parts at the death of the men who made them. And then the work of accumulation must be begun over again if there are to be millionaires in Georgia. I look, unless some of the old veterans have either already proved the work or should live long enough to do so, to see some of the Inmans reach that glittering point. They are young, careful, sagacious and devoted. They have the best connections, ample capital and are dealing heavily but safely, in the royal staple.

And as for the great mass of workers—the youngsters in the professions—the small men of business—the men whose eyes are fixed on $25,000 as an ultimatum—why we must peg along in the humdrum way. When we get restless beyond endurance we may make a dash for glory with a lottery ticket or speculate in "cribs" or wheat. And when we get tired of our snug and comely houses and sigh for castles, we must quarry materials from some glowing sunset, and build our castle in Spain.

52

Henry W. Grady,
Atlanta Constitution,
April 18, 1880.

"LEVELED LANDMARKS"

I don't know that it will concern the public, but I can't help saying a word or two about the destruction of the old building on the corner of Broad and Alabama.

As young as the city is, that building is an old landmark, and there are many associations clustered about its falling brick and its dismantled rafters. It was built out of the ashes at the close of the war, and was rented first as a larger beer saloon. After awhile it was deserted, and then became the home of newspapers—from which time it may be fairly said to have commenced making history—though I suspect it wrought the history of many a blighted life and broken heart while in use as a saloon.

The first newspaper to occupy its walls was the *New Era*. It was in these walls that Sam Bard with owl-like wisdom and cheery stammer, forged the paragraphs that made him famous, and established Bullock's top-boots as an issue in Georgia politics. Here Wallace Read made gentlemanly fun of the young democracy, and Joe Nall balanced the cash, when there was any to balance, and then balanced his pen on the bridge of his nose. It was to this sanctuary that gallant Billy Blalock retired to dress his wounds after his frequent combats, and here the dainty Scruggs allowed choice English to drip from his gloved fingers. These and others toiled in the old building, working at less than wages, and finally scattered when the *Era* gave up the fight.

The ghost of the dead newspaper had hardly time to make itself at home among the old rafters, and to weave its seat in the dusty corner, before a brisk young fellow full of bustle and excitement, spiced with a foreign flavor, and suggesting a Frenchman from the clubs, flung the door open and let in the sunshine. Announcing himself to the ghost, and all others concerned as Alex. St.-Clair Abrams (and bidding them be careful of the hyphen), he planted himself behind a hastily-made counter, cocked his hat on one side, gave his goatee a nervous stroking, whistled a stave of the Marseillaise, and announced that the *Atlanta Herald* was ready for business.

The *Herald* was a journalistic success from the first issue. If it had died at the end of the first week, it would have established Abrams as the best journalist, pure and simple, Georgia ever had. There was a city air about it that was a revelation to us all. The first "hit" the *Herald* made was in the matter of the Force-Townsend duel, which it wrote up in such style as to sell a second edition of 1,500 copies— a feat then unprecedented in Atlanta. I have often wondered why Abrams never succeeded in maintaining a great paper. The first reason was that he never had proper backing from the counting-room. In the next place I think he put too much of the journalist and too little of the man in his paper. In small cities there must be provincial touches in the journals—concessions that the journalist must make to circumstances. There was none of this in Abram's work. He wrote and edited as if he were running the *London Times*, and the result was a perfect piece of journalism—that appeared cold and unsympathetic though, to the mass of its readers. This belied Abrams' real nature, too. He was tender, easily affected, full of good impulses, and clinging as a woman in his friendships. He found no pleasure in the terrible writings he used to do, and his best work was in the half-playful, half-tender articles that he used to write for Sunday editions. We have never had a writer of purer English on the Georgia press—I doubt, excepting Colonel Albert Lamar, if we ever had his equal.

I bought an interest in the *Herald* by accident, and I account it a very lucky accident, despite the way it turned out. I was on my way to Rome, where I had a daily paper, and missing connection stopped for the night at the Kimball. Walking to the register, a gentleman met me and introduced himself as Bob Alston. He stated that he had been thinking of telegraphing me to come and buy an interest in the *Herald*. A short time before General Toombs, Dunlap

Scott and myself had about closed a trade for a half interest in the *Constitution*, when the price was advanced, and I was still anxious to come to Atlanta.

In an hour after I had met Alston the trade was closed. No papers were drawn up that night, and the details were fixed over a bowl of oysters in Thompson's. Alston and I returned to the Kimball at midnight and took the same room. After arranging to make about one hundred thousand dollars the first week we dropped to sleep. During the night I was awakened by Alston's calling me. I remember so well the tones of that soft quizzical voice as it came through the darkness: "Grady, is there any insanity in your family?"

"None at all! Why do you ask me?"

"Well, I've been thinking over this *Herald* trade for a week. You've only known of it a few hours. Now, I know that a man that's quicker on a trade than I am must be crazy, and I was afraid I'd gone in partnership with a lunatic!"

I remember the first night I entered the *Herald* office and the first thing that occurred. Ed Murphy, then as now, the best of detectives, was in the office talking to Abrams. I sat down in the corner and Murphy was very polite to me. At length he rose and said half-confidentially to me:

"I understand that there are some wolves in town and that there's some sugar on them. So I believe I'll go and pull them!"

I don't think I ever felt so discouraged before in my life. Despite his serious manner I felt that he was either crazy or poking fun at me. Abrams, however, said quickly:

"If you do, let us know!"

Then I felt that Atlanta was too big for me, and that I was not fit to edit one of its papers. I could comprehend the idea of a wolf or two being in town, for I had seen them in Rome tied under country wagons, but I was utterly unable to comprehend the saccharine suggestion regarding them, and equally unable to see how they could be pulled like ripe fruit. The thing threw a damper over my first week in the city, and led me to regard Ed Murphy as a foreigner, until I learned that wolves meant thieves, that sugar meant a reward, and the pulling meant arresting.

I don't think I was ever happier than during the few years we suffered along in the old building. It was hard work, of course, and full of desperate chance—but we were young, sanguine and fond of the profession. And the *Herald* won more than enough success to be happy. The income was enormous. We frequently had $2,000 worth of advertising in one day's issue and once had $2,700 in a quintuple sheet, such as the *New York Herald* sends out. The receipts in cash had gone over $5,000 a week, and this was enough to give any man hope. Our outlay was of course ahead of our income. For over three months an eight-page paper, larger than the *New York Herald*, was published, and the whole of the fourth page was devoted to editorial matter. The bill for special telegrams was sometimes $200 a week, and for more than a month $150 a day was spent for a special train to carry the *Herald* mail, and for the next month $75 a day went to the same source. And so we jogged on inside these old walls fighting like the devil for existence, but always chipper, saucy and well-contented—as glad to see the sheriff or the constable as we were to see an advertiser or subscriber.

The *Herald* had many a hard campaign. When I came to it, it was fighting for O'Conor against Greeley, and supporting Stabo Farrow for mayor against Spencer, and trying to beat an alderman's ticket headed by Frank Rice. From that day onward it was a continued scuffle. It was in that building that we tackled Joe Brown, and received encouragement in our fight against him from people who requested that we should not let him know they had encouraged us. I never knew exactly what we were fighting him for—and I do not think I exactly understood the fight, though I went into it heartily, until he smashed the paper out of existence, and we had time to reflect over it. It was there we helped Gordon in the Senate, and there that we enlisted in the series of campaigns through which Ben Hill returned to public life. The first campaign for Colquit was opened and there many another campaign was fought through. It was in that building, too, that we prepared to fight all the duels, that were afterwards not fought. Those were awful times! The consultations we did have—the dueling pistols we did borrow—the volumes of the code we did thumb, and the number of solemn suppers we did eat, having them served from the restaurant because we did not dare venture on the streets for fear of arrest. It's a wonder to me that we did not slaughter several men. No paper ever went through the preliminaries of so many duels. There is not a field of honor on the borders of the state, or any other state, for that matter, we did not intend at some time or other to dye with the life blood of some one of our enemies. We enjoyed them just as much as if they had come to the most bloody termination, but I can't help wishing that we had shot at somebody and missed him, or that somebody had shot at us and missed—missed by a big margin. I didn't see how all the men we got mad with escaped, or how we escaped them. It's all over now though, and would God that all differences between men and friends had been settled as we settled our hot, foolish disputes of those days. Hearts that are now broken would then be happy!

Many of the best workers of the profession worked in that old building. Bill Moore wrote there his famous "police court reports" that for broad and genuine humor have seldom been surpassed. John Goodwin and Jim Anderson worked the local columns and exasperated Abrams by coloring their reports of city politics to nullify his editorials. Thornton ran his legs off and tapped the English language on the head in behalf of the *Herald* and made the best reporter I have ever seen before or since. Tom Burney was the apostle of the paper and went over the state like a new Peter the Hermit, waking the masses with his eloquence and earnestness. One of the most interesting men on the force, was Dr. Craig—a gentle, amiable, loyal man of talent, whose only ill luck was that his hands were not strong enough to get a grip on success. It was a game, gallant crowd, that stuck to the *Herald* above everything, and loved it passing well.

And where are all these workers now? Scattered far and wide. Poor Bob Alston is dead and his grave is now growing green with its first summer's rains. Abrams is in Florida steadying his impetuous nature, in the seclusion of an orange grove, and is listing the days away on the edge of tideless lakes. What editorials and paragraphs must run through his fancy, as he thinks over the days that are gone. Does he still stroke his goatee, with that peculiar nervous stroke of old? and does he still whistle the Marseillaise? Does his pulse throb as fiercely, and his blood heat as quickly? I saw the other day that he had written some antagonist down as "the wild ass of the Apopka." That stroke shows that his thumb and forefinger can still pinch.

Craig, poor fellow, after his womanly fingers had slipped from all else, gently let go life itself, and sleeps out at Oakland.

Bill Moore, after a varied experience, has put on a gingham

bonnet and edits the best of evening papers—the delight of the
ladies and the aversion of small politicians.

Sam Bard, in the minority for a long time, has at last gone over
to the majority. Wallace Read is writing lazily but brilliantly. Joe
Nall has charge of more than cash enough, as money man at the
post-office. Goodwin has put on a paunch and is an alderman, and
Anderson, though still lean, has had honors put on him. Scruggs is
in China, probably handling rice sticks with the fingers erstwhile
so deft with the pen, and here I am basking in the sunshine, my
memory warming to the old crowd, and half-happy, half-sad thoughts
swarming about my heart as I watch the workmen knocking down
the bricks of the old house, with careless hands and rude jest. Ah!
well, we must all go as the old house is going, and we may be thankful if there is some one to sit by the way in the sunshine and give
even a passing regret, as the gaunt workmen of death remove us
from the face of the earth.

53

Henry W. Grady,
Atlanta Constitution,
August 15, 1880.

"SELF-MADE MEN"

To the deuce with politics!

Light your cigar! lift your feet over the banister so your brains
may settle well down toward your middle, and let me tell you the
story of self-made men! Of men that have wrought their lives with
their own hands—whose brain and brawn their home have builded—
men who, big-hearted and brave, with cool heads and steady nerves
have marched to the front rank.

I have the greatest interest in these self-made men. Atlanta is
the home of this sturdy genus, and I have thought that this was one
secret of· the wonderful vigor and advancement. To me the most
interesting period of Joe Brown's life—and it is a study all the way
through—is the time when he used to ride into Dehlonega on a load
of wood, and sell a basket of vegetables to good Mrs. Choice of the
hotel who never failed to add to the price she paid a warm dinner
for the barefoot boy, and before whom when he was made governor,
long afterwards, she appeared with a most sacred and touching petition. It is a tribute to the manliness and independence of our character, that none of our great are prouder than when they refer to
their days of labor and privation. Joe Brown smiles with pride
when he is reminded of the historic bull-yearling that listened to his
persuasive "gee" or his impatient "haw." Governor Milt Smith
glows with pride when the echoes of hammer and anvil of his old
blacksmith shop ring through his brain. Alex Stephens is proud of
the fact that he owed his education to a charity, nobly repaid by an
illustrious life. I have heard it boasted that Ben Hill was a plough-
boy. If so, what a magnificent furrow he must have turned—if indeed
he did not, in scorn of limit, plough the whole field at once. It is
also stated—possibly for campaign purposes—that Governor Colquitt
once ploughed somewhere, though Major Stanley, of Athens, describes
"young Colquitt" to me as a boy of unusual long and white-ruffled
shirt cuffs that were once the admiration of the women and the envy
of the men. If Governor Colquitt ever did plough, I know that he
cut a straight, neat, honest furrow, skimped nowhere, but faithful
all through and to the end. Bob Toombs is only one of our great
men that I never heard mixed up with manual labor. He is a

patrician all through—in tradition and instinct—born a Prince Bountiful, and living all his life a prodigal gentleman.

But about our self-made men of Atlanta. Do you remember how in slavery-time, the patrols used to walk the streets at night, and as the town clock struck each hour, called, "all well," that rang through the darkness and entered the dreams of the sleeping city making them assured and peaceful? Persons living here twenty-seven years ago may have heard every night from the Norcross corner, faithful to the minute, the cheery call of a young patrol walking his beat for $30 a month. That was young Dave Dougherty, now the great dry goods merchant, who sells nearly half a million a year, and employs half a hundred men. Many a night through storm and danger, did this poor country boy patrol our streets and discipline himself for the life that was to follow. After awhile he became a clerk for a year for $100, and afterwards the great merchant that he is. As to Mr. C. W. Hunnicutt, now prosperous and rich and growing richer, he came to Atlanta in yellow copperas breeches, barefooted and topped with a wool hat. His history is interesting and so interwoven with that of other prominent men that he may fairly be called the veteran of them all. Mr. Hunnicutt came here, as I have said, a poor country boy of country boys. He applied for work, but was unable to get it. At length, Mr. Levi, a merchant, offered him his board for six months if he would work for him. He was to get no wages, but simply bread and meat. After he had been at work for a month, Mr. Levi wanted to send him to Cartersville to work in a store he had there. It soon became known that he was going, and a tall, awkward boy with a frank, honest face and determined look, applied for his place and got it. This was Mr. Jett Rucker, who is now one of our leading custom merchants and most estimable men. Young Hunnicutt, now prosperous and rich and growing richer, he came to Cartersville, being induced to stay there by the extravagant offer of $12 a month. In three years Mr. Hunnicutt had laid up about $250, when he met a poor young fellow who had been to California and had by years of labor got together about $700. This was John Silvy, now the wealthy wholesale dry goods merchant. This firm of young men took young Dougherty out of patrol service and gave him work at $100 a year.

But my tired fingers call a halt to suggestion, and my pencil drags wearily while a hundred histories similar to these etched above crowd for expression. The truth is, Atlanta is full of these self-made men. They enrich her blood, quicken her pulses and give her vitality, force and power. I have always honored them in my heart. They have won fame and fortune by no accidents of inheritance, nor by capricious turn of luck, but by patient, earnest, heroic work. They have wrought much out of nothing—have compelled success out of failure—have been examplars to their fellows, and have set hope in the hearts of struggling youth. They have sunk the corner-stones of the only aristocracy that America should know—the distinction of honest and intelligent labor crowned with its inevitable results. And to those named, and hundreds just as worthy who are unnamed— the self-made men of Atlanta—this hasty tribute is tendered by one who, starting life ready-made, speedily unmade himself and is now hopefully rambling along the road of regeneration.

54

Henry W. Grady,
Atlanta Constitution,
November 7, 1880.

"I Told You S'o"

One week ago this morning the *Constitution* printed a dispatch from me in which I stated that I had seen little chance of Hancock's election. I might have sent a hurried dispatch, but I saw there was literally no hope for the democrats. Had I misled my readers, I should have been enduring the indignation of those who bet on my opinion. But let that go.

In electing Garfield the republicans have elected the worst man in my opinion, that has offered for the presidency since the days of Aaron Burr. They have beaten the purest man that has offered since the days of Madison. They have paved the way for Grant in 1884, have divided the Union into two sections, and have established the central authority of the republic as supreme.

As for the future two things seem certain: 1. The solid South will always be met by a solid North. What ever man or party is so distinctly Southern as to be able to count on the vote of the solid South is doomed to defeat in the North. Seymour was beaten in 1868 because the "passion of war had not died out." Greely was beaten four years later "because the South was massacreing the negroes." Tilden was opposed four years later "because the negroes were not allowed to vote freely"—and Hancock is beaten sixteen years after the war, when the passions have died out; when the negroes are living in perfect peace and voting as they please—simply because the South "is solid."

I have been through the North frequently during the campaign and it is not too much to say that the issues presented to the North by the solidity of the South has dwarfed and even absorbed every other issue. "S'olid on what?" the Northern voter would ask. "Solid on antagonism to the North," was the reply his leader would give. And on this answer he acted. I was talking just before the election with a prominent democrat of New York who was going to vote for Garfield. I said to him:

"How can a sensible man like you believe that the South has any sinister designs when we have voted for Greely and now vote for Hancock, who led your armies against us?"

"That is just the trouble," he replied, "I have no doubt that you would allow John Sherman to write your platform and let him put Conkling on it, and then would give it every electoral vote in the South if you only thought you could get possession of the government by so doing. After you took Greely, and yielded one plank in your platform after another, we began to believe that the only sentiment necessary to unite the South was hostility to the North, and the only purpose of your campaigns to get possession of the government. This is what alarms us, and it is what will make us practically solid against you."

It is in consequence of this that we see every Northern state with the possible exception of New Jersey banded against the South and by enormously increased majorities. Ohio gave Hayes 5,000 majority and give Garfield about 30,000. Massachusetts has swelled her majority from 13,000 to 40,000 and so on through the list. The cause of this cannot be found in the candidates, for Hancock was professedly the better and the stronger candidate of the two. It cannot be found in the platform for there has been no general principles discussed in the campaign. The North was called upon to rally against the solid South in something of the same spirit that inspired the people in 1861. A conquered section, solid in the attempt to recover by ballot what it had lost by bayonet—this was the issue as the Northern people understood it and voted on it.

Under the present organization the republican party grows stronger in votes as it lengthens its hold on power. Its office-holding personality—a machine, the mere mention of which is tremendous gives it a skilled army of veterans, billeted in every nook and corner of the country and dependent for spoils upon the alertness with which it meets every crisis and the decisiveness with which it whips its fights. The 20 per cent assessment levied upon these officials runs into the millions and gives a force that is virtually irresistible.

This advantage, it must be perceived, deepens with every triumph and strengthens with every succeeding year of power. With a quarter of a century of uninterrupted patronage, with the treasury at its back, the money power in its service, the republican party holds the republic well-nigh helpless in its grasp.

There is another manifestation that though personal to the superficial observer has a deep and terrible meaning to the student of history of the past twenty years. I refer to the unscrupulous manner in which the people of the North are led and driven and bullied into the worship of Ulysses S. Grant. There is no denying that Gen. Grant is today the strongest man in the United States, and even stronger than any party or platform. Never has there been a more disgraceful exhibition of subserviency of party to power than was exhibited in the late campaign. The republicans, alarmed at the disfavor with which Garfield's nomination was met, and the enthusiasm with which Hancock was greeted saw that there was only one man who had the power to save them. This man was Grant—there sulking in his tent. To coax him into the field, the leaders who had fought his nomination at Chicago now fawningly declared that they would probably favor his nomination in 1884,—and the leader of his forces at Chicago had a meeting with Garfield, for whom he had previously expressed the greatest contempt, and doubtless drove a bargain by which the succession was secured to Grant. Certain it is that after his interview Grant and his friends went into the fight heart and soul, and won it.

Now mark a prediction. The next thing we hear of will be the running of Grant on a platform of national reconciliation, with some Southern democrat as vice-president. We shall hear of Grant and Brown, Grant and Colquitt, Grant and Hampton, Grant and Gordon, Grant and Lamar. All this will be wicked and stupid, for no Southern man can afford to run with a man who has proved himself so brutal and so false as Grant. If no other guide were offered to his dangerous character than the contrast between his speeches made when traveling through the South seeking nomination, and those made for Garfield whose only hope was in raising antagonism to the South, there is enough to keep any man who loves his country from aiding in his elevation.

The South has but one thing to do, and that is to stand firm to the principles upon which true democracy is based—the rights of the states—to supremacy of civil law—a free ballot and honest money. It is better to be beaten forever upon this platform than win by abandoning it. With these principles surrendered there is nothing left worth fighting over, and our party contests will then become mere struggles over patronage. We have lost too much already by compromise. Point after point has been yielded, this man and that has been followed, until it has really looked as if we only wanted to get into power and did not care under what leadership or what platform. If the South is true to her traditions, she is brave enough to stand by the right regardless of the results. If she is worthy of herself, she will stand firm even if the national democracy should dissolve—and amid that dissolution will see this faction or that depart, with tranquil determination, and when the last has gone will raise the flag of eternal protest against the destruction of the states, and will stand the old guard of constitutional liberty.

One thing is certain: the South can never hope for anything from Garfield, Grant or any of their belongings. Any alliance with those men will only bring us their contempt. If principles for which we have voted were ever essential and right, they are so now.

We are able to do without federal patronage. The defeat of Hancock will be a blessing in disguise if it only tends to turn our people from politics to work. We have the best country in the world. The sun shines on us kindly, the soil yields us abundant crops, the earth gives us gold, iron and coal at every fissure. How grander a mission it is to develop this section into its full power and production than to win a share of public patronage. What we need is fewer stump-speakers and more stump-pullers—less talk and more work —fewer gin-mills and more gins—fewer men at the front and more men at the hoe. One plow is worth twenty politicians. In the old days of slavery it was a passion with us to lead in politics—these days of close competition, he should be the best man who can lead in the corn row. Let us crystallize within our heart the sacred principles of our faith—and then turn about bravely and build up the South; make it thrill and swell with growth until it has compassed the full measure of the destiny for which God intended it.

55

Henry W. Grady,
Atlanta Constitution,
November 28, 1880.

"JOHN H. INMAN"

A short time ago I printed an article on "self-made men." This hasty sketch took the rounds of the press, and I am led to believe did some good. It certainly kindled fresh hopes in some young hearts that were despairing, set aright some designs that were going awry, anchored some lives that were drifting, and lifted the eyes of some young fellows that were groping about blindly. The article was effective because it taught by example and not by precept.

I have become acquainted with the history of a man and a family that is a fit supplement of that sketch. How I got the facts that I detail need not be known—it is enough to say that I am perfectly sure of their correctness. I will not stop to consider with what relish those interested will see their affairs put into print—I merely know that it is an instructive and interesting history, and I set it out as a pattern of life.

In 1865, a young Tennessean, after an honorable and arduous service of four years, in which he was always at the front, brave and uncomplaining, with his parole in his pocket came out of the confederate ranks, and returned to Dandridge, with less than $100 in money, and no property. In 1870 he married a charming and intelligent Tennessee girl, and then his wealth was reckoned at about $75,000. Last year his net income for the year was $190,000 and his fortune now is about $1,500,000. He is just 36 years of age, in perfect health and is just entering the prime of life. And now to the details.

The other night I was introduced to Mr. John H. Inman, a youngish looking man, with a ruddy complexion, high, broad and unruffled forehead, finely cut features, a mouth in which decision and kindness were singularly mixed, and a head very much like that of our Mr. Sam Inman. The first glance betrayed the perfectly well-bred man, quiet, attentive and winning—but the suggestion that held me was one of great reserve power—the hint that beneath that untroubled and decorous face, there was a forceful and earnest brain that had done notable things, which led me to push an investigation so to speak, when shortly afterwards I fell in with one who knew the points in Mr. Inman's life.

What an exemplar is here for our young men. What a brilliant promise to draw them away from the arid ways of politics and the hardly less arid ways of professional life! Just look at the chapters in this one man's history. At twenty out of the dust and heat of battle, penniless and alone; at twenty-five worth $75,000, happily married, and at the head of a prosperous house; at thirty-six worth a million and a half, in good health and heart, and with a net income of over $200,000 per year! Follow the probabilities. At forty-six worth five million dollars and possessed of an income of over a million a year, and just in the prime of a well-ordered life. How this example should draw its followers! How completely it should teach that in the wrangling of public life and the pretentious ways of the professions there is not all the honor of usefulness. Ah! but it is impossible to attain such dizzy heights as this. To be sure, there will be few who can hope for such success—but nothing surer than that a young man who starts with clean habits, a clear head and a faithful soul, and works earnestly and devotedly can get far enough along this road to come into sunshine, while yet the flowers on the way-side are wet with the dew and the air of the morning embalms the earth.

As for me, I should be charged with irreverence if I wrote down how many politicians, in my opinion, this one young merchant is worth. The mere computation gives me some hint of the severe contempt with which solid men of business look out from their world upon the babbling orators who declare that paralysis or prosperity waits alternately upon the victory or defeat of a faction of salary-mongers. I should like to strike a balance between the lives of John Inman, merchant, and some one of our eminent latter day states-men, when both are dead, and see which had done most and better work. Then we should see how much speeches counted against deeds —prophecy against performance—boasting against fulfillment. To drop into metaphor, we may say that the farmer and the mechanic create the blood which enriches the body corporate—the merchant stationed in the heart, supplies the vital force that sends it coursing through the veins—the professional man tempers the flow, gauges its current and defines limitations while the politicians, camped along its channels, fattens on its exhalations and puts the whole body in a fever by swearing that the veinous is superior to the arterial blood, or vice versa—not hesitating to spill either to disprove the excellence of the other.

56

Henry W. Grady,
Constitution,
January 1, 1881.

"DIRECT QUESTION"

I went up to the Fifth Avenue the other night to see Mary Anderson—that divine girl with slouching stride of a race horse, play the Countess in "Love." I found her the same thoroughbred she always was—the best product of the blue grass region. Her neck arches as prettily as ever—her lips flicker and tremble just as they used to do, and the same dewy spring-like freshness hangs as the breath of morning about her garments. She has the same crude inartistic movements as free and as easy as a young filly running down the wind—that the prigs used to criticise and the audience applaud. Her arms are quite as long as ever, and she flings them about just as carelessly. I suppose she has the longest arms in the world—though white and virginal wanton in their very length and loveliness. I thought so sweet a necklace had never been designed for the bliss of one man and the envy of all others.

But it was not concerning the charming actress that I started to write, but a very different person. In the stage box on the left, watching every curve of the milk-white neck, every uplifting of the glistening arms and every tremor of the red lips, sat Gen. W. T. Sherman, sternest and most grizzled of soldiers. A handsome bouquet found its way from this box to the stage, and a dazzling smile was flashed toward the box that would have paid for all the flowers in the garden of Babylon. All through the play the General led the applause with all the zeal that he ever led his veterans. He has long been one of the staunchest and truest friends of the fair Kentuckienne, and I marvelled that the bright-eyed old veteran that sat there, clapping his hands to the echo of a girl's voice, was the most merciless invader since Alaric, and the man who swept through Georgia like a scourge of God.

After the play was over I called at the Fifth Avenue hotel and spent a pleasant half hour with General Sherman. I found him in a jaunty sack coat and pants cut trimly giving his body a youthful look, that the grizzly beard scarcely denied and the bright eyes, mobile mouth and quick affable motions most decidedly affirmed.

I doubt if there was a more conscientious soldier in the Northern army than General Sherman. There is no sentimentalism about him. To his nation war meant cruelty—it meant death—destruction—and the sooner this was realized the sooner there was a chance for peace. The heaviest, sharpest and most decisive blows, he contended were the most merciful, and the real scourge, he held, was he who connived at the prolonging of the war with its inexorable desolation, by glossing its horrors over with a show of pity. This was his argument severe and savage—but perhaps logical and just. On this argument he fought; and with this argument he expected to be confronted in turn. He struck with a mailed hand, and sowed desolation in his path. From the terror and suffering of his own creation, he appealed from the hideous aspects of the war, for a speedy and all-embracing peace. Those who agreed with him, hold that the relentless severity with which he marched through the heart of the confederacy, first brought the people to know what was really meant, and hastened peace. Be this as it may, we need not judge Gen. Sherman. History will bring him to its bar—and after history—God! (From this point on are a series of questions and answers concerning the burning of Atlanta. I give only the last paragraph.)

It was nearly midnight when I left General Sherman. A brainy, cordial, direct man—a great man in a special sense of the word, and the best type, perhaps, of the tremendous energy and courage that has built up that great west, to which his thoughts turn always and in which his heart is to be found. As I left his presence I fell to wondering why he and his brother, who are to be credited with the grandest and most decisive feats of the late war and the legislation that followed it—the march through Georgia and the resumption of specie payment—have neither reaped the full reward of their enterprise, but have been overtopped by other and weaker men.

57

Henry W. Grady,
Atlanta Constitution,
January 12, 1881.

"THE STAGE"

Suppose we take a turn through the theaters, if for nothing else to look up some old friends, see what they are doing and how the world moves with them.

Of course, sweet Mary of the blue-grass, deserves and shall have the first attention. She is the puzzle of the stage—the despair of critics. She is not as good an actress as she was when I saw her three years ago. She has mannerisms that then imperfections, are now grievances. She has an amateurish accent, which is simply to throw in emphasis wherever she catches her breath. She dismisses a scullion with the same grandeur of tone and gesture that she defies a queen, and drops as many luscious thrills into her voice when she coos to the hawk on her wrist as when she confesses to the lover at her feet. She is so intense and dramatic in small things, that she loses naturalness, and discounts her really great scenes. Her mouth has actually become so sensitive that she can't hold it still, and an ugly frown has cut its deep furrows on her virgin forehead. I am afraid she could not eat an oyster without the same dilated eyes, quivering mouth and panting nostrils with which she greets the poison or the dagger on the stage. She has over-acted herself. Her gasping paroxysms have none of the power that Clara Morris shows when she is swept along shuddering and broken in the throbs of some great passion, but have an automatic and periodic recurrence that suggest a nervous disorder.

And yet how charming she is—and how the people flock to see her. I saw her last night as "Ion"—the young boy who sacrifices himself for his country—and a daintier picture than she made I have never seen on the stage or off of it. Her figure is perfect, and her step is as that of the fawn. As I contrasted her slender, natural form, with its maidenly curves and graces, with the tight, plump, exact curves and calves of the Pomeroys and Daveports, I could not help thinking how much more cunning is nature than artificer, and the flesh and blood, than springs and pads. She is the best Parthenian I ever saw, and the best Evade, I believe, that ever powdered her downy neck. In these classical impersonations she is steadier, happier, and purer, and she looks the Grecian maiden to the life. A thousand times have I held out my hand in grasping sympathy with that wild-eyed, loose-collared son of the west, who after seeing her play Ingomar, wrote it down, that "if she'd a turned her great limpid eyes on us, and held out her lovely arms, and cried, Ingomar. In-g-omar, with her juicy voice, we'd crawled to her feet, if we'd a had to wriggle over an acre of red-hot coals to get there." And so the people think, for they go in shoals to hear her. If she would only take a year of rest, and make it a year of reflection, and study and quiet, she would reappear on the stage incomparable. But she is playing to $900 a week now, and Stepfather Griffin sits up with the cash box, so I suppose she will go on as she is. The ladies may be interested to know that her diamonds bought in Paris and London and St. Louis, have not been over-described, but are superb and a fitting crown to her toilets; and the men may be interested in knowing that she is not married and is not likely to be. She is wedded to her art, and she may follow Boucicault's advice indefinitely, and not spoil the prettiest picture of the stage, nor rob it of the auroral freshness that envelopes it like a charm.

I have never read "Uncle Tom's Cabin." I have avoided that classic of hate and slander just as I have the "Fool's Errand" and similar spawn of later day passion. But I went the other night to see "Uncle Tom's Cabin" acted at Booth's theater, and I confess that I am astonished no longer at the effect it has had on the anti-slavery sentiment. A more unfair and yet vivid statement of the case cannot be imagined. The air was rent during all the play with the hissing of the slave-whips and the shrieks of slaves. Mothers were sold away from their children, and husbands from their wives. Bloodhounds were put on the track of flying women and children, and longhaired men with their cravats tied across their stomachs swore their New England oaths with the twang of Bowery roughs, cut plug tobacco as types of Southerners. It was very exciting and kept me busy remembering that it was all a false picture of a system that, wrong in itself, had been made tolerable by the people on whom it was saddled. There was no hint on the stage of the real ante-bellum life of the South that made the old plantation darkey the happiest laborer on all the earth. No touch of that strange tenderness that bound the old slave to his old "massa" and "missus," in a bondage safer and yet stronger than slavery. But while we may condemn New England greed for abolishing the slave trade, and curse New Englandship for bringing the slaves to us, we must not let it be forgotten that the men and women of the South, on whom these slaves were saddled, gave the poor creatures for a century a happiness and contentment to which the servants of New England were utter strangers, and which we fear the negro will never see again. There was one little touch on the stage that spoke the truth and let in some light. There was on the stage a host of real negroes who filled up the scenes. In the death of little Eva, the room in which she lies dying projects on the stage and the bed, the father, Uncle Tom and the girl can be seen through the windows. About these windows, moving like shadows in the dark and the reverent hush are the negro children, old women and field hands, gazing through the curtains, or moving vaguely around the house, their kindly faces wearing a grief that is mingled with tender unrest and anxiety. Who that has ever lived on the plantation does not recall some such scene as this? Who does not remember, whenever the shadow of death fell upon the house of their master how these poor creatures came from the fartherest cabin on the place, bringing rough but sincere consolation of their presence, until the whole yard was filled with dusky forms, and their tearful and sorrowing faces were pressed against every glass, and their rude but reverent comment was heard beneath every oak tree? I could not help thinking that the counterfeit presentment of the stage stirred memories in the hearts of many of those humble actors, until the lights and glare become a mist and film beyond which they saw a starry night, full of balm and gentleness—the silent fields beyond, lying asleep in their fullness and peace—a darkened house about which men and women moved sorrowing, and over which the spirit of death swung its ghostly pinions.

I was struck with the distinctness with which every type of negro that we see in a community was represented in that haphazard group of a hundred or so, on the stage. There was the chipper little old woman, with a pair of spectacles on her nose, and her features soft and complacent, usually the seamstress, promoted to house-keeper and general gossip. There was the sharp-eyed, straight-nosed dapper little man, with an abundant head of gray hair—always the preacher. There was the straight-backed, kinky-haired, starchy girl, ready for a "rascal" or a race—alternating between the disgrace of the cotton patch, and the glory of dining-room. There was the broad-shouldered, simple-faced, flat-nosed, good-natured fellow, with his hair tied in strings, who always goes to town on training days, and on the slightest provocation pulls out a set of reeds and blows you a primitive tune. There was the fat old cook, with benevolent face, and glorious amplitude of body, herself an advertisement of her art; the dandy buck, a swiveller cut in ebony, and the "nus gal" with her ill-mixed finery and her flirty ways. They were all there—any type of darkey that the stable, the field, the kitchen, the house or the "quarters" could suggest—and above all, the peculiar negro without which no community is complete, the negro whose legs bend in until his knees cross beyond each other when he walks; a sort of knock-kneed negro whose knees don't knock, but simply bow and pass. I have never seen a village in which there was not such a one, and I believe if there were such a village, one of these limber-legged negroes would come down to it in the rain. There are two peculiarities about these fellows—they are always clever, and they never die. I now call to mind seven, not one of whom has ever died or ever will die. I suppose they are saved up to keep the gray mules company, when everybody and everything else has perished from the face of the earth.

58

Henry W. Grady,
Atlanta Constitution,
February 22, 1881.

"A NOBLE LIFE"

For a model life let me commend you to that of Peter Cooper.

Ninety years of age, enthroned in the bosom of his family and the love of his people, he waits in his peace and content for the end. He lived to see all the dreams of his youth realized. His inventions have been made useful, his philanthropy has proved a mercy and a profit, his schemes have all prospered, his children have grown up in honor and prosperity around him and their children have clambered on his knees, and with a stingless conscience and a heart that still glows beneath the snow of age, he will round a noble life with a Christian's death.

Mr. Cooper is probably the oldest New Yorker who was observant in his youth and is intelligent enough to tell in his old age what he saw when he was young. He remembered when New York had only 27,000 inhabitants, and when the ground where the Astor house and the *Herald* building now stand were cornfields. He rode one mile down the river from Bellevue Hospital, and he saw but one house in the mile which is now a solid front of buildings. He has seen New York grow from half the size of Atlanta to be the metropolis of America, with about as many inhabitants as the entire state of Georgia.

Peter Cooper began life as an apprentice to a coachmaker and received only $25 a year. He was an industrious young fellow, and gave his whole mind to his business. He invented while in his apprenticeship a machine for mortising hubs in carriage wheels, out of which his employer made a fortune. His first money was made by the invention of a machine for shearing cloth. He made the machines and sold them. This was prior to the year 1812. Before he was twenty-one years of age he had mastered three trades—that of a brewer, coachmaker and machinist. At the end of three years of apprenticeship he worked a year at $1.50 a day.

He is connected with the development of some of the greatest inventions of his age. He built the first locomotives ever made in this country. The tubes for the boiler were made of old gun-barrels, and the engine made thirteen miles in one hour and thirteen minutes. This saved the Ohio and Baltimore road from bankruptcy and encouraged its projectors to go ahead. When the first Atlantic cable was being laid the company's credit was gone, and Mr. Cooper ordered the contractors to draw on him personally, and thus carried the enterprise through. The first monitor that repelled the Merrimac in Hampton Roads and saved the federal navy, was built at Mr. Cooper's foundry. Among things he invented a torpedo boat that would run six miles by steel spring, and exploded on touching an enemy's vessel.

His life has been one of magnificence and philanthropy. The first money he ever earned he used it in lifting the burden of debt from his father's shoulders. Since then he has given freely and wisely. His great charity was in founding the Cooper Institute. He says of this institute: "An old friend of mine was telling me of the benefit that poor boys of Paris received from the Ecole Polytechnique. A young man living on a crust a day could get the best scientific education at the Ecole free. I had felt the need of such a school in my youth, and I determined when I became able to establish a free scientific school, open free to every young working-man in America.

Henry W. Grady,   59
Atlanta Constitution,
March 9, 1881.

"CARPING CRITICS"

I am proud to be able to say that in the ten years of my active service, I have never done any man a wilful injustice. It has been my pleasure to help rather than retard any fellow-journalist struggling side by side with me along a road that is tedious enough even when enlivened by courtesy and sympathy; to entertain my readers rather than gratify spleen or cultivate mlaice—to help build up our city and state and country, rather than tear down even the humblest character or hinder the slightest progress. I have had nothing but courtesy and kindness from the real journalist of Georgia—men who have steady place and interest in the profession—who labor to build up their journals as corner stones in the fabric we are all so proud of. When these men disagree with me or each other, it is an open and manly way that adds to the respect of all concerned. But it is the fellows who swarm on the skirts of journalism, dip in wherever they can get a job or justify a spite—who can neither command the confidence of employers or the public, and are consequently casuals one week and loafers the next. These are the men that make it their business to jig at me. Well, as I said before, I have not gone very high up the hill, but I thank God that I am high enough to look above these journalists and their petty malices into the faces of the men and women of Georgia who for years have read my work and theirs—have watched my course and theirs, regardless of any special plea or protest!

60

Henry W. Grady,
Atlanta Constitution,
May 29, 1881.

"A LIFE WORTH LIVING"

It is this lesson that Mr. Seney teaches that is more valuable than his donations. How many men fall under the influence of this greed of which he speaks, and live and die in its blighting shadow! It will be worth while for any man who reads this article to look about him and see how many really rich men of his acquaintance are happy and contented men. He will see that the few he selects are men who have done good with their money—who have helped public enterprise, and dealt in private charity—who have fought off the miserliness that too often comes with wealth.

To illustrate, who will weigh the happiness of Peter Cooper, who at the close of a long and honorable life, meets death placidly and without a fear, and goes into the next world with the consciousness of having done his duty in this, with the life of a man who, having pinched and starved himself for years, crouched among his money bags at the approach of death, and finds the pangs of his dissolution sharpened with the knowledge that he has never soothed a human sorrow or gladdended a human heart. Which has lived the happier life? To which has money brought the most joy? Which man leaves the best legacy to his children—the man who dies with the blessings of a people on his life and leaves a moderate fortune, an honored name and beloved memory, or the man who leaves a mass of money and the taint of a selfish and miserly life?

There are many lessons that may be learnt from this life—so hearty, sincere, cheerful and prosperous. It teaches that a man may be liberal and at the same time grow rich; it teaches that a man may be a philanthropist and at the same time a capitalist; it teaches that money can buy no happiness like that which comes of doing good, and that the miser has no joy to live by and no hope to die with like that of the man who does his duty to his fellow-men—and above all, it teaches that a man may be a Christian and at the same time successful in business. It has come to be a saying—and many excuse under this suggestion what they would otherwise condemn—that the ways of the world are so sharp and devious that a Christian must lay aside his nicer scruples when he goes out into active business. Through a long life, active all the time, involving huge schemes and competition with the shrewdest men, Mr. Seney has carried his Christian character above reproach—stood by the principles on which his faith is founded—and brought honor and repute to the cause he represents.

61

Henry W. Grady,
Atlanta Constitution,
November 30, 1881.

"PULLMAN'S PALACES"

How many people ride in a Pullman car year after year without thinking of the history that is back of it—just as we meet folks every day, and look in their faces without thinking of what lies below the surface.

To my mind back of the monogram—"P. P. Co." that looks down at me from my berth just now, is the happiest man in America.

Right in front of me sits Senator John Sherman—gray and care-worn with political strife, his life clouded, high as he has risen, because he failed to get the presidency. Back of the monogram I am looking at, is a man happier and more useful than Mr. Sherman could have been, even if he had won the great prize on which he staked his life.

I suppose few people will deny that the great problem of the world—from the days when the Israelities served Pharaoh to the present—has been to properly adjust the rights of labor to the rights of capital. Certainly the most engaging work to which man has ever put his hand has been the founding of a community in which all the citizens shall be prosperous and contented, and all their conditions felicitous. No experiment has such fascination for the public as one made in this direction whether by co-operative societies, by governments, or by individuals, whether by some strong-handed practical worker, or by some new Plato, dreaming amid the clouds. How many experiments toward this ideal have been made, and how surely they have all failed. All over the world are found the wrecks of these hopeful ventures—the dead town of this high ambition.

And yet there are men still consecrated to the work. I believe that the man back of my sleeping-car monogram is working out to-day the most promising experiment ever made in this direction, and has better chances of succeeding. Hence I say he is or ought to be the happiest man in America.

Was I not right in saying that Mr. Pullman is or ought to be the happiest man in America? What more could any man want than this opportunity of doing good? He certainly has charge of the most important experiment now being worked out in this country. In his new city he can give trial to every reform in education, in social economy, in building, in labor, in city government.

The philosopher can there test his theory, the architect his design, the gardener his art, the teacher his skill, the inventor his improvement. Here can be adjusted finally, if anywhere, the great question of labor and capital, and the model set for masters and employes. Mr. Pullman· is an enthusiast on all that promises to make the city built out of his brain better than any other, the workman happier, thriftier and contented, and the product of his shops superior. So that we may look for many things to be settled in this great enterprise—this experimental city—so to speak, in which will be tested the value of the contending theories, and out of which may come rules for the betterment of us all.

After he has finished this great work—and I repeat in closing this hasty scroll that it is a greater and more useful work than Mr. Sherman, in front of me, there, could do if he were president over and again. I have it from a friend that he has been nursing for some time. This plan is to put on the Atlantic a fleet of the finest ocean steamers ever built, to ply the waters between New York and France and England. He is carefully making up his plans, and the time will come if he keeps his health when the name of Pullman will be as familiar on the seas as it is on the land, and he will revolutionize ocean travel almost as thoroughly as he has revolutionized along our lines of steel.

62

Henry W. Grady,
Atlanta Constitution,
January 14, 1882.

"ON TO FLORIDA"

Nothing further need be said of the ladies than to remark that palm trees are already lifted above their horizon and the bloom of magnolia already softens the skies that lie beyond. But I cannot forbear noting the fine vigor with which the sportsmen are preparing their work. I should be an unfaithful scribe if I failed to depict Ben Hill, as, up to his throat in rubber boots, and clad in corduroy duck, he walked up and down the sleeper with the impatience of one who would be afield with the game, or Frank Rice, as, with a liver-colored pointer by his side, he sweeps the passing landscape with his shotgun leveled through the window or adjusted to his broad shoulders the dip net with which he declares he will catch some oranges if he cannot kill any birds. As for myself I do not see why I should not bag considerable game. My preparations have been ample. I have a hunting vest exactly similar to one that Willie Venerable wore through a very successful season, and a coat that could hardly be told from Captain Gay's. My hunting pants are borrowed from a re-doubtable hunter, and my cartridges were loaded by the same man who loaded Judge Hillyer's. With these accessories I have little fear of the result. Our party is perfectly equipped. Frank Rice having even brought along a hunting knife with which he fought Indians in the early days of Atlanta, and which he now carries on his person against a hand to hand engagement with a bear.

Already we have swept out of the murky atmosphere that overlaps Atlanta into sunshine. The muddy streets are replaced by brown slopes and forest full of rusting leaves.

And on we go to Florida. Our little party with high hopes and its gayety, traveling against the future and building against the morrow, is but a type of all enterprise—one pilgrimage of thou-sands—with the humblest and proudest, with small affairs and great ones, with the army marching against a king or a beggar seeking alms in a new field—with any and all of the sons of earth, it is the same venture and the same chance. It is God's mercy that he lights the heart with hope, even while the seeds of failure have taken root in the future, and disappointment is vailed by but a day. In the meantime the ladies and children of our party have set their faces resolutely to the sunshine. Ben Hill has girded his boots yet more tightly about his loins and let out another reef of corduroy. Frank Rice's gray eyes closely follow the barrel of his gun as it menaces every hamlet on the wayside, and the writer reads over once the guarantee that his cartridges are compounded by the same receipt that makes Judge Hillyer's so deadly.

The train on which we are riding is filled with consumptives seek-ing a new lease of life in the tropics. They are in all the cars and traveling under all conditions. In the second-rate cars you see here and there an invalid too poor to afford a sleeper, crowded and hemmed in, his pale face made still paler, and his weak lungs irritated con-stantly as he breathes the heavy air made foul with smoke and dust. He is traveling alone—tottering about the car and waiting on him-self—shouldered this way and that getting little sympathy or kind-ness, reeling at last into the worst corner of the car because he is too weak to contend for the best one. In the sleepers you see the rich invalid, reclining upon soft pillows, surrounded by friends who min-ister to every wish before it is spoken—wealth hastening to console where it cannot relieve and brighten the approaches to death it can-not avert.

There are all sorts of parties on the train. Here is a worn, merry looking wife, with love in her patient eyes, ministering to her husband, whose hectic flush tells too plainly that her labors are nearly ended. There a father with a brood of children, are gath-ered about a dying mother, whose sweet smile and loving words, even impending death cannot still or subdue. Yonder is a father and mother watching a son, and reading in each other's anxious looks the truth that either is afraid to speak.   An interesting pair is a father on whose life this dread disease has fastened itself, traveling alone with his boy—a chubby youngster of ten years, surrendered possibly by a mother to watch over a life that is precious to her, but that she cannot follow.   Right across the car from me is one of the most touching figures in the car.   A young woman of perhaps thirty years—with plain, resolute face—alone.   She wears the indescribable air of reserve and sadness that invest women who have lived their lives apart.   She is dressed plainly and her well worn habit tells of privation and struggle.   She is probably a teacher, who, walking to and from her work in some bleak New England village, thinly clad and illy protected, the winds and storms of winter whipped into her slender form the seeds of disease.   She had remained at her post too long—so long that death has already set its seal on her cheeks, and looks gaunt and exorable out of her great clear eyes. It was probably poverty that kept her there—probably demands of a mother or a sister upon her small resources pinched them so that they pinned her to her martyrdom.   And now at last, on the savings of many years, the price of her life, she comes to find balm and healing in the South.   There is despair in her face, but there is no trouble there.   Her great eyes are cloudless—her thin lips are peacefully closed—her brow is calm, and there is gentle resignation in every feature.   Perhaps she looks with little regret to the end of life that has been hard and laborious and lonely and feels that God will give her at last the rest and peace so long denied her.   Just beyond her there is a strong man chafing uneasily in the thralls of disease.   His face is knotted with suffering and dread.   His wealth, his strength, his resources—none of these give him peace and content that has come to this frail, slender girl.   Truly, there is no power like the consciousness of a life well spent, a duty fully performed, a mission accomplished, a martyrdom endured.   To the girl across the way, death is but a falling to sleep—sweet, dreamless rest after a long and weary work.

63

Henry W. Grady,
Atlanta Constitution,
June 22, 1882.

"GOLD IN GEORGIA"

Suppose we now run hurriedly through the process by which gold is mined—follow it from hill to mint!

Here we are on top of a hill—say 2,500 feet above tide water. Around is a scene the grandeur and beauty of which even the painter's brush could not put on paper.   To the front, right and left of us are endless mountain ranges, their azure heads lost in the clouds.   Breaking green surfaces of the outlying foot-hills are tiny gashes or miners' huts or swift and slender streams "dropping like a downward smoke." To the rear of us is Dahlonega, showing up like a toy village in the skies.

At our side is a huge reservoir dug into the mountain top, and supplied with water forced from below.   At our feet is an enormous gulch.   The heart of the mountain has indeed been cut out.   The gulch has been cut irregularly but in its vast depths you might drop twenty Kimball houses and scarcely miss the space.   About 150 feet below us on a smooth level surface is a force of men at work with picks and hammers.   Crawling like children in the depths of the gulch, they are simply loosening bits of rocks.   Already behind them, is a rough surface that looks as if it were covered with crumbs. At the lower end of the gulch is a crack a few feet wide cut through the solid hill.

Along the walls of the great gulch here and there were holes like swallow's nests in the banks. These were pockets into which exceptionally rich veins had been followed, until they were exhausted. In time these will be obliterated as the gulch is widened.

At any rate I shall look with interest for news from Dahlonega— that quaint and hospitable old town, perched on a mountain side as an eagle's nest—where the goodly citizens carry lanterns when they walk abroad by dark, and where the stores are all closed and the men put on their best clothes when there is a funeral—where the clouds hang above the house-tops by day, and the outstanding peaks lift themselves among the stars at night. And I shall often think of that strange war of man against the mountain. I hear, even now, the ceaseless pulse of the mills, the sudden roar of the torrent, the quickening ring of the machinery, and the pretty laugh and prattle of miners, as the assault closes in on the everlasting hills. I see their great bodies gashed and pierced, their verdure stripped away piecemeal, their elixir stolen from their veins, their very hearts rifted and torn. And I see the depths where silence has reigned since men first found voice, and with eager hands rifling the newly-opened veins of the slow-gathering wealth of ages! And all for

"Gold! Gold! Gold! Gold!
Bright and yellow—hard and cold."

64

Henry W. Grady,
Atlanta Constitution,
August 13, 1882.

"SURF-BATHING"

I noted at one of the resorts several days ago the handsomest woman I ever saw on the beach. She was tall and slender, but divinely formed. Her flesh was firm and dazzling in its whiteness. Her pretty head was poised like a queen's upon a swan-like neck that swelled into snowy bust and shoulders. A bathing shirt loosely tied about the neck and without sleeves, gave perfect play to her superb body. Black silk stockings encased a leg of equisite proportions, and feet that left perfectly outlined foot-prints set regularly in the sand at about thirty degrees divergence. There was something royal in the unconscious grace and beauty of this woman as she walked into the water the cynosure of a hundred eyes. Utterly dwarfing her escort, she seemed disregardful of his presence, and when the foam was clustering about her knees, raised her gleaming arms above her head, and went like a flash into the body of an incoming breaker. The vision of that woman shines to this hour, as a serene star amid the crowding memories of this month, nor does the vision lose its luster when I reflect that she was an employe in the hotel; and her graces was the result of hard work and constant exercise.

But I might fill the *Constitution* with gossip of the sights and incidents of a month at the seaside, and then barely turn the little page of what written would be a most delightful volume.

It is an enchanting pastime for young folks, fair, joyous, and innocent. For older people it is exhilarating and healthful, and for children it is simply better than anything. No medicine for the little ones can compare with an hour's scamper on the beach morning and evening in loose bathing suits, so that it doesn't matter whether the waves tumble them or not. As for a man who is tired of work, etc., and of the bustle and dust of the city, it is incomparable. Just think of this schedule for an August day. A tumble in the waves in the morning, a shower bath in the spray, and ride on the billows, a swing out to the buoy, tossing pretty girls about in the salt water, a header or two under the surface for a finisher. A walk to the bath house with an indescribable glow pervading the whole body and tingling every nerve. A leisurely toilet with the salt spray drying on the flesh and making it acrid and cool. Across to the bar for a little apollo-naris and claret. Upstairs to a bed standing across a window, through the half-closed shutters of which comes a crisp salt breeze, drying and fanning the glow out of the body. There, with half-shut eyes, to muse on the mercies and goodness of the Lord, until all the senses have yielded to the delicious drowsiness that overpowers them and the slumberous roar of the surf, beats through a tissue of dreams, and the waves that break on the beach conjure from the heart of a deep and sweet sleep the memory of a baby cradled in the mother's swinging arms and soothed with a lullaby from her loving lips.

65

Henry W. Grady,
Atlanta Constitution,
August 17, 1882.

"Ben Hill"

To write of Ben Hill dead!

What a sorrow is that—and in spite of the dull forebodings of the past year was a surprise!

Inscrutable indeed are the ways of Providence that demand a life so richly endowed as his, and still forever a tongue so eloquent. To the very last, in spite of all reason, there was a hope that by some miracle of mercy the great Senator would be spared to his people. Against inexorable logic of nature there was a hope that his life, so potential in all things else, and so grandly calm in this, would stand unmoved against the assaults of death itself. Therefore it is that the end so definitely foretold brings a strange sense of surprise.

In the disquiet that always comes with death, emphasized by the shock that comes with this death against which all finite reason rebels, I am to write of his life. I would dishonor the emotion that fills my heart in this sad hour if I attempted any study of the life that has just closed so solemnly or any analysis of a character that is idolized by universal grief, I shall write as one who loved him living and who mourns him dead, and as I look over the years through which he has passed and in which I know him so well, I feel as one who has seen the sun move down the western sky, and after it has gone, stands gazing on the banks of clouds still luminous with its glory, and finds that it lives in the quivering afterglow, even after it has passed into the infinite.

The first time I ever saw Mr. Hill was in the winter of '67. I had gone to LaGrange to spend my Christmas vacation with young Ben Hill, who was then named Cicero Hill. I have never seen a happier home than that into which I was welcomed that winter day. I have never seen one more unaffectedly happy and affectionate than was this husband and father. Mr. Hill, lovely, no less in face and figure than in character, was full of goodness and courtesy. Miss Hill, now Mrs. Thompson, charming, accomplished and brilliant, was the idol of her father's heart—the two sons were smart manly young fellows, and the youngest daughter interesting and pretty. As for Mr. Hill nothing was too trivial to engage his attention if it only related to any member of his family. He was playful, genial and affectionate always. He made companions of his children and was as ready to romp with his boys as to advise with them as to their future. Emory Speer and myself were added to the family group that gathered in the library night after night—and charming nights were they. Mr. Hill usually led the conversation, though there was restraint upon no one. He was deeply interested in the reconstruction problem, and would discuss it earnestly and eloquently—then just as earnestly interested himself in the details of the day's hunting or assisted in the plans for the morrow, or go over the town gossip with his wife or discuss with his daughter a pair of $1,500 horses that he had just sent out from Kentucky for her special use. Before the family separated for the night there were, earnest Christian prayers, at the close of which each son and daughter kissed the father and mother "good night."

66

Henry W. Grady,
Atlanta Constitution,
February 11, 1883.

"A Pauper Colony" and What Became of It

Just one hundred and fifty years ago this morning, a seventy-ton sloop and five boats sailed into the Savannah river.

This little fleet beat its way slowly, and by the afternoon of the next day anchored opposite a bluff on which a small Indian trading post was perched. A company of about 125 persons—men, women and children—disembarked. As they reached the shore a crowd of Indians headed by a medicine man waving a huge fan of white feathers and jingling a staff strung with bells, came to meet them.

After friendly salutations were over, the visitors pitched four large tents, and hurriedly landed their bedding, clothes, provisions and utensils. That night they slept in open air on the ground. Thus was the city of Savannah founded, and the first colony planted on the soil of Georgia.

There is a strange fascination for me in the history of that little settlement, in the traditions of the vague and misty centuries, against which its story is but as a tale of yesterday, and in the years of its struggles and development to which we are knitted with actual sense of kinship.

If the leisurely readers of *The Constitution* who have an hour to spare, will give me that much of their time, we will have a talk of old and new Georgia—a subject that should interest all Georgians— and that will interest all men and women who are interested in the heroic, the pathetic or the curious.

Such are some of the suggestions, written as they come, that spring from a contemplation of these old, heroic, pathetic, hopeful days. But crowding out of these half-melancholy thoughts, a final sense of contrast between the Savannah of that day and this.

What a work has one hundred and fifty years wrought!

Up the same river this morning, through whose unknown waters a century and a half ago a sailing vessel stole its timid way, came thronging ships on the deck of which the fleet of '33 could have been stowed with ease. Where there was a single trading post, dropped like a single mustard seed in the unbroken wilderness, is now a great and populous city. From all parts of a prosperous country thousands of visitors are hurrying to the point, where then a few naked Indians gathered to witness the landing of the colonists.

Few men there are in this world who realize fully the purport of their work. Little did Oglethorpe dream when in very mercy and compassion he brought a ship load of people to our shore, he should live to see that colony in successful rebellion against his king, or that his grandchild might live to see it a part of a republic with double the population of the united kingdom. All men work blindly. We may be laying today in our busy and vaunting way, the cornerstone of a future more glorious than the past century and a half would suggest —or we may be staggering unconscious toward some vast catastrophe beneath which we may be buried, and behind which our monuments may stand, voiceless and melancholy reminders to a coming and nameless people of a race that is gone and forgotten. Be this as it may, the lesson of the founders of this state—of the men who followed Oglethorpe and Wesley, and Habersham, and Whitfield, and in whose presence we stand by courtesy this morning—is that we shall be brave, and patient, and steadfast, and upright, keeping our souls stainless, our consciences void of offense and leaving the rest with God that orders all things for the best.

67

Henry W. Grady,
Atlanta Constitution,
May 12, 1883.

"One Day's Fishing"

What a night that was! Out under the great live oak trees, that were drowsy with the hum of the cricket and the katydid. The stars gleaming in their tranquil depths—farther away and more steadfast than the city stars ever seem to be; the lake lisping on the shore at the feet; the old house, larger than cluster of modern houses, silent and desolate save where the overhanging boughs of the trees swept caressingly against it; the whippoorwill calling from the outlying woods, from vague and indeterminate points, as if some restless spirit of a bird were calling from shifting impalpable perch—the cows moving uneasily in their slumbers, and the geese, sweeping as spectres through the pale byways of the night—the dogs crouching near where we sat—two city bred youngsters huddled in our arms—and above all the ineffable hush, and peace, and expansion, depth, and breadth, and stillness of the starlit night in the country, into which no bustle can reach, and about which no limit is set. The stars, the trees, the earth, the lake, the house, the sky, water, brutes and birds, and the watchers who sat beneath the trees seemed to be of one piece, and of one substance. The air that bound all these things together throbbed with one pulse and rose or fell with one breath. All things held kinship with all things else, and the incomparable quiet of the stars, the whispers of the lake and the tree, and all the sounds and the silence of that restless night sank into the soul of men who lay beneath them and filled them with a peace that passes all understanding.

BIBLIOGRAPHY

Adamson, J. E.: The Individual and the Environment.
Albright, Evelyn May: Descriptive Writing.
Avery, I. W.: Co-editor of Henry W. Grady (H. C. Hudgins & Co.).
Bagehot, Walter: Literary Studies.
Baker & Huntington: Principles of Argumentation.
Bleyer, Willard Grosvenor: The Profession of Journalism.
Clark, S. H.: Interpretation of the Printed Page.
Dana, Chas. A.: Recollections of the Civil War.
Editorial, English Journal, 1925.
Emerson: Self-Reliance.
Flint, Leon Nelson: The Conscience of the Newspaper.
Gardiner, J. H.: The Forms of Prose Literature.
Greenough & Kittredge: Words and their Ways.
Harris, J. C.: Life and Writings and Speeches of Henry W. Grady.
Hillis, Newell Dwight: Great Books as Life Teachers.
Howe, P. P.: The Best of Hazlitt.
Knight, L. L.: Reminiscences of Famous Georgians, I: 425.
Krock, A.: The Editorials of Henry Watterson.
Lee, Dr. J. W.: Henry W. Grady, Editor, Orator, Man; *Arena*, 2: 9-23, Je. 1890.
Mabie, Hamilton Wright: Short Studies in Literature.
Matthews, William: Words; Their Uses and Abuses.
Merriam, George S.: The Life and Times of Samuel Bowles.
Neal, Robert W.: Editorials and Editorial Writers.
O'Rell, Max: Lively Journalism, *North Am. R.*, 150: 364-69.
Painter, F. V. N.: Elementary Guide to Lit. Criticism.
Papers of Madison, I; 1020.
Payne, George Henry: Hist. of Journalism in the United States.
Phillips, Arthur Edward: Effective Speaking.
Pritchard, F. H.: Training in Literary Appreciation.
Quiller-Couch, Sir Arthur: On the Art of Writing.
Saintsbury, George Edw.: A History of the 19th Cent. Literature.
Sherman, L. A.: Analytics of Literature.
Shuman, E. L.: How to Judge a Book.
Shuman, E. L.: Practical Journalism.
Spencer, M. L.: Editorial Writing.
Rhodes, Chas. Elbert: Effective Expression.
Rolph, Julian: The Making of a Journalist.
Trent, William P.: The Authority of Criticism.
Wilson, Jas. H.: The Life of Chas. A. Dana.
Wilson, John: Modern British Essayist.
Winchester, C. T.: Some Principles of Literary Criticism.
The Files of the *Atlanta Constitution* from 1869 to 1883.
The Files of the *Atlanta Herald* from 1873 to 1875.